Laurence Oliphant

Episodes in a Life of Adventure

Or, Moss from a rolling Stone

Laurence Oliphant

Episodes in a Life of Adventure
Or, Moss from a rolling Stone

ISBN/EAN: 9783337177799

Printed in Europe, USA, Canada, Australia, Japan

Cover: Foto ©ninafisch / pixelio.de

More available books at **www.hansebooks.com**

EPISODES

IN

A LIFE OF ADVENTURE

OR

MOSS FROM A ROLLING STONE

BY

LAURENCE OLIPHANT

AUTHOR OF 'PICCADILLY,' 'TRAITS AND TRAVESTIES,'
'ALTIORA PETO,' ETC.

NEW EDITION

WILLIAM BLACKWOOD AND SONS
EDINBURGH AND LONDON
MDCCCXCVI

All Rights reserved

CONTENTS.

CHAP.		PAGE
I.	THE OVERLAND ROUTE FORTY-SIX YEARS AGO, AND AN ASCENT OF ADAM'S PEAK IN CEYLON,	1
II.	REVOLUTIONARY EPISODES IN ITALY IN THE YEAR 1848, AND AN ADVENTURE IN GREECE,	23
III.	MY FIRST EXPERIENCES IN DIPLOMACY,	39
IV.	POLITICS AND INDIAN AFFAIRS IN CANADA,	60
V.	CRIMEAN AND CIRCASSIAN EXPERIENCES,	79
VI.	ADVENTURES IN CENTRAL AMERICA,	107
VII.	CALCUTTA DURING THE MUTINY, AND CHINA DURING THE WAR 1857-1859,	125
VIII.	SOME SPORTING REMINISCENCES,	139
IX.	AN EPISODE WITH GARIBALDI, AND AN EXPERIENCE IN MONTENEGRO,	165
X.	THE ATTACK ON THE BRITISH LEGATION IN JAPAN IN 1861,	185
XI.	A VISIT TO TSUSIMA: AN INCIDENT OF RUSSIAN AGGRESSION,	212

XII. POLITICS AND ADVENTURE IN ALBANIA AND ITALY
IN 1862, ... 228
XIII. CRACOW DURING THE POLISH INSURRECTION OF 1863, 243
XIV. EXPERIENCES DURING THE POLISH INSURRECTION:
WARSAW, ... 264
XV. A VISIT TO AN INSURGENT CAMP, . . . 302
XVI. TWENTY-FOUR HOURS IN VOLHYNIA, . . . 333
XVII. A VISIT TO THE CONVENTS OF MOLDAVIA, . 355
XVIII. THE WAR IN SCHLESWIG-HOLSTEIN: THE BATTLE OF
MISSUNDE, ... 381
XIX. THE MORAL OF IT ALL, ... 416

EPISODES

IN

A LIFE OF ADVENTURE.

CHAPTER I.

THE OVERLAND ROUTE FORTY-SIX YEARS AGO, AND AN
ASCENT OF ADAM'S PEAK, IN CEYLON.

THE proverb that a rolling stone gathers no "moss" is, like most proverbs, neater as an epigram than as a truth, in so far as its application to human existence is concerned. Even if by "moss" is signified hard cash, commercial and industrial enterprises have undergone such a change since the introduction of steam and electricity, that the men who have made most money in these days are often those who have been flying about from one quarter of the world to another in its successful pursuit—taking contracts, obtaining concessions, forming companies, or engaging in speculations, the profitable nature of which has been revealed to them in the course of their travels. But there may be said to be other kinds of moss besides money, of which the human rolling stone gathers more than the stationary one. He meets with adventures, he acquires new views, he undergoes experiences, and gains a general knowledge of the world, the whole crystallising in after life into a rich fund of reminiscences, which becomes the moss that he has gathered. The journal of such a one in after years, if he has been careful enough to record his experiences, becomes amusing reading to himself, and may serve to refresh his memory in regard to incidents which, as matters of history, may not be devoid of interest to the public generally.

I was a very young stone indeed when I began rolling —a mere pebble, in fact; but some of the moss which I collected then has stuck to me with greater tenacity than much that has gathered itself upon my weather-worn surface in later years. The impressions of early travel are generally so deeply stamped at the time, that the memory of them does not easily fade. Thus I have made the overland journey to the East, backwards and forwards, eight times, but the recollection of the first one continues the most vivid; and it is the same with my passages across the Atlantic,—but perhaps that is because it lasted seventeen days, was made in the depth of winter, and under circumstances calculated to cause themselves to be remembered. My first voyage to the East was by the overland route in the winter of the years 1841 and 1842; it was made in company with my tutor, and so imperfect were the arrangements in those days, that it took us two full months to reach Ceylon. At Boulogne, where we arrived in a steamer direct from London Bridge, my companion and I seated ourselves in the *banquette* of an old-fashioned diligence—for very few miles of railway had been built in France in those days; and from our elevated perch, which we preferred to retain throughout, we had abundant opportunity for a survey of "La belle France," as we rumbled across it from one end to the other, accomplishing the journey from Boulogne to Marseilles in eight days and five nights of incessant diligence travel; our only adventure being that we stuck for some hours of the night in the snow near Chalons, and had to be dug out. At that time there were no passenger-steamers from Marseilles to Malta, and the mails were conveyed in a man-of-war, which was also compelled to submit to the humiliation of having to take passengers. The only incident of which I have any recollection during the voyage was that of pitching head-foremost from the quarter-deck on to the main deck, in the course of a race in sacks, and the flash of thought which suggested instant death as I went over. From this accident I remained insensible for twenty-four hours, but was otherwise none the worse. At Malta we changed steamers for Alexandria, where the East burst for the first time upon my surprised senses. The foreign population was probably not a quarter of what it is now; carriages had not been introduced; the streets were narrow, ill-paved, and crowded with camels, donkeys, veiled women, and the traffic characteristic of an Eastern city, but all was life and bustle: the place was just beginning to quiver under the impulse of the movement which the invention of steam was imparting to the world, and one of the earliest evidences of which was the direct route to India, which Lieutenant Waghorn had just opened through Egypt.

One of the pleasantest experiences of the journey, was the voyage along the Mahamoudich Canal in canal-boats towed by horses, as far as Atfeh. This was a perfect picnic while it lasted; the culinary arrangements being extemporised to meet the difficulties of the situation, principally by the passengers themselves, for the organisation was still so defective that they had largely to trust to their own resources and exertions to secure their comfort. The morning of "Cook" had not yet dawned, and we were still in a sort of twilight of ignorance and dragomans. We had been looking forward to a sail up the Nile in *dahabeeyahs* to Cairo, but the first steamer had just been put on the river; notwithstanding which, owing to various delays, which I for one did not regret in a country where all was so new and interesting, it took us three days to get from Alexandria to Cairo. Here, as there was no civilised hotel—for Shepheard's had not yet sprung into existence—we had to go to a native khan, where a number of bare unfurnished cells opened upon a corridor, enclosing four sides of a square, which was filled at all hours of the day and night with a mob of grunting, munching camels, and their screaming, quarrelling drivers; and here we found Mr Waghorn himself, indefatigable in his exertions for our comfort, and in a constant struggle with the authorities, which, considering that only a few months before we had bombarded the Egyptians out of Acre, and had handed Palestine over to the Turks, was by no means to be wondered at. Looked at by the light of subsequent events, we should probably have done better had we left things as they were; but in that case subsequent events would have been so different that we might have had occasion to regret them still more. No doubt there were reasons why it seemed best at the time to separate the interests of Palestine from those of Egypt: but the fate of each country must ever be powerfully influenced in the future, as it has been in the past, by the destiny of the other; and their relative position towards each other, topographically and commercially, must always cause the influence which is paramount in Egypt to be powerfully operative in Palestine. And this will become the case, in a still more marked degree, when the two countries are united, as they must be before long, by a railway from Cairo to Damascus. There is no line probably in the world, except perhaps between the populous cities of China, more certain to pay than one which should connect Egypt and Syria, and which would convey the greater part of that produce which is now carried in native boats by sea, or transported wearily across the intervening desert on the backs of camels. The Eastern question will have, however, to be reopened and closed again before we can hope to see it constructed. Meantime we were almost as unpopular in Egypt in 1841 as we are now; but then, at all events, we had a clear and definite policy, and knew distinctly what we were aiming at. What we lost in one direction we gained in another, instead of losing all round, as we do in these days, and which we shall continue to do in the degree in which the British mob is invited by subservient statesmen to dictate to them the policy to be pursued in foreign affairs. However, these are merely the views of a rolling stone, with which it is impossible that stones which form a part of the pavement of London streets, and can see no farther than the houses on either side, can sympathise; but of this they may feel sure, that if they were picked out of their political gutters, and sent rolling about the world for a few years, they would get rid of a good deal of the dirt of party, and gather a little of the moss of patriotism.

Forty-six years have worked a far greater change in Cairo than they have in Alexandria. In fact, they have transformed the city to an extent which makes it no longer recognisable. From the most oriental of oriental cities, which it was when I saw it first, it has become the most European—the broad *boulevards* and miles of roads and streets, the hundreds of carriages plying for hire, the magnificent hotels and handsome villas with their surrounding gardens, have superseded all that was quaint, Eastern, and picturesque. The Ezebekeyeh, where in old days one sat in the still evenings, and smoked *chibouks* and *narghilehs*, and drank coffee and sherbet, and listened to the twang of native instruments, in company with groups of venerable Moslems, is now a park where nursemaids and babies and *petits crevés* go and listen to a military band. And one has to make an expedition expressly into the native quarter to know that it exists. We were detained a couple of days in Cairo, while Mr Waghorn was arranging for our transport across the desert to Suez, and we were never tired of exploring its narrow streets on donkeys, and spending money on articles which could never be of any manner of use to us, in its crowded and well-stocked bazaars.

We crossed the desert in several four-horse vans—horses having been recently substituted for the camels which were at first attached to these vehicles—and found waiting for us at Suez the steamer India. The journey from the Mediterranean to the Red Sea, including two days' stay at Alexandria, had occupied eight days. The last time I crossed from one sea to the other it was by an express train without any delay at Cairo, and the time occupied was nine hours. Before the establishment of the Peninsular and Oriental Steam Company, the mails were conveyed from Suez to Bombay by one of the East India Company's men-of-war. The first merchant-ship which carried passengers and mails direct from Suez to Calcutta was the India, and this was her first voyage. She was commanded by a Captain Staveley, and was considered a large ship in those days, though she was not over 1500 tons. The survey of the Red Sea was also, I imagine, imperfect. At any rate, on the second night after leaving Suez we were all nearly thrown out of our berths by the ship running full speed upon a coral-reef, on which the scene of panic usual on such occasions occurred. All the passengers, male and female, were on deck in the lightest of attire in a moment, and were somewhat reassured by the fact that the sea was as calm as a mill-pond, and the ship as motionless as a statue—so much so, indeed, that one weak-minded cadet, who had been the butt of the younger members of the party all the way, thought the opportunity a good one in which to write his will, which he proceeded with great earnestness and good faith to do in the saloon, assisted by several of his friends, whose good faith was not so obvious. When he had finished it, we took charge of it, and promised that in case any of us were saved from the wreck, which he thought imminent, the survivors would see that it was executed. I have often wondered since whether this youth ever rose to command the regiment he went out to join. We stuck on this reef several hours, and then with the help of the little tide there is in the Red Sea, and the boats, we floated off, with, as it afterwards turned out, a severely damaged bottom. However, we steamed slowly on for two or three days more, and then ran out of coal. As there was not a breath of wind when this discovery was made, the prospect of lying for an indefinite time, "like a painted ship upon a painted ocean," was not encouraging. However, the ocean was fortunately a very narrow one, and with the aid of a puff of wind which ultimately sprang up, we managed to work our way into Mocha. As I was not in the slightest hurry to reach my journey's end, I was delighted at this *contretemps*, as it gave me a chance of seeing a very rarely visited place.

We lay off Mocha for three days, taking in wood. Its aspect from the sea is not particularly inviting. It is merely a row of white flat-roofed houses, with a minaret or two rising above them, glistening in the broiling sun, with a palm-grove at either end, and a desert beyond. Some of us went on shore to explore the town and pay a visit to the Governor or Shereef. We then found that the white houses looked far grander at a distance than on nearer acquaintance; and that there was a bazaar behind them, in which a large proportion of desert Arabs mingled with the Moslem townspeople, bringing in strings of camels with dates, coffee, and other produce for sale. I was told that, though the country immediately surrounding Mocha was barren and unprepossessing, there was a fertile, well-watered hill-region behind, where the celebrated coffee called after the town is produced, but which, even to this day, has been only very partially explored. At present, the obstacles to exploration are even greater than when I was at Mocha. At that time it was virtually, if not technically, the capital of Yemen, a rich and fertile province about 400 miles long by 150 wide; and though the Sultan of Turkey cast covetous eyes upon it, and even attempted to lay some claim to sovereignty over it, it was practically an independent country,—the supreme authority being the Imaum, whose palace was at Sana, a town equidistant from Aden and from Mocha, being about 160 miles from each, and the centre of a trade which found its way to the sea-coast at Mocha. Now all this is changed. There is no longer an Imaum at Sana: after a protracted war, which has lasted over several years, and which never raged more fiercely than it did last year, though we heard very little about it, Yemen has been annexed to the Turkish empire and constituted into a Vilayet, with a Turkish pasha resident at Sana, where, however, his authority does not extend beyond the bayonets of his soldiers, of whom a large force is kept under his orders. I have conversed with many of these men who have returned from service in Yemen, and they all tell me that the country is in a state of chronic revolt; that the Arabs are intensely hostile to the authority of the Porte; that they are very brave, and that their conversion into peaceful subjects seems an almost hopeless task. I have also met in Jerusalem a very interesting set of Jews, who only arrived there as refugees a little more than two years ago from Yemen, where they say they were settled long before the final dispersion, for they claim to be descended from the tribe of Dan : they are learned in the Scriptures, and more devout and unsophisticated than those who have been in contact with Western civilisation. They say they were compelled to leave Yemen in consequence of the war between the Turks and Arabs, where they found themselves between the upper and the nether millstone.

So far as I was able to gather, there is, however, a strong tribe of nomads, all pure Jews, who have sided with the Arabs in the late war, and who have retired into fastnesses, where the Turks have had a difficulty in following them, for parts of the country are very mountainous. I have also heard from more than one source of the existence of a valuable gold-mine somewhere in Yemen, and conversed with those who have seen the ore that has been extracted from it.

The creation of Yemen into a Turkish Vilayet brought the frontier of the empire almost to the gates of Aden; and the native Arab tribes, who, on the occasion of my first visit, made it unsafe to venture a hundred yards from the fortification, were glad to seek our protection rather than fall under Turkish rule. The result has been a certain tension between the Turkish authorities and British officials, arising out of this newly born propinquity; and the fear lest our influence should spread into the interior, has induced the Ottoman Government strictly to prohibit Englishmen from entering Yemen. When I was at Mocha, it was only necessary to enlist the favour of the Shereef of that place, and obtain permission from the Imaum of Sana to get into the interior, which, although it was never thoroughly explored, had already been visited by Wellstead, Cruttenden, and other travellers.

Meantime Mocha has suffered severely under all these changes; and from having a population of 10,000 inhabitants, has dwindled down to a mere village, all the trade of Yemen finding its outlet at Aden, which is only eighty miles distant from it by sea.

The Shereef of Mocha, when we visited him, was a great personage, and received us with much ceremony, gave us excellent coffee, which, under the circumstances, was only to be expected, and was delighted with the present of a ship's musket, which the captain gave him to enlist his influence in the wood question. He immediately loaded it, and took a shot at a mark on the opposite wall of the street, which was not more than a foot or two above the heads of the people, by whom it was crowded. Their alarm and astonishment, as the ball whistled close to their ears, were ludicrous to behold, and highly amused the Governor, who I don't think would have been much affected even if the consequences had been serious.

The indifference of the natives to human life was remarkably illustrated while we were here. From morning till night our ship was surrounded by boats loaded with wood, their crews keeping up a most discordant din of screaming refrain while engaged in the process of discharging their cargoes into us. The abundance of this article was a strong evidence of its existence in the interior; but as it had all come on camels' backs, it must have been an expensive commodity. One of these boats, with a couple of men in it, got capsized, the boat turned over, and the men scrambled on to the keel. There must have been a strong current, as they speedily drifted out to sea, without any efforts being made by their comrades to rescue them, though the accident took place at mid-day, in full view of everybody. I suppose our captain thought that it was the business of the natives to look after each other. We watched them with our glasses until they disappeared on the horizon; but as the sea is very narrow at this part, it is to be hoped they drifted ashore on the opposite side.

From Mocha, with our wood fuel and our rickety bottom, we steamed slowly round to Aden, where the ship was laid up for repairs, and I was kindly received as a guest by Captain Staines, then Commissioner at that place. Forty-six years have worked a great change at Aden, as at all the other places on the route. It had then been only two years in our possession, and was held like a post in an enemy's country. Every morning and evening long strings of camels were to be seen passing into the camp from the interior with supplies, and returning again to the desert, every Arab who accompanied them being compelled to have a pass, and none of them being permitted to sleep within the gates for fear of treachery.

We have now reduced all these unruly tribes to subjection, and within a certain radius of Aden the petty sultans by whom they are governed have been placed under our protection—notably the Sultan of Lahaj, whose village is a day's ride distant into the interior, and who can now be visited with perfect security. We have annexed a small district adjoining the peninsula, and upon it, three miles from the fortifications, have established a town called Sheikh Osman, which has a population of 12,000, composed of Somaulis, Hindoos, Abyssinians, and Arabs. Each of these nationalities has its own quarter, and perfect peace and order are maintained without the intervention of any European—there being no white man in the place. Aden itself has now a population of at least 50,000, and is a growing commercial emporium, while large sums are about to be spent upon its fortifications. When I first visited it, the resident population, outside the garrison, were to be counted by hundreds; and both at the "Camp" and the "Point," into which the settlement was divided, the residences were of the most flimsy description. To me, however, their quaint and unsubstantial character possessed all the charm of novelty; and the conditions of existence generally were so strange and unlike anything to which I had been accustomed, that I enjoyed my week's stay immensely, and was quite sorry when the repairs of the ship were completed, and we were called upon to bid adieu to its hospitable society.

The remainder of the voyage was only remarkable for our slow rate of speed, and we reached Ceylon without further incident, sixty days after leaving England.

I read a very interesting article in 'Blackwood's Magazine' not long since on sacred footprints, in which the writer suggested that many of them were originally coronation-stones, and in which he offered some ingenious suggestions as to the religious character which attaches to them among the various races in the different countries where they are found. They seem, indeed, to possess a peculiar fascination to the devotional mind among oriental races; and we not unfrequently find the same footprint invested with a traditional sanctity by the adherents of religions which have no relation to each other beyond one or two of those broad ideas which are more or less common to all worship. This is notably the case with the print on Adam's Peak, the Sripada of the Buddhists; the penitential mountain of our first parent, of the Mohammedans. It was from here that Gautama is supposed to have stepped across the Bay of Bengal into Siam—a gigantic stride, but not so wonderful a performance as that attributed to Adam, as described by a devout Mussulman to a friend of mine, when discussing the means by which he transported himself to Ceylon, after his expulsion with his wife, according to Moslem traditions, from the Garden of Eden. It seems that poor Eve, after being separated from Adam for two hundred years, and reunited with him on Mount Ararat, died before he left Arabia; for her tomb, which is regarded with great veneration by Moslems, is pointed out to the pious pilgrims on their way to Mecca, at Jeddah. According to this tradition, it was at the former place that Adam knelt down to ask forgiveness upon that stone, which has been invested with the utmost sanctity from a period long anterior to Mohammed—the sacred Caaba of Mecca; and there he had his penance imposed upon him. Then, travelling to the coast, Eve died, and was buried about a mile from Jeddah, in a tomb 200 feet long; for she was a tall woman. The human race seems steadily to have degenerated after her time, for Noah occupies a tomb which was pointed out to me near Zahleh, in the Lebanon, only 104 feet long by 10 wide.

If Eve was 200 feet high, her husband, to judge by the present proportions of the sexes, must have been a good deal taller, say 25 or 30 feet. Now the difficulty which my friend suggested to his Moslem disputant was—how, in those early days, a man 220 or 230 feet high could find a *sambook*, or craft such as are now used in those seas, big enough to carry him on a long voyage?

"There was no difficulty at all about it," replied the Moslem; "he went over to Ceylon in *several sambooks!*"

After performing such a wonderful feat as this, the fact that he should have been able to stand on the top of Adam's Peak on one leg for a thousand years, and leave his footprint there deeply embedded in the rock, dwindles into insignificance. Moslem traditions vary considerably in regard to the proceedings of our earliest ancestors, and I by no means pin my faith to this one. According to another, Ceylon itself was the Garden of Eden, and in that case Adam's post of penance was handy, while his enormous height would enable him to reach the top a great deal more easily than I did, and then Eve must have gone over in "several *sambooks*" to Jeddah. Again, the most commonly accepted version of the origin of the Caaba is, that it was originally a white stone given by the angel Gabriel to Abraham, and has since been blackened by much kissing; while others again say that Hagar rested there with Ishmael, when, after being turned out of house and home, they drank at Mecca at the sacred spring Zem-zem. These are all fertile themes of discussion among Moslems, and the reader may take his choice of them. Meantime many pilgrims go annually to the top of Adam's peak, which is about 7500 feet above the sea-level, both

Moslem and Buddhist; and must feel not a little indignant with each other at finding it appropriated by two such very different characters as Adam and Buddha. By far the greater number, however, are Buddhists.

There are two paths of ascent: the one most commonly taken by pilgrims is from Ratnapoora, a place which owes its importance chiefly to its trade in precious stones. The sand-washings of the river which flows past it, yield rubies, sapphires, amethysts, cat's-eyes, besides cinnamon stones and others of less value, and furnish a fair source of profit to the inhabitants. While watching the washers one day, I bought on the spot a cat's-eye from one man I saw find it, which, when polished, proved to have been a good bargain.

As it is rather a fatiguing day's journey from Ratnapoora to the top of the Peak, I made an early start with a friend from the house of the hospitable judge who was at that time exercising his functions in this district, attended by our horsekeepers—as grooms are called in that country—and some natives, who acted as guides and carriers of the provisions we required for a three days' trip. To say that our way led us through beautiful scenery is to use a platitude in connection with the central and mountainous districts of Ceylon, where the luxuriance of tropical vegetation merges, as we reach higher altitudes, into the heavy forests peculiar to them—where the villages are no longer embowered in groves of cocoa-nut trees, or nestle beneath the broad leaves of the plantain, but where they are surrounded by coffee-bushes red with berry, and are shadowed by the feathery bamboo; while the valley bottoms are terraced for the irrigation of rice, another variety of which, called hill-paddy, clothes the steep hill-sides where these are not already occupied by forest. Now, these once heavily-timbered slopes are for the most part covered with coffee plantations up to a certain elevation, beyond which coffee gives place to tea and cinchona. But forty years have made a difference in this respect; and when I ascended Adam's Peak, the villages became fewer and farther between as we increased our elevation, while our path often led us up the steep mountain-flank, through a dense jungle, as yet untouched by the hand of the foreign capitalist. We passed the night at a native house in one of the higher villages, and leaving our horses there, on the following morning pursued our way on foot amid scenery which at every step became more grand and rugged, the path in places skirting the edge of dizzy precipices, at the base of which foamed brawling torrents. The way was often rendered dangerous by the roots of large trees, which, having become slippery by the morning mist, stretched across the narrow path, and one of these nearly cost me my life. The path at the spot was scarped on the precipitous hillside; at least 300 feet below roared a torrent of boiling water,—when my foot slipped on a root, and I pitched over the sheer cliff. I heard the cry of my companion as I disappeared, and had quite time to realise that all was over, when I was brought up suddenly by the spreading branches of a bush which was growing upon a projecting rock. There was no standing-ground anywhere, except the rock the bush grew upon. For some time I dared not move, fearing that something might give way, as the bush seemed scarcely strong enough to bear my weight. Looking up, I saw my companion and the natives

B

who were with us peering over the edge above, and to their intense relief shouted that so far I was all right, but dared not move for fear the bush would give way. They, however, strongly urged my scrambling on to the rock; and this, with a heart thumping so loudly that I seemed to hear its palpitations, and a dizzy brain, I succeeded in doing. The natives, of whom there were five or six, then undid their long waist-cloths, and tying them to each other, and to a piece of cord, consisting of the united contributions of all the string of the party and the packages they were carrying, made a rope just long enough to reach me. Fastening this under my armpits, and holding on to it with the energy of despair, or perhaps I should rather say of hope, I was safely hauled to the top; but my nerve was so shaken that, although not in the least hurt, it was some moments before I could go on. This adventure was not a very good preparation for what was in store for us, when not very far from the top we reached the *mauvais pas* of the whole ascent. Here again we had a precipice with a torrent at the bottom of it on one side, and on the other an overhanging cliff—not metaphorically overhanging, but literally its upper edge projected some distance beyond the ledge on which we stood; it was not above forty feet high, and was scaled by an iron ladder. The agonising moment came when we had mounted this ladder to the projecting edge, and had nothing between our backs and the torrent some hundreds of feet below, and then had to turn over the edge and take hold of a chain which lay over an expanse of bare sloping rock, to the links of which it was necessary to cling firmly, while one hauled one's self on one's knees for twenty or thirty yards over the by no means smooth surface. My sensations, at the critical moment when I was clinging backwards on to the ladder, remind me of a subsequent experience in a Cornish mine. I was some hundreds of feet down in the bowels of the earth, crawling down a ladder similarly suspended; and feeling that the temperature was every moment getting warmer, I said to a miner who was accompanying me—

"It is getting very hot down here. How far do you think it is to the infernal regions?"

"I don't know exactly, sir," he promptly replied; "but if you let go, you will be there in two minutes."

Thus did he meanly take advantage of my precarious and helpless position to reflect upon my moral character! which was the more aggravating as I afterwards discovered that the remark was not original.

It was my companion's turn, after we had safely accomplished this disagreeable feat of gymnastics, to pant with nervousness. And here let me remark that the Alpine Club did not exist in those days, and we were neither of us used to go about like flies on a wall. He was a missionary, in fact; and he was so utterly demoralised that he roundly declared that nothing would induce him to make the descent of the same place. Now the prospect of imitating Adam, and staying permanently on the top of the peak called after him, was so appalling, that I proposed opening a bottle of brandy, which we had brought with us, and fortifying our nerves by taking a light repast there and then—a measure which was further recommended to us by the fact that the spot commanded an extensive and magnificent bird's-eye view of the whole southern portion of the island, with the sea distinctly visible in the extreme distance, and thousands of feet below us the forests from which we had so abruptly ascended. We had one or two pretty steep places after this, but nothing comparable to the *mauvais pas*, and reached the summit an hour or so before sunset. Here we found the solitary inhabitant of a single hut to be a Buddhist, who was guardian of the sacred footprint, over which was a wooden erection something like a light arbour, and which was secured to the rock by chains riveted into it. The print itself was about four feet long and nearly three wide, so far as I can recollect, and was so misshapen that it required some stretch of imagination to detect in it a resemblance to a human impression on a gigantic scale, more especially as the toes were almost undefined. The whole area of the summit, which was almost circular in shape, was not more than twenty yards in diameter: and the sensation of being perched up at so great an elevation on such a relatively minute point of rock, was an altogether novel one. One felt as though a violent gale of wind might blow one off it into space; and that there was some such danger was evident from the fact that the two flimsy erections upon it were fastened to the rock.

We now congratulated ourselves on having brought up thick blankets; for, accustomed as we had been for some time past to the heat of tropical plains, we felt the change to the sharp night air of such an elevation,—the more especially as the priest's hut was too filthy-looking for us to occupy, and we preferred taking shelter under its lee. We had no inducement, after a night on the hard rock, to sleep late; and by getting up an hour before sunrise, I was fortunate enough to witness a spectacle which was well worth all the fatigues and perils of the ascent.

As Adam's Peak rises from a comparatively low range of hills in the form of a perfect cone, it presents a far grander aspect than its rival Pedrotallagalla, which, although more than 1000 feet higher, neither stands out from its neighbours with the same solitary grandeur, nor does it furnish anything like the same extent of panoramic view, while it is easy of ascent on horseback. When I awoke to look about me, by the light of a moon a little past the full, in the early morning, I looked down from this isolated summit upon a sea of mist which stretched to the horizon in all directions, completely concealing the landscape beneath me. Its white, compact, smooth surface almost gave it the appearance of a field of snow, across which, in a deep black shadow, extended the conical form of the mountain I was on, its apex just touching the horizon, and producing a scenic effect as unique as it was imposing. While I was watching it, the sharpness of its outline gradually began to fade, the black shadow became by degrees less black, the white mist more grey, and as the dawn slowly broke, the whole effect was changed as by the wand of a magician. Another conical shadow crept over the vast expanse on the opposite side of the mountain, which in its turn reached to the horizon, as the sun gently rose over the tremulous mist; but the sun-shadow seemed to lack the cold mystery of the moon-shadow it had driven away, and scarcely gave one time to appreciate its own marvelous effects before the mist itself began slowly to rise, and to envelop us as in a winding-sheet. For half an hour or more we were in the clouds, and could see nothing; then suddenly they rolled away, and revealed the magnificent panorama which had been the object of our pilgrimage. Even without the singular impression which has captivated the religious imagination of the devotees of two faiths, the peculiar conditions under which this remarkable mountain was exhibited to us were calculated to inspire a sentiment of awe, which would naturally be heightened in the minds of the ignorant and superstitious by the discovery on its summit of a resemblance to a giant's footprint.

We heard that there was another and much easier way down, but it led in the wrong direction. Fortunately my companion having taken counsel with himself during the sleepless hours of the night, had now screwed up his courage for the descent, which we accomplished without further adventure; and we reached the hut where we had left our horses, in time to proceed on our journey the same day to visit some coffee plantations which had been recently opened in the neighbouring district of Saffragam.

CHAPTER II.

REVOLUTIONARY EPISODES IN ITALY IN THE YEAR 1848,
AND AN ADVENTURE IN GREECE.

IN the year 1846, my father, who was then Chief-Justice of Ceylon, came on a long leave to England. I was on the point of going up to Cambridge at the time, but when he announced that he intended to travel for a couple of years with my mother on the Continent, I represented so strongly the superior advantages, from an educational point of view, of European travel over ordinary scholastic training, and my arguments were so urgently backed by my mother, that I found myself, to my great delight, transferred from the quiet of a Warwickshire vicarage to the Champs Elysées in Paris; and, after passing the winter there, spent the following year roaming over Germany, Switzerland, and the Tyrol, by rail in the few cases where railways existed, but more often by the delightful but now obsolete method of *vetturino*; while, for a couple of months, fishing-rod in hand, we explored on foot the wild and then little known valleys of the Tyrol. I often wondered, while thus engaged, whether I was not more usefully and instructively employed than labouring painfully over the differential calculus; and whether the execrable *patois* of the peasants in the Italian valleys, which I took great pains in acquiring, was not likely to be of quite as much use to me in after life as ancient Greek.

Meantime, mutterings of the coming revolutionary storm had been heard all over Europe, and it was just bursting over Italy as we descended into that country at the close of 1847. Indeed, Italy has always proved an excellent field for moss-gathering since the day when, as I entered Rome for the first time, I passed cannon pointed down the streets, and found the whole town seething with revolution—to the year 1862, when, as the guest of a regiment of Piedmontese cavalry, I hunted brigands in the plains of the Basilicata and Capitanata. The incidents of my first visit are so long ago now, that I only remember their most salient features, but these are indelibly stamped upon my memory. I shall never forget joining a roaring mob one evening, bent I knew not upon what errand, and getting forced by the pressure of the crowd, and my own eagerness, into the front rank, just as we reached the Austrian Legation, and seeing the ladders passed to the front, and placed against the wall, and the arms torn down; then I remember, rather from love of excitement than any strong political sympathy, taking hold, with hundreds of others, of the ropes which were attached to them, and dragging them in triumph to the Piazza del Popolo, where a certain Ciceroachio, who was a great tribune of the people in those days, and a wood-merchant, had a couple of carts loaded with wood standing ready; and I remember their contents being tumultuously upset, and heaped into a pile, and the Austrian arms being dragged on the top of them, and a lady—I think the Princess Pamphili Doria, who was passing in a carriage at the time—being compelled to descend, and being handed a flaming torch, with which she was requested to light the bonfire, which blazed up amid the frantic demonstrations of delight of a yelling crowd, who formed round it a huge ring, joining hands, dancing and capering like demons,—in all of which I took an active part, getting home utterly exhausted, and feeling that somehow or other I had deserved well of my country.

And I remember upon another occasion being roused from my sleep, about one or two in the morning, by the murmur of many voices, and looking out of my window and seeing a dense crowd moving beneath, and rushing into my clothes and joining it—for even in those early days I had a certain moss-gathering instinct—and being borne along I knew not whither, and finding myself at last one of a shrieking, howling mob at the doors of the Propaganda, against which heavy blows were being directed by improvised battering-rams; and I remember the doors crashing in, and the mob crashing in after them, to find empty cells and deserted corridors, for the monks had sought safety in flight. And I remember standing on the steps of St Peter's while Pope Pio Nono gave his blessing to the volunteers that were leaving for Lombardy to fight against the Austrians, and seeing the tears roll down his cheeks—as I supposed, because he hated so much to have to do it. These are events which are calculated to leave a lasting impression on the youthful imagination. Unfortunately, in those days newspaper correspondence was in its infancy, and posterity will have but a comparatively meagre record of the exciting scenes and stirring events of the great revolutionary year.

If it was disagreeable to the Pope to bless the Italian patriots in their struggle against Austria, it was still more hateful to the King of Naples to have to grant a constitution to his subjects, and swear to keep it upon crossed swords, which I saw him do with great solemnity in a church, after a revolution which had lasted three days, and in which at length the troops refused to fire upon the people. It was true that he had no intention of keeping his oath, and broke it shortly afterwards, but the moment was none the less humiliating; and his face was an interesting study. Some idea of the confusion which reigned in all parts of Italy about this time may be gathered from an incident which happened to my father and myself at Leghorn on the day of our arrival in that town. It had been more or less in a chronic state of revolution for some weeks past. The Grand Duke still reigned in Florence, but he had lost control of Leghorn, which was practically in the hands of the *facchini* and the scum of the population. Considering themselves the masters of the situation, the porters who carried our luggage from the quay to the hotel made such an exorbitant charge that we refused to pay it. They accordingly summoned us before the magistrate. After hearing the case, that worthy decided that the charge was reasonable, and that we must pay it. With the instinct of resisting extortion to the last, which is characteristic of the Briton, we persisted in our refusal notwithstanding this judgment; upon which the magistrate said that in that case it would be his painful duty to commit us to prison. We replied that we were travelling for information—moss-gathering, in fact; that we were much interested in Italian prisons; that we could not have a better opportunity of examining into their management and internal economy than by being committed to one; and that we were quite ready to go, provided that he would take the consequences. And we reminded him that we had still a British Minister at Florence. It will be seen from this that we were of that class of tourists who are a perfect pest to unhappy diplomats. We were conscious of this at the time, but reconciled ourselves to it by the reflection that a great principle was at stake. Moreover, we had a suspicion, which proved well founded, that matters would never be allowed to reach that point. Our refusal to satisfy the demands of the *facchini* completely nonplused the poor judge: he now appealed to them to moderate their claim, but this they sternly refused to do; upon which, after a few moments' sombre reflection, he thrust his hand into his pocket, and, to our intense astonishment, paid them the full amount of their extortionate charge himself. We suggested to the hotel-keeper, who had accompanied us to the court, that the dispensation of justice on these principles must be an expensive operation; but he said that, on the contrary, it simplified justice very much, for the judge always gave judgment in favour of the mob, knowing very well that, if he did not, he would be stabbed on his way home the same evening, and that few ever thought of resisting any demand which was backed by an institution then existing at Leghorn similar to the Camorra at Naples. The course we had taken had left him no other alternative but to satisfy the claim out of his own pocket.

So we gave the amount to our host, and told him at once to reimburse the unhappy functionary.

We had scarcely reached the hotel before we had the satisfaction of seeing our *facchini* friends receive a lesson which our late experiences with them enabled us keenly to appreciate. A boat approached the quay containing two young Englishmen. Not only was their nationality unmistakable, but they appeared—what they afterwards turned out to be—university men in the prime of "biceps." On the boat touching the quay, it was boarded by half-a-dozen *facchini*, each one attempting to grab something, were it only an umbrella, for which to claim payment. In vain did the travellers struggle to select two, which was more than enough for all their requirements. Each porter obstinately clung to what he had seized, and refused to part with it. One of them at last sprang on shore, followed by a young Englishman, who, finding he could not regain possession of his property, incontinently knocked his man down. This was the signal for a general assault upon the travellers, who, from the beautifully scientific way in which they handled their fists, must have been pupils of some great master in the noble art of self-defence. In less time than it takes to write it, six porters were lying in a heap on the quay: they were so taken by surprise, they had not even time to draw their knives, and so demoralised that those who were not too much stunned to do so crawled off, leaving the two travellers to carry their own baggage triumphantly into the hotel.

I think, however, it is better to be in a town which is completely in the hands of the mob, than in one which is half held by the people and half by the Government.

This happened to us at Messina. The Mole and fort at the end were held by the Neapolitan troops, but the town was in the hands of the populace. It was difficult to land except at night, because during the day even a foreign flag ran the risk of being fired upon from the Mole. However, we succeeded in doing so without mishap—though we had not been long on shore before we began to repent of our curiosity, and to wish ourselves at sea again.

We had hardly taken up our quarters at an hotel, before a Neapolitan man-of-war entered the harbour and began to bombard us—one ball entering the wall so near our window, that by making a long arm one could touch it, which illustrates the folly of going to an hotel on the quay of a town which is liable to bombardment. We found all the streets by which the enemy were likely to attempt an assault defended by sandbag batteries, in many of which cannon had been already placed. While the work of fortification was being pushed forward energetically, at one point I came upon a party of Messinese in despair at being unable to haul a gun up to a battery which had been erected on the hillside behind the town, when their difficulty was solved by a party of British tars, apparently on shore for a spree, who laid hold with a will, and in a few moments had placed the gun in position. Pushing my explorations rashly in the direction of the Mole, I heard a shot fired and a bullet whistle past me, and had just time to throw myself flat behind a low wall to escape the volley which followed. I had strayed unconsciously on to the neutral ground between the fort and the town, and had crossed unobserved an open space which intervened between the wall under which I was lying and the nearest street, which was barricaded. I had not approached the wall from this direction; but this, I observed, was the nearest shelter, and I calculated that it was at least a hundred and fifty yards back to the town— an unpleasantly long distance to run the gauntlet of a heavy fire. So I lay still for at least a quarter of an hour pondering. At the end of that time I saw a sympathetic citizen waving to me from the corner of a house where he was concealed from the fort in an opposite direction. Indeed I now perceived that I was an object of interest to a good many of the townspeople, who had discovered my unpleasant position, and were watching me from sundry safe corners. As the friendly signaller indicated that I was to keep along the wall in the opposite direction from which I had come, although it seemed to slant somewhat towards the enemy, I followed it on my hands and knees to a point where it turned off straight towards the fort: here I perceived a ditch turning towards the town, in which, by lying flat on the bottom and wriggling along snake-fashion, I thought I could escape observation. It took me a long while to accomplish this operation, and as the ditch was muddy in places, dirtied me considerably. At last I thought I was at long enough range to risk a rush across the open for the remaining distance, and this I accomplished successfully, a harmless bullet or two being sent after me by the garrison, who were not expecting my appearance in this direction, and who still supposed me crouched behind the wall. I was warmly welcomed by my rescuer, who was by this time surrounded by a small group of spectators, by whom I was accompanied back to the hotel a sort of mild hero, their interest being increased by the fact that I was a sympathetic Englishman.

We afterwards went on to Catania and Syracuse, and at the latter place were present a tthe peaceable transfer of the town from the royal to the popular authorities,—all the officials, finding further resistance hopeless, handed over their functions in the most amiable way to those appointed by the people, and the small garrison vacated their premises to the national guard without firing a shot. Indeed, wherever there were sentries posted, they were relieved with all due military ceremony by the new troops; and the royal soldiery, together with the civilians, were embarked in a transport which had been sent to convey them away. So complete was the popular success at one time throughout the kingdom, that it was difficult to believe that in a few months the country would lapse into a worse condition, if possible, than that from which it had emerged, and have to wait for another twelve years for its deliverance.

If, in presenting my moss to my readers, I am compelled to have recourse to personal narrative, it is because at this distance of time I can thereby best illustrate the political and social conditions of the country in which I happened to be at the time. Here is a little bit of Greek moss characteristic of the year 1848 in Athens. The newly constructed little country which had just before been erected into an independent monarchy, felt a ripple of the wave of revolutionary sentiment which swept over Europe in that eventful year. In order to overawe the population of the capital, King Otho had quartered in it a regiment of Mainotes—a reckless, dare-devil set of men, recruited in the most lawless province in his kingdom, imperfectly disciplined, and still more imperfectly educated in any moral code. One morning at six o'clock I went with my sketch-book to the tomb of Socrates, intending to take a sketch of the Acropolis from the neighbourhood of that lonely spot, before breakfast. I had not been above a quarter of an hour at work, when a burly figure approached me, and addressed me in Greek. I was sufficiently fresh from school to be able to make out that he asked me what o'clock it was. I looked at my watch and told him, when he put out his hand as though to take it. I instinctively sprang back; upon which he laughed, threw back his big cloak and displayed the uniform of a Mainote soldier, at the same time drawing his bayonet. He did all this with rather a good-natured air, as though not wishing to resort to violence unless it was absolutely necessary; at the same time, he stooped, picked up a rather expensive many-bladed knife, with which I had been cutting my pencil, and put it in his pocket. In the meantime I had folded my camp-stool, which was one of those used by sketchers, with a sort of walking-stick end, and which, in default of a better weapon of self-defence, I thought might be turned to account. I expected every moment to be attacked for the sake of my watch, which he told me to give up, but which I had determined to make a struggle for; on my pretending not to understand him, he stood watching me, while I put up my drawing things with as much *sang froid* as I could assume, with the view of beating a retreat. When I walked off, he walked behind me in most unpleasantly close proximity.

I did not like to take to ignominious flight for fear of precipitating matters, as I could not feel sure of outstripping him; but on the other hand, he trod so closely on my heels, that I felt a constant premonitory shiver down my back of six inches of his horrible bayonet running into it. I certainly never had a walk so full of discomfort in my life. Nor could I account for his conduct. He had got my knife, and evidently wanted my watch; then why did he not use his bayonet and take it? As I was thus unpleasantly ruminating, I perceived in the distance the king's coachman exercising a pair of his Majesty's horses in a break. I knew it from afar, for it was the only turn-out of the kind in Athens. I hesitated no longer, but started off for it at my best pace across country. I need not have been in such a hurry, for the soldier did not follow me, but continued calmly to walk towards the town. On reaching the break, I eagerly explained to the coachman, who was a German, what had happened. He told me at once to jump up beside him, and as the plain happened to be tolerably level, put his horses into a gallop across it, so as to cut off the soldier. The latter no sooner saw himself pursued than he took to his heels; but we overtook him before he could reach the town. He did not attempt to deny the theft, overawed by the royal equipage, but at once gave up his plunder.

"Now," I said to my good-natured Jehu, "let us insist upon his accompanying us to the police; the man deserves punishment."

"Rest satisfied with having got your property back," he replied. "In the first place, he would not consent to come, and I doubt whether we could make him; and in the second, it is not my business to mix myself up in such an affair."

So, to my great disgust, we let him walk off.

I then asked the coachman why he had been satisfied with taking my knife: he knew I had a watch, and if he had searched me, he would have found that I had money. I was unable to account for his forbearance.

"I will show you how to account for it," he replied,— with which enigmatical response I was obliged for the moment to be satisfied.

A few moments later we passed a piece of a ruined wall, behind which three or four soldiers were standing.

"Do you see those men?" said the coachman; "they are his comrades. They saw you go out alone to a solitary place—a thing you should never do again while you are in Athens—and they sent one of their number after you, so as to prevent your escaping them by going back some other way; but this was the place where you were to have been robbed on your return, and the plunder equally divided. The thief could not resist pocketing the knife on his own account; but he saw no reason why he should incur all the risk of committing a murder, if he could not keep all the spoil to himself afterwards."

As I felt sure I could recognise the man, I called on the British consul to consult him as to the expediency of prosecuting the matter further. But he took very much the same view of it as the king's coachman.

"If you get the man punished," he said—"which, as you are a foreigner, you will very probably be able to do —you will have to leave Athens the next day, for your life will not be safe—and the punishment will be light, for these troops are kept here for the express purpose of intimidating the population, and as soon as you are gone he will be released. If you are bent upon going to solitary spots alone, take a pistol with you: you might have shot that man, and nothing would have been said."

The present Sir Aubrey Paul, who was travelling with us at the time, and who was about my own age, was delighted when he heard of this advice.

"Let us devote ourselves," he said, "to the pleasing sport of trying to get robbed, and of shooting Mainote soldiers. We shall be conferring a benefit upon the inhabitants, and amusing ourselves." So we armed ourselves with our revolvers, and at all hours of the day and night used to prowl about in the most secluded localities, in the hope of finding sport. We were very young and silly in those days; and though we often encountered Mainote soldiers, both alone and in company, a merciful Providence deprived us of any valid excuse for shooting any of them.

But if Athens was in a lawless condition at this time, we had experiences illustrating the reverse of the picture in other parts of the country. My father chartered a native schooner at the Piræus, and had her nicely cleaned out, her hold partially filled with white sand, over which were spread carpets; in fact, we fitted her out as a yacht with such humble appliances at were at our disposal, and started for a cruise amid the Isles of Greece, our party consisting of four gentlemen and two ladies.

After the first day, however, the weather and the accommodation combined proved too much for the ladies. The cook, I remember, always would make the salad in his old straw-hat. So we put into the exquisite land-locked little harbour of Poros, the memory of which still rests upon my mind like a dream, to consider in calm water what should be done—for we men did not at all like the idea of abandoning our cruise. We had happened to cast anchor just off an extensive orange-grove; and when we landed with the ladies to explore its beauties, they became completely fascinated by the ideal charm of its position. There was a delightful wooden summer-house—in fact, almost a summer cottage, except that it had only trellis walls, over which crept heavy vines; and there was a gurgling brook of crystal water rippling past it, and wide-spreading umbrageous trees, besides oranges and lemons, and a lovely view over the Bay and the Island of Poros opposite—for this orange-garden was on the mainland.

"Can't you land us here, and leave us?" exclaimed the younger and the fairer of the ladies. "It will be quite, too awfully quite, delicious!" I don't think those were the words she used, but they would have been had she spoken seven-and-thirty years later. Ah me! she is seven-and-thirty years older now, and has gathered moss of all sorts. We had a most willing and intelligent Greek dragoman, by name Demetri—all Greek dragomans are Demetris—and he assured us that he could guarantee the safety of the ladies, if we liked to leave them under his charge. It seemed rather a rash thing to do; but that was a matter for the consideration of the person responsible for them—and he was willing to take the risk, as were the ladies themselves; so we landed them, bag and baggage. We made a beautiful bower of bliss for them under the orange-trees, with canvas and carpets and shawls, and landed mattresses and cooking utensils, and everything needful for a week's camping. Demetri, with the assistance of a boy, undertook not merely to protect them, but to procure supplies, cook for them, and wait upon them generally; and so, with a parting injunction to these deserted fair ones to betake themselves to the summer-house in case of rain, we sailed away without having seen a human being during the whole process of their installation on shore. We visited Hydra, and Poros, and Naxos, and sundry other islands, landing at quiet coves where there were no inconvenient officials to ask for our passports, and make us pay port-dues,—shooting and fishing and bathing; and so to Argos, from whence we made an excursion to Tiryns and Mycenæ; and so back to Poros, feeling rather nervous and guilty as we approached that port, and speculating upon the possible chances of mishap which might have occurred to the ladies during our week's absence. Our fears were set at rest as we neared our anchorage, and perceived a great waving of pocket-handkerchiefs; but lo! we discerned also the waving of a hat! This was the more remarkable as the Greek costume was at that time almost universal, and a stove-pipe hat did not form part of it; so we pulled ashore full of curiosity, and were introduced by the ladies to a gentleman in irreproachable Western costume—the proprietor of the garden, in fact. His residence was about two miles distant, and he had been much surprised, on visiting his garden the day after our departure, to find it occupied by two errant damsels, protected only by a dragoman. Fortunately he had spent some years of his life in civilised Europe, and had now returned to his native land with a fortune;

so he could appreciate a lady when he saw one—even in unlawful occupation of his garden. So far from resenting it, he was perfectly enchanted with an act of trespass which had provided him such guests, and he had danced attendance upon them from morning till night during all the time of our absence. He had invited them to his residence, where he had a wife and family; but was evidently so much relieved at his invitation being declined, that it is probable that he kept the whole affair a secret, as he seemed to enjoy the monopoly of his self-imposed service. The result was that the camp was supplied with every delicacy which the resources of the country could supply in the way of comestibles, and numerous articles of furniture were added to the slender stock of those we had left behind; so that, in spite of the waving of pocket-handkerchiefs, I believe our reappearance, which was to put an end to this romantic sojourn among the Greek orange-groves, was viewed with regret rather than otherwise.

CHAPTER III.

MY FIRST EXPERIENCES IN DIPLOMACY.

FROM Greece we went to Egypt, and spent a month on the Nile, finally riding across the desert to Suez by the route then supposed to have been the track of the Israelites—a theory which subsequent investigation has entirely exploded. By this time all idea of Cambridge had been given up, and I returned to Ceylon as my father's private secretary. Here I spent three years, devoting my time largely to sport as well as to law, my avocations and amusements enabling me to travel over the island pretty thoroughly. My residence here was further enlivened by the excitement incident on what was called a rebellion in the Kandyan Province—a very trumpery affair, to which I shall have occasion to refer later—and by an expedition which I made on the invitation of Jung Bahadoor, who spent a few days in Ceylon, and whom I subsequently accompanied to Nepaul. This visit into a little-known and most interesting country, and the trip through India which I afterwards made with the present Duke of Westminster, the Hon. Mr Leveson Gower, and the Hon. Captain, now Admiral Egerton, formed the subject of a book which

I published a year later in England. Meantime I had got called to the Ceylon bar, and had some curious legal experiences, not the least of which was that at the age of twenty-two I had been engaged in twenty-three murder cases. This success, and the desire I had to bring out my book, induced me to return to England for the purpose of being called to the English bar. While I was engaged in this very uninteresting operation, my journey to Nepaul was published by Murray, with such satisfactory results that I became bitten with a mania for authorship. The difficulty was to find something to write about: this I solved by deciding to go to some out-of-the-way place, and do something that nobody else had done. Unfortunately, I had only the long vacation at my disposal. The only part of Europe within reach, fulfilling the required conditions, seemed to me to be Russian Lapland, for I heard from an Archangel merchant that the Kem and other rivers in that region swarmed with guileless salmon who had never been offered a fly, and that it would be easy to cross over to Spitzbergen and get a shot at some white bears; besides, too, it appeared probable that I should come across other uncommon varieties of game. I propounded this scheme to my friend Mr Oswald Smith, who agreed to accompany me; and, well-equipped with the necessary tackle, we started one day in August 1852 for the shores of the White Sea. On our arrival at St Petersburg we found, to our dismay, that we had to deposit the whole value of our equipment in cash before we were allowed to bring our guns and rods into the country, and then only on the express condition that we should leave Russia by our port of entry. This disgusted us so much that we packed our whole sporting apparatus back to England without entering them at all, and thus found ourselves stranded in Russia, and unable to carry out the object of our journey. We therefore bent our steps southwards, visited Moscow, the great fair at Nijni Novgorod, went down the Volga, through the country of the Don Cossacks, across the Sea of Azof, and all over the Crimea, finally leaving Russia at Odessa, and returning home by way of the Danube. As it turned out, I owed the Russian authorities at St Petersburg a debt of the deepest gratitude for the journey thus forced upon us in default of a better, as the book which I wrote describing it, and especially the Crimea, appeared at the moment that war was declared by England against Russia, and a military expedition, which should have for its objective point the Tauric peninsula, had been decided upon.

Thus it happened that in the early part of the year 1854, I was startled one morning by the clattering of a mounted orderly, who reined up at the door of my modest lodging in Half-Moon Street, and impressed my worthy landlady with a notion of my importance which she had not hitherto entertained, by handing her a letter which required an immediate answer. I found it to contain a request from Lord Raglan's chief of the staff, that I should repair at once to the Horse Guards. As may be imagined, I lost no time in obeying the summons. I was ushered into a room containing a long table covered with maps, and round which were standing several officers of rank, among whom the only two that I remember, were Lord de Ros and Sir John Burgoyne. The Commander-in-Chief himself was not present. The Crimea was at that time almost a *terra incognita* in England, and travellers who had ever been actually inside the forbidden precincts of Sebastopol itself were rare.

It so happened that we had spent two or three hours within the walls of that celebrated fortress, and I was now summoned to tell the chiefs of the expedition all I knew about it. Sir John Burgoyne told me that he had just been examining a Pole, who had given him an account of the serious character of the fortifications on the land side which did not altogether tally with other information he had received, and he begged me to give him the result of my observations. I assured him that if any such fortifications on the land side existed, they must have been erected since my visit. We had entered the town from Balaclava, and I must certainly have remembered passing through them. I was therefore prepared most positively to assert that, in October 1852, there was no more impediment to an army, which should effect a landing at Balaclava, from marching into Sebastopol, than there would be for an army to march into Brighton from the downs behind it; and I felt sure that my travelling companion, Mr Oswald Smith, would, if further evidence were required, confirm this statement. At the same time, I had, without any pretension to a knowledge of military tactics, amused myself, as soon as a hostile invasion of Russia was determined upon, in forming quite another plan of campaign, which consisted in a combined attack upon the Isthmus of Perekop, by way of the Gulf of Perekop on the west and the Sea of Azof on the east. The capture of the small fort there would have cut off the whole of the Crimea, to which very few troops had yet been transported. It would have been impossible for Russia to reinforce Sebastopol, either by sea or land, and the fall of that fortress, provided that the Allies could have maintained their position at Perekop, would simply have been a question of time. We should have stood upon the defensive against Russia at a position of great natural strength, instead of on the offensive against her, at the point where, as it afterwards turned out, the genius of Todleben made her impregnable for a year.

The capture of Kertch and Theodosia would have given us command of the resources of the Crimea; and the defeat of the garrison of Sebastopol, had it ventured out to attack us, would not only have sealed the fate of that garrison, but would have given us the whole peninsula, which we should have held as a permanent guarantee; and then if Russia still refused to come to terms, we should, by leaving a sufficiently strong force to defend Perekop, have been free to transfer the scene of our operations to the Caucasus and the provinces beyond it. I ventured, after giving Sir John Burgoyne all the information in my power as to the defences of Sebastopol, the apparent strength of its garrison, and so forth, to point to Perekop as a weak spot; but, of course, could only do this with the greatest diffidence. So far as I can remember, he listened without making any remark; at all events, I soon felt so much impressed with a sense of my own presumption in volunteering a plan of campaign, that I confined myself to a mere hint of it; but I have often wondered, if the whole thing had to be done over again, whether it would be attempted the same way as before.

The immediate prospect of a war in the East had the

effect of utterly unsettling my mind, so far as my legal studies were concerned. I had determined in my first enthusiasm to come to the Scotch bar as well as the English, and was indeed ultimately called to both; but the world at large seemed such a much bigger oyster to open than my neighbour's pockets, that I never even went to the expense of buying a wig and gown, while the absurdity of perpetually paying for dinners at Lincoln's Inn that I never ate, induced me at last to disbar myself. Meantime I was extremely anxious to take part in the Crimean campaign in some capacity or other, and should have accepted an offer of the late Mr Delane to go out as 'Times' correspondent, had not Lord Clarendon kindly held out hopes that he would send me out when an opportunity offered. It was while anxiously awaiting this that Lord Elgin proposed that I should accompany him to Washington on special diplomatic service as secretary, and as the mission seemed likely to be of short duration, I gladly accepted the offer, in the hope that I might be back in time to find employment in the East before the war was over.

The mission to which I was now attached arose out of the unsatisfactory nature of the commercial relations existing between Canada and the United States, and the futile attempts, lasting over a period of seven years, which had been from time to time made to put them upon a better footing, and which finally determined the English Government to send the Earl of Elgin, then Governor-General of Canada, to Washington, with instructions to negotiate a treaty of commercial reciprocity between the two countries. Our party, on leaving England, consisted only of Lord Elgin; Mr Hincks, then Prime Minister of Canada, afterwards Sir Francis Hincks; Captain Hamilton, A.D.C.; and myself: but at New York we were joined by the Hon. Colonel Bruce, and one or two Canadians, whose advice and assistance in the commercial questions to be treated were of value.

We happened to arrive at Washington on a day which, as it afterwards turned out, was pregnant with fate to the destinies of the republic, for upon the same night the celebrated Nebraska Bill was carried in Congress, the effect of which was to open an extensive territory to slavery, and to intensify the burning question which was to find its final solution seven years later in a bloody civil war.

We found the excitement so great upon our arrival in Washington in the afternoon, that after a hurried meal we went to the Capitol to see the vote taken. I shall never forget the scene presented by the House. The galleries were crammed with spectators, largely composed of ladies, and the vacant spaces on the floor of the House crowded with visitors. The final vote was taken amid great enthusiasm, a hundred guns being fired in celebration of an event which, to those endowed with foresight, could not be called auspicious. I remember a few nights afterwards meeting a certain Senator Tombs at a large dinner given by one of the most prominent members of Congress—who has since filled the office of Secretary of State—in Lord Elgin's honour. It was a grand banquet, at which all the guests were men, with the exception of the wife of our host. He himself belonged to the Republican, or, as it was then more generally called, the Whig party. Notwithstanding the divergence of political opinion among many of those present, the merits of the all-absorbing measure, and its probable effects upon the destinies of the nation, were being discussed freely. Senator Tombs, a violent Democrat, was a large pompous man, with a tendency, not uncommon among American politicians, to "orate," rather than to converse in society. He waited for a pause in the discussion, and then, addressing Lord Elgin in stentorian tones, remarked, *apropos* of the engrossing topic—

"Yes, my lord, we are about to relume the torch of liberty upon the altar of slavery."

Upon which our hostess, with a winning smile, and in the most silvery accents imaginable, said—

"Oh, I am so glad to hear you say that again, Senator; for I told my husband you had made use of exactly the same expression to me yesterday, and he said you would not have talked such nonsense to anybody but a woman!"

The shout of laughter which greeted this sally abashed even the worthy senator, which was the more gratifying to those present, as to do so was an achievement not easily accomplished.

When the war broke out, Senator Tombs was among the fiercest and most uncompromising partisans of the South. He was one of the members of Jefferson Davis's Cabinet, and I believe only succeeded with some difficulty, at the conclusion of hostilities, in making his escape from the South. He remained to the last a prominent political figure, and only died quite recently.

It was the height of the season when we were at Washington, and our arrival imparted a new impetus to the festivities, and gave rise to the taunt, after the treaty was concluded, by those who were opposed to it, that "it had been floated through on champagne." Without altogether admitting this, there can be no doubt that, in the hands of a skilful diplomatist, that beverage is not without its value. Looking through an old journal, I find the following specimen entry:—

"*May* 26.—Luncheon at 2 P.M. at Senator F.'s. Sat between a Whig and a Democrat senator, who alternately poured abolitionism and the divine origin of slavery into the ear they commanded. I am getting perfectly stunned with harangues upon political questions I don't understand, and confused with the nomenclature appropriate to each. Besides Whigs and Democrats, there are Hard Shells and Soft Shells, and Free-Soilers, and Disunionists, and Federals, to say nothing of filibusters, pollywogs, and a host of other nicknames. One of my neighbours, discoursing on one of these varied issues, told me that he went the whole hog. He was the least favourable specimen of a senator I have seen, and I felt inclined to tell him that he looked the animal he went, but smiled appreciatively instead. There were, however, some interesting men present,—among them Colonel Fremont, a spare wiry man with a keen grey eye, and a face expressing great determination, but most sympathetic withal; and a senator from Washington Territory, which involves a journey of seventy days each way; and another from Florida, who, from his account of the country, represents principally alligators; and Colonel Benton, who is writing a great work, and is 'quite a fine man'; and the Governor of Wisconsin, whose State has increased in population in ten years from 30,000 to 500,000, and who told me that he 'met a man the other day who had travelled over the whole globe, and examined it narrowly with an eye to its agricultural capabilities, and who therefore was an authority not to be disputed; and this man had positively asserted that he had never in any country seen fifty square miles to equal that extent in the State of Wisconsin—and therefore it was quite clear that no spot equal to it was to be found in creation.' As various other patriots have informed me that their respective States are each thus singularly favoured, I am beginning to feel puzzled as to which really is the most fertile spot on the face of the habitable globe. After two hours and a half of this style of conversation, abundantly irrigated with champagne, it was a relief to go to a *matinée dansante* at the French Minister's."

Here follow remarks upon the *belles* of that period at Washington, which, though they are for the most part complimentary, are not to the purpose, more especially as they were the result of a crude and youthful, and not of a matured judgment.

"Got away from the French Minister's just in time to dress for dinner at the President's. More senators and politics, and champagne, and Hard Shells and Soft Shells. I much prefer the marine soft-shell crab, with which I here made acquaintance for the first time, to the political one. Then with a select party of senators, all of whom were opposed in principle to the treaty, to Governor A.'s, where we imbibed more champagne and swore eternal friendship, carefully avoided the burning question, and listened to stories good, bad, and indifferent, till 2 A.M., when, after twelve hours of incessant entertainment, we went home to bed thoroughly exhausted."

Meantime, to my inexperienced mind no progress was being made in our mission. Lord Elgin had announced its object on his arrival to the President and the Secretary of State, and had been informed by them that it was quite hopeless to think that any such treaty as he proposed could be carried through, with the opposition which existed to it on the part of the Democrats, who had a majority in the Senate, without the ratification of which body no treaty could be concluded. His lordship was further assured, however, that if he could overcome this opposition, he would find no difficulties on the part of the Government. At last, after several days of uninterrupted festivity, I began to perceive what we were driving at. To make quite sure, I said one day to my chief—

"I find all my most intimate friends are Democratic senators."

"So do I," he replied, drily: and indeed his popularity among them at the end of a week had become unbounded; and the best evidence of it was that they ceased to feel any restraint in his company, and often exhibited traits of Western manners unhampered by conventional trammels. Lord Elgin's faculty of brilliant repartee and racy anecdote especially delighted them; and one evening, after a grand dinner, he was persuaded to accompany a group of senators, among whom I remember Senator Mason—afterwards of Mason and Slidell notoriety—and Senator Tombs figured, to the house of a popular and very influential politician, there to prolong the entertainment into the small hours. Our host, at whose door we knocked at midnight, was in bed; but much thundering at it at length roused him, and he himself opened to us, appearing in nothing but a very short night-shirt.

"All right, boys," he said, at once divining the object of our visit; "you go in, and I'll go down and get the drink;" and without stopping to array himself more completely, he disappeared into the nether regions, shortly returning with his arms filled with bottles of champagne, on the top of which were two huge lumps of ice. These he left with us to deal with, while he retired to clothe the nether portion of his person. He was a dear old gentleman, somewhat of the Lincoln type, and had the merit of being quite sober, which some of the others of the party were not, and though thus roughly roused from his first sleep, expressed himself highly delighted with our visit. He was, moreover, evidently a great character, and many were the anecdotes told about him in his own presence, all bearing testimony to his goodness of heart and readiness of wit. At last one of the party, in a fit of exuberant enthusiasm and excessive champagne, burst out—

"As for our dear old friend the Governor here, I tell you, Lord El*gine*,"—the accent was frequently laid on the last syllable, and the *g* in Elgin pronounced soft,—"he is a perfect king in his own country. There ain't a man in Mussoorie dar say a word against him; if any of your darned English lords was to go down there and dar to, he'd tell them——" here followed an expression which propriety compels me to omit, and which completely scandalised our worthy host.

"That's a lie," he said, turning on his guest, but without changing his voice, as he slowly rolled his quid of tobacco from one cheek to the other. "I can blaspheme, and profane, and rip, and snort with any man; but I never make use of a vulgar expression."

The impoliteness of the allusion to the British aris-tocracy, in Lord Elgin's presence, which called forth this strong asseveration on the part of the Governor, also evoked many profuse apologies from some of the others present, who maintained that, if all English lords were like him, and would become naturalised Americans, they would "run the country"; and that, so far as he was individually concerned, it was a thousand pities he had not been born an American, and thus been eligible for the Presidency. Certainly it would not have been difficult to be more eligible for that high office than the respectable gentleman who then filled it. Of all Presidents, I suppose none were more insignificant than Mr Pierce, who was occupying the White House at the time of our visit; while in his Secretary of State, Mr Marcy, we found a genial and somewhat comical old gentleman, whose popularity with his countrymen seemed chiefly to rest on the fact that he had once charged the United States Government fifty cents "for repairing his breeches," when sent on a mission to inquire into certain accounts in which great irregularities were reported to have taken place.

Thirty-two years have doubtless worked a great change in Washington society, as indeed it has upon the nation generally, and more especially upon the eastern cities, since I first knew them. Then, Washington, "the city of magnificent distances," struck me as a howling wilderness of deserted streets running out into the country, and ending nowhere, its population consisting chiefly of politicians and negroes. Now, it is developing rather into a city of palaces, and becoming a fashionable centre during the winter for the *élite* of society, from all parts of the United States. Its population is growing rapidly under the new impetus thus received, and it will in all probability ultimately become the handsomest and most agreeable place of residence in the country. At the time of our visit Sir Philip Crampton was British Minister at Washington, and under his hospitable roof I remember meeting Lincoln, and being struck by his gaunt figure, and his quaint and original mode of expression.

I cannot convey a better idea of the effect produced upon society by our festive proceedings at Washington than by quoting the following extract from a paper at the time describing the ball given by Sir Philip Crampton in honour of the Queen's birthday:—

"As for the ladies present, our pen fairly falters in the attempt to do justice to their charms. Our artists and *modistes* had racked their brains, and exhausted their magazines of dainty and costly fabrics, in order to convince the world in general, and the English people in particular, that the sovereign fair ones of Washington regarded their sister sovereign of England with feelings, not only of 'the most distinguished consideration,' but of downright love, admiration, and respect,— *love*, for the woman—*admiration*, for the wife of the handsomest man in Europe—and *respect*, for the mother of nine babies. More was accomplished last evening in the way of negotiation than has been accomplished from the days of Ashburton to the advent of Elgin. We regard the fishery question as settled, both parties having partaken freely of the bait so liberally provided by the noble host.

"Amid the soft footfalls of fairy feet — the glittering of jewels — the graceful sweep of $500 dresses — the sparkling of eyes which shot forth alternately flashes of lightning and love — there were two gentlemen who appeared to be the 'observed of all observers.' One was the Earl of Elgin, and the other Sir Charles Gray. Lord Elgin is a short, stout gentleman, on the shady side of forty, and is decidedly John Bullish in walk, talk, appearance, and carriage. His face, although round and full, beams with intellect, good feeling, and good-humour. His manners are open, frank, and winning. Sir Charles Gray is a much larger man than his noble countryman, being both taller and stouter. He is about sixty years of age, and his manners are particularly grave and dignified.

"The large and brilliant company broke up at a late hour, and departed for their respective homes,—pleased with their courtly and courteous host; pleased with the monarchical form of government in England; pleased with the republican form of government in the United States; pleased with each other, themselves, and the rest of mankind."

At last, after we had been receiving the hospitalities at Washington for about ten days, Lord Elgin announced to Mr Marcy, that if the Government were prepared to adhere to their promise to conclude a treaty of reciprocity with Canada, he could assure the President that he would find a majority of the Senate in its favour, including several prominent Democrats. Mr Marcy could scarcely believe his ears, and was so much taken aback that I somewhat doubted the desire to make the treaty, which he so strongly expressed on the occasion of Lord Elgin's first interview with him, when he also pronounced it hopeless. However, steps had been taken which made it impossible for him to doubt that the necessary majority had been secured, and nothing remained for us but to go into the details of the tariff, the enumeration of the articles of commerce, and so forth. A thorny question was intimately associated with the discussion of this treaty, which was settled by it for the time; and this was the question of the fisheries off the coasts of British North America, claimed by American fishermen. This vexed subject, which was reopened by the abrogation of the treaty, has recently been the matter of protracted negotiation between the English and American Governments; which, however, has proved so imperfect that serious disputes are daily arising, which it will require all the tact and forbearance of the English and American Governments to arrange amicably.

For the next three days I was as busily engaged in work as I had been for the previous ten at play; but the matter had to be put through with a rush, as Lord Elgin was due at the seat of his Government. And, perhaps, under the circumstances, we succeeded better so than had longer time been allowed the other side for reflection. As it was, the worthy old Secretary of State was completely taken by surprise. I will venture to quote the description I wrote at the time of the signing of the treaty, and ask the reader to make allowance for the style of mock heroics, and attribute it to the exuberance of youth:

"It was in the dead of night, during the last five minutes of the 5th of June, and the first five minutes of the 6th of the month aforesaid, that four individuals might have been observed seated in a spacious chamber lighted by six wax candles and an Argand lamp. Their faces were expressive of deep and earnest thought, not unmixed with suspicion. Their feelings, however, to the acute observer, manifested themselves in different ways;

but this was natural, as two were in the bloom of youth, one in the sear and yellow leaf, and one in the prime of middle age. This last it is whose measured tones alone break the silence of midnight, except when one or other of the younger auditors, who are both poring intently over voluminous MSS., interrupts him to interpolate an 'and' or erase a "the.' They are, in fact, checking him as he reads; and the aged man listens, while he picks his teeth with a pair of scissors, or cleans out the wick of a candle with their points, which he afterwards wipes on his grey hair. He may occasionally be observed to wink, either from conscious 'cuteness or unconscious drowsiness. Presently the clock strikes twelve, and there is a doubt whether the date should be to-day or yesterday. There is a moment of solemn silence, when the reader, having finished the document, lays it down, and takes a pen which had been previously impressively dipped in the ink by the most intelligent-looking of the young men, who appears to be his 'secretary,' and who keeps his eye warily fixed upon the other young man, who occupies the same relation to the aged listener with the scissors.

"There is something strangely mysterious and suggestive in the scratching of that midnight pen, for it may be scratching fortunes or ruin to toiling millions. Then the venerable statesman takes up the pen to append his signature. His hand does not shake, though he is very old, and knows the abuse that is in store for him from members of Congress and an enlightened press. That hand, it is said, is not all unused to a revolver; and it does not now waver, though the word he traces may be an involver of a revolver again. He is now Secretary of

State; before that, he was a judge of the Supreme Court; before that, a general in the army; before that, governor of a State; before that, Secretary of War; before that, minister in Mexico; before that, a member of the House of Representatives; before that, a politician; before that, a cabinet-maker. He ends, as he began, with cabinet-work; and he is not, at his time of life and with his varied experiences, afraid either of the wrath of his countrymen or the wiles of an English lord. So he gives us his blessing and the treaty duly signed; and I retire to dream of its contents, and to listen in my troubled sleep to the perpetually recurring refrain of the three impressive words with which the pregnant document concludes—'Unmanufactured tobacco. Rags!'"

Thus was concluded in exactly a fortnight a treaty, to negotiate which had taxed the inventive genius of the Foreign Office and all the conventional methods of diplomacy for the previous seven years, and which, as it has since proved, has been of enormous commercial advantage to the two countries to which it was to be applied. A reference to figures will furnish the most satisfactory evidence on this point.

In 1853, the year prior to our mission to Washington, the trade of Canada with the United States amounted to $20,000,000, as recently given from correct data, by the 'Toronto Mail.' In 1854 the treaty commenced to operate, and the volume of trade at once increased to $33,000,000. In 1855, it was $42,000,000; in 1857, $46,000,000; in 1859, $48,000,000; in 1863, $55,000,000; in 1864, $67,000,000; in 1865, $71,000,000; and in 1866, the year the treaty was abrogated by the action of the

American Government, it had reached the high figure of $84,000,000. It had thus nearly quadrupled in the course of twelve years under the action of the treaty, which the Americans erroneously believed to be so much more to the advantage of the Canadians than of themselves, that they seized the earliest available opportunity, after the term fixed for its expiry, to abrogate it,—a measure dictated, I fear, rather by sentiments of jealousy than of political economy, and from which the States suffer certainly as much if not more than Canada, whose trade with the mother country has latterly undergone considerable development in consequence.

The brilliant and dashing manner in which Lord Elgin achieved this remarkable diplomatic triumph, apparently certain of his game from the first, playing it throughout with the easy confidence of assured success, made a profound impression upon me—an impression which I had no reason to modify throughout a subsequent intimate association with him of three years in two hemispheres—during which he was nearly all the time engaged in confronting difficulties and overcoming obstacles which I used to think to any other man would have seemed insurmountable. As one by one they melted before his subtle touch, my confidence in his profound sagacity and his undaunted moral courage became unbounded; and I could enter into the feelings of soldiers whose general never led them to anything but victory. It was both a pleasure and a profit to serve such a man; a pleasure, because he was the kindest and most considerate of chiefs—a profit, because one could learn so much by watching his methods, which indeed he was always ready to discuss and explain to those who occupied confidential relations towards him. By his premature death the country lost one of its most conscientious and ablest public servants— one whose services, and whose great capacity for rendering them, have never received their just recognition at the hands of his countrymen.

Our progress from New York to Canada was triumphal. On our arrival by a special train at Portland, Maine, we were received with the thunder of salutes, and went in procession to the house of one of the leading citizens, with bands of music, and flags, and escorts, mounted and on foot, the whole of the gallant militia having turned out to do Lord Elgin honour. A characteristic incident occurred prior to our starting for a banquet at the city hall. While we were assembled in the drawing-room of our host, a tray with various kinds of wines and spirits was brought in, and our hospitable entertainer remarked—

"You'll have to take your liquor in here, gentlemen; for I guess you'll get none where we're going to. We've got a liquor law in Maine, you know," he added, with a sly look at the tray.

Drinking all you want before dinner is not a satisfactory way of "taking it in." However, we made the best of it, and soon found ourselves seated at a table plentifully supplied with tumblers of water, at which were two hundred guests. I am bound to say, considering the absence of stimulants, there was no lack of noise and merriment; and when dinner was over, speeches followed in rapid succession, in response to toasts and sentiments. Lord Elgin was *facile princeps* in this respect, and his speeches provoked enthusiastic applause. He brought down the house by a retort upon one of the speakers whose good taste was not equal to his patriotism, and who took the opportunity of comparing the position and functions of the governor of a State with those of the Governor-General of Canada, much to the disparagement of the latter. Alluding in one of his speeches to the uncomplimentary parallel thus drawn, Lord Elgin said he would, narrate an anecdote. In the course of his travels in the United States he had one day found himself next a stage-driver, with whom he entered into conversation as to the political parties in the States. The driver informed him that the majority in the State was Whig, but that the governor of it was a Democrat.

"How comes that about, if the majority are Whigs?" inquired Lord Elgin.

"Oh," replied the driver, "we traded the governor off against the land agent."

"Now, gentlemen," pursued his lordship, amid loud laughter, "you could not trade the Governor-General of Canada off against any land agent."

All the way from the Canadian frontier to Montreal arches were erected, addresses presented, and all the paraphernalia of a triumphal progress exhibited. British troops lined the streets of Montreal, and a large procession attended the party to the hotel; we did not linger here, however, but pushed on without delay to the seat of Government.

CHAPTER IV.

POLITICS AND INDIAN AFFAIRS IN CANADA.

I DO not remember ever having been more vividly impressed by the beauties of nature than on that lovely spring morning, when, in order to avoid any more demonstrations, we landed unostentatiously from the steamer in which we had descended the St Lawrence, at the foot of the beautiful grounds which encircle Spencerwood, then the residence of the Governor-General. Although it was the 11th of June, the trees were still in their spring garb of tender green; there was a delicious stillness in the air, and a peculiar clearness and brilliancy in the light with which the landscape was flooded, which enhanced its own rare beauty; and as I now knew that I was to be a dweller here for some months, I was enchanted by the sort of fairyland that was to be my future residence. For within the last twenty-four hours a new prospect had dawned upon me. Although our Washington treaty was completed, I was not, as I had originally anticipated, to return at once to England, after accompanying Lord Elgin to Canada, but to enter upon new functions for which I was altogether unprepared. The exigencies of the service compelled Lord Elgin's brother, Colonel Bruce, who had hitherto filled the office of Civil Secretary of Canada and Superintendent-General of Indian Affairs, to join his regiment in the Crimea, and I was appointed to succeed him. The department of Indian Affairs was then under imperial control. It has, since confederation, been handed over to the Dominion.

The novelty of the functions I was now called upon suddenly to assume, invested my new position with great interest. I soon began to realise this by the style of the correspondence which poured in upon me. First came a letter to the Queen from an Indian tribe, expressing to their "Great Mother across the Big Lake" their sympathy with the war in the Crimea, and the desire of the warriors to participate in it; and another addressed to myself, in which the "red skins" write to their "great brother who lives towards the sunrising, to express their confidence in his administrative talents, which alone reconciles them to the loss of their good brother [Colonel Bruce], who is now upon the war-path." The colonel's paternal administration had rendered him very popular. No doubt his being a "warrior" by profession was also a point in his favour; and I feared that they would consider me little better than a "squaw," while their confidence in my administrative talents had about as solid a basis of knowledge as their sympathy with the objects for which the Crimean war was undertaken. The important political events which transpired immediately on our arrival at Canada, obliged me, however, to suppress for the present the desire which began to consume me to make a closer acquaintance with my red brothers, to visit the industrial schools which my predecessor had established, and to smoke the "calumet of peace" with them in their wigwams.

Lord Elgin's first act upon arriving at Quebec was to open Parliament in state. The number of British troops in those days quartered in Quebec rendered this a very imposing ceremony, as the streets were lined with them. The striking feature in the procession was the state carriage, in which I accompanied the Governor-General to the House, and the panels of which were gaping with cracks and splits, inflicted upon them by the mob of Montreal on the occasion when they stoned his Excellency some years before, and burned down the Parliament Houses. The carriage had never been repaired since that event, in order that it might serve to remind the populace of the measure to which they had resorted in order to give vent to their feelings. Until that time the party in power had been the Tories, or loyalists, who found themselves in a minority on the occasion of the passing of the Rebellion Losses Bill, and who expressed their indignation on being turned out of office to make way for those who commanded the parliamentary majority, by these acts of violence. They had been out of office for about six years, during which time the leaders of the party had resented the constitutional conduct of the Governor-General so keenly, that many of them had ever since refused to set foot in Government House, and even neglected to salute his Excellency in the street. It was only as the result of the somewhat exciting events upon which we were now entering, that they finally came to understand that Lord Elgin did not allow himself to be influenced by personal sympathies, and was determined to give effect to a parliamentary majority, of whomsoever it might be composed. After several days' debate the Government was beaten on an amendment to the address, and Ministers determined to go to the country. Lord Elgin came down a week after he had opened the House to prorogue it, when a somewhat exciting episode occurred. When the Commons were sent for, they refused to come. The pause was in the highest degree embarrassing. The Legislative Chamber, filled with an audience *en grande tenue*—Lord Elgin seated on the throne—a silence, broken only by a whispering and tittering, which did not add to the dignity of the situation,—all contributed to form a unique political situation. At last, after the lapse of nearly half an hour, the Speaker of the Lower House, who had been engaged drawing up a protest against the course which was being adopted, appeared, supported by a large body of members, and read it—a proceeding which the Governor-General promptly met by declaring the House dissolved; and for the next few days a state of feverish excitement pervaded political circles, the Opposition declaring the whole course of proceeding to be unconstitutional, and the local Opposition press teeming with abusive articles denouncing a tyranny which had deprived them of their liberties.

Altogether the month had been in the highest degree exciting and eventful; for in the short space of four weeks, Lord Elgin had negotiated and signed a treaty with the American Government, made a triumphal progress from Boston to Quebec, opened the Canadian Parliament, prorogued and dissolved it. But though the difficulty had been overcome, so far as any opposition to the treaty at

Washington was concerned, it had still to receive the assent of all the Colonial Legislatures. In Nova Scotia especially it was unpopular, owing to the fishery clauses; and it required the exercise of all the authority and tact of the Governor-General to force the adoption of a measure to which, as it afterwards turned out, that colony owed a greater degree of prosperity than it has ever enjoyed before or since. In 1869, or four years after the Reciprocity Treaty of 1854 was abrogated, the 'Halifax' remarks:—

"From the making of the Reciprocity Treaty until its abrogation, Nova Scotia increased in wealth and population at a most extraordinary rate. From its abrogation until the present, we have retrograded with the most frightful rapidity. Want of a good market has depreciated the value of our coal-mines—has nearly pauperised our fishermen, farmers, and miners; and should this want not be supplied in the only way it can be, by a new treaty with the United States, Nova Scotia will in five years be one of the least desirable countries to live in on this continent."

This quotation affords an interesting illustration of the incompetence of the popular judgment to arrive at accurate conclusions in matters affecting the public interests; for I can bear personal testimony to the furious opposition which the treaty encountered from all classes in the province, from the Lieutenant-Governor downwards, at the time it was proposed, and of the conviction generally entertained that it would prove the ruin of the colony. Under these circumstances the final result was satisfactory beyond our most sanguine expectations, as may be gathered from the fact that the treaty ultimately passed through the Congress of the United States, and through the Colonial Legislatures of Canada, New Brunswick, Nova Scotia, Prince Edward Island, and Newfoundland, with a total of only twenty-one dissentient votes. Had Canada then been confederated, as it was fourteen years later, the task would have been much easier. Unfortunately the reaction predicted in the Nova Scotia newspaper has occurred in that province, and the decline in its prosperity is attributed to confederation. It is really due to the unsatisfactory state of our relations with the United States on the subject of the fisheries; and if those were placed upon a sound footing, the outcry against confederation which has recently been raised in Nova Scotia would soon die away. What is needed in Canada is an imperial officer, who might still be called Civil Secretary, and be attached to the Governor-General's staff, and whose functions should be partly political and partly diplomatic. At present, when delicate questions arise between the confederated provinces, involving a special mission and local treatment, the settlement has necessarily to be intrusted to an agent appointed by the Dominion Government— which means an agent of the political party then in power; and whatever arrangement he may make is certain to be objected to by the Opposition.

This consequence of party government is unfortunately not confined to Canada, and receives daily lamentable illustrations in our own political performances at home. So, in questions arising between Canada and the United States, our Minister at Washington is necessarily guided by the information and advice of the Canadian politicians sent to assist him. And as whatever they do must be wrong, in the opinion of the other side, the result is sure to be severely and unfairly criticised. Whereas, if negotiations of this character, whether as between the provinces or with the United States Government, were intrusted to an imperial officer thoroughly conversant with the questions at issue, outside of all local politics, and who could not be suspected of being influenced by them, they would meet with far less opposition on the part of local politicians, and be arranged on a broader and more satisfactory basis. Had such an officer existed, it is probable that neither the British Columbia nor the North-West questions would have assumed the proportions they did; that Newfoundland would ere this have been included in the confederation; that the discontent now existing in Nova Scotia might have been appeased; and that the fishery and other questions which are still outstanding with the United States would have obtained a satisfactory solution. I received assurances from leading members of the Dominion Government only a few years ago, that so far from being opposed to the idea of availing themselves of the good offices of an imperial functionary of this kind, they would even be prepared to contribute to his salary, which could be added to from funds drawn from the Foreign and Colonial Offices at home. The amount required would be very small, and would simply constitute an increase on the present salary of the Governor's secretary, whose position would naturally qualify him for the exercise of these functions. In these days, when the idea of imperial federation has assumed such prominence, such appointments, calculated rather to soothe than to wound sensibilities, would form additional *traits d'union* between the mother country and her dependencies.

The excitement into which the whole country was thrown by a Ministerial defeat, and a general election so unexpected, created a social and political lull in Quebec itself, which I was thankful to avail myself of, in order to pay a round of visits to my "red children." This duty was eminently to my taste; it involved diving into the depths of the backwoods, bark-canoeing on distant and silent lakes or down foaming rivers, where the fishing was splendid, the scenery most romantic, and camp-life at this season of the year—for it was now the height of summer —most enjoyable. It was a prolonged picnic, with just enough duty thrown in to deprive it of any character of selfishness. There were schools to inspect, councils to be held, tribal disputes to be adjusted, presents to be distributed, and, in one case, a treaty to be made. At nearly all the stations there was a school or mission-house of some kind, and here the meeting of the "warriors" and the "young braves" with their "father" took place; and as I had barely attained the age of five-and-twenty when these paternal responsibilities were thrust upon me, the incongruity of my relation towards them, I am afraid, presented itself somewhat forcibly to the minds of the veterans on these occasions. It was a novel and exhilarating experience to paddle up in a sort of rude state at the head of a train of canoes, and to be received by volleys from rifles and fowling-pieces by way of a salute from all the members of the tribe collected on the margin of the lake or river, as the case might be, to receive me. Then they would form in line and file past me, every man, woman, and child shaking hands as they did so, and in solemn procession escort me up to the place of meeting,—

when, if it was a chapel, I mounted into the pulpit, and solemnly lighting a pipe, waited till my audience were all seated on their heels and had lighted theirs, before entering upon the business of the hour. This generally terminated in a lecture upon temperance and industry; for their love of spirituous liquors and their inveterate indolence are the curse of these poor people, and render them an easy prey to the more unscrupulous class of white settlers, who systematically carry on a process of demoralisation, with the view to their extermination, a result which is being rapidly achieved. I do not know whether my efforts to convince them that they were themselves their own worst enemies, procured for me the name of Pah Dah Sung, or "The Coming Sun"—possibly from the light I was expected to throw upon the subject.

My two most interesting experiences in connection with my brief administration of Indian affairs in Canada, were the distribution of annual presents upon the island of Manitoulin, and a treaty which I succeeded in negotiating with a tribe which owned an extensive tract of territory upon the shores of Lake Huron. Manitoulin, which is over a hundred miles in length, is said to be the largest fresh-water island in the world, and was destined by a former Governor-General of Canada—Sir Francis Bond Head—as an eligible territory on which to make the experiment of collecting Indians, with a view to their permanent settlement and civilisation. It has not succeeded, however, and at the time of my visit was the rendezvous of thousands of Indians belonging to many different tribes, who, with their whole families, congregated here to receive blankets, agricultural implements, and other presents which it was hoped would conduce to their welfare. These, correctly speaking, were not presents, as they were purchased from funds in the hands of the Indian Department, whose principal function it was to invest the large sums of money which had accrued to the Indians from the sale of their land to white settlers, and to apply the interest to their advantage. The collection of birch-bark wigwams which surrounded the little harbour where I landed looked like a huge camp, and in these were huddled a swarm of dirty occupants, some of them having travelled hither from a great distance, miserably clad in frousy blankets and skins. Here and there were fine-looking picturesque figures, more gaudily decorated with paints and feathers; but, taking them as a whole, I know of no nomads—and I have seen Calmuck Tartars, Kirghiez, Bedouins, and gipsies—who presented a more poverty-stricken and degraded appearance than did the majority of my red children! I was the more disappointed with them in their savage state, because I expected an improvement upon their semi-civilised brethren, with whom I had hitherto come in contact. I believe the annual congregation of Indians on this island, and distribution of presents among them, has been discontinued by the Dominion Government.

The occupation by the Indians of large tracts of country eligible for settlement by whites, which they reserve as hunting-grounds, from which they got nothing but a few foxes and musk-rats, was a fruitful source of trouble to the Department, as settlers were constantly unlawfully squatting upon them, who had to be driven off. The largest and only remaining one of these in the immediate vicinity of a thickly settled district, was called the Saugeen Peninsula, a promontory extending into Lake Huron, and containing about half a million of acres of fine land. I determined to try and induce the tribe to which this extensive tract belonged, and who practically derived no revenue from it, to make a cession of it to the Government for the purpose of having it sold in lots to white settlers, the whole of the proceeds to belong to the tribe, which would thus become one of the wealthiest in the country. In order to do this, it was necessary to undertake an expedition to a remote, and, in those days, very inaccessible spot. My journey involved sundry adventures by flood and fell, for I was nearly wrecked in a small boat coasting along the shore of Lake Huron, and lost in a swamp while endeavouring to follow the Indian trail through the forest, where sometimes we only had the "blaze"—or places where the trees had been scored with an axe—to guide us.

On my arrival at my destination, I found all the males of the tribe collected in a chapel where a native catechist acted as interpreter, the tribe being a branch of the Chippeways. In order not to lose time, the meeting was convened for 7 P.M., on the evening of my arrival. As usual I opened the proceedings with a pipe and a speech from the pulpit, the twelve elders of the tribe sitting immediately below me on the ground, each with his pipe, and forming the front row of a crowd of squatting men, all smoking. My address was frequently interrupted by what Fenimore Cooper calls "expressive ughs"; and the grunts and murmurs of the audience, expressive of their disagreement with my proposal, were not encouraging.

A pause of at least ten minutes ensued after I had finished, during which they all smoked vigorously. Then their principal chief rose, and in an energetic speech set forth his objections, which were received with grunts of approval by the majority. Then another chief rose, who seemed to be a man of some weight, and delivered himself forcibly in the opposite sense. In the course of his remarks he made some observations apparently of a character uncomplimentary to the previous speaker, for a fierce wrangle ensued, in which many took part, and in which, when I came to understand it, I occasionally joined, adding, by the advice of the catechist, fuel to the fire. When the atmosphere had become sufficiently stormy,—it was already so smoky that I could not see across the room, but perhaps that was partly owing to its being illuminated only by a couple of tallow-dips,—I, again by the advice of my interpreter, retired, "to let them fight it out," which, as he afterwards assured me, they did literally with their fists. As he believed himself to be pecuniarily interested, he remained to take part in the *mêlée*—a course of proceeding which I left him to reconcile with his own conscience as a religious teacher. I reconciled it to mine by the fact that my efforts were being directed entirely in the interests of the Indians themselves, which they were too stupid to understand.

It was past midnight when the catechist summoned me from the little outhouse in which I had been waiting, with the welcome intelligence that all the difficulties had been overcome, and that the chiefs expressed themselves ready to consent to the proposed arrangement. It seemed to be my fate, while in America, to assist at the signing of midnight treaties; but on this occasion the scene was infinitely more novel and picturesque than on the previous one. Round a table below the pulpit, which was covered with papers and maps, crowded a wild-looking group of Indians, in blankets and leggings and mocassins, with their bare arms and long straight black hair. Twelve of these placed their totems opposite my signature, each totem consisting of the rude representation of a bear, a deer, an otter, a rat, or some other wild animal.

It was one o'clock in the morning before I set out with a light heart, for I had the treaty in my pocket, on a two-mile tramp through the forest in pitchy darkness to the rude tavern at Southampton, then the extreme outpost of civilisation, which did duty for a lodging; but it was not to find rest. The Indians all followed me; and my host, in anticipation of my triumphant return, had exhausted the resources of the place in preparing a grand meal for me, to which we—Indians and all, with a sprinkling of whites attracted by the excitement of the event—sat down at 4 A.M. The Indians, so lately at loggerheads, now became reconciled over copious libations of whisky, under the influence of which there was a general fraternisation with the whites as well, who were in high spirits at the prospect of so much new territory being opened up to settlement, and who offered to give me a banquet if I would only prolong my stay a day; but on my declining this, the whole crowd, red and white, when day broke, accompanied me to the river, and gave me three cheers as I ferried across it on my return journey.

By means of the revenue derived from this cession of Indian territory, I was enabled to reorganise the whole financial system of the Indian Department, and to effect a clear saving to the imperial exchequer of £13,000 a-year, —an economy with which Lord Taunton, then Colonial Minister, expressed himself so well satisfied, that he was kind enough to offer me a small lieutenant-governorship in the West Indies, which I should have gratefully accepted had it not been for my preference for diplomatic work, and desire to go to the seat of war in the Crimea.

The most distant Indian settlement I visited was in the immediate neighbourhood of Lake Superior. Finding myself so far west, I determined to return by a very roundabout way, for the purpose of seeing some of the country to the west of the lake. My companions were Lord Bury, who had been for some time previously Lord Elgin's guest at Quebec, and Messrs Petre and Clifford, whom we met on Lake Superior, and with whom we made a bark-canoe voyage from the western end of the lake to the head-waters of the Mississippi, coming down that river to Dubuque, from which place we crossed the prairies of Illinois to Chicago, then a rising young city of 75,000 inhabitants, and so by way of Niagara back to Quebec,—a trip which afforded me material for a book at the time,[1] and which is interesting now to look back upon as furnishing the recollection of a country in which the Indian and the buffalo still roamed, where the scream of the locomotive was then unheard, and where not an acre of land was taken up by a white settler. It is now a thickly peopled region, from which Indians and buffaloes have alike retired, and where the traveller, instead of poling up

---

[1] Minnesota and the Far West. By Laurence Oliphant. William Blackwood & Sons: 1855.

a river in a bark-canoe can fly across the country by train, and look forward at night to a comfortable hotel, instead of the turf for a bed, and a lean-to of pine-branches for a shelter.

In view of the future which I saw for the country, I bought a town lot at the city of Superior, which then consisted of one log-shanty and a tent, and to find which I had to wade up to my knees in water, and cut my way to it with a billhook. The city of Superior rose at one time to contain about 1200 inhabitants; then was victimised by a political intrigue, and, to use the expressive phrase of a citizen, "bust up flat," so that the cottage which I had built upon my lot, and which, had I been wise enough to sell it at one moment, would have realised a handsome profit, became worthless, and I had to sell the doors and windows to pay the taxes, for the place was deserted. Five years ago a slow upward movement commenced, and I accepted an offer which exactly covered the money expended upon it during the previous five-and-twenty years. Since then, I believe it has come under the influence of what is called "a boom," and the purchaser is in possession of a property which will yield him a large return. Such are the ups and downs of western towns, and of people who speculate in them.

The Canadian elections had been completed during my absence from Quebec, and Lord Elgin opened the new Parliament a few days after my return. I found that I arrived just in time for another political crisis, as the elections had resulted unfavourably for the Government. The two great questions which it was Lord Elgin's great ambition to settle before closing his term of office, were the abolition of Seigneurial Tenure and the Secularisation of the Clergy Reserves, which, in his speech from the Throne, he recommended to the attention of the House. To the settlement of both these questions in the popular sense, the Opposition, or Tory party, had been vigorously opposed. When, therefore, the Government was beaten on the election of the Speaker, the fate of these measures seemed somewhat critical. I was fortunately situated for watching the progress of the parliamentary proceedings, and the crisis resulting therefrom. By virtue of my office, I had a seat on the floor of the House, without, however, the right of voting or of speaking, except to offer explanations in the event of any question affecting the Indians coming up. I was thus present at all the debates, and on excellent terms with the leaders of both parliamentary parties. In fact I had practically all the fun of being a member of the House without any of the responsibilities, and after the vote on the Speaker was taken, had sundry confidential meetings in the small hours of the morning with the prominent men on both sides, the result of which was, that I could not resist, in my excitement, waking the Governor-General up at 5 A.M. to inform him of the defeat of the Government, and what I had learned since. The day following, the Prime Minister placed his resignation in his Excellency's hands; and to the great astonishment of the public, as well as to his own, Sir Allan M'Nab, who had been one of his bitterest opponents ever since the Montreal events, was sent for to form a Ministry—Lord Elgin by this act satisfactorily disproving the charge of having either personal or political partialities in the selection of his Ministers. After some little delay, Sir Allan succeeded in forming a Coalition Ministry, which adopted the address of their predecessors *in toto*, and thus committed themselves to passing the two important measures alluded to in it, in exactly the same sense as their opponents intended to do—a sense which they had always resisted. Meantime the Reciprocity Treaty also passed unanimously, and the Governor-General went down in state to give it the royal assent.

We immediately afterwards started on a tour through Upper Canada, which was a triumphal progress throughout—the people, many of whom until lately had been his Excellency's bitterest opponents, turning out *en masse* to do him honour; while at sundry banquets, and on other numerous occasions when he was called upon to speak, he explained to the people the advantages of the treaty he had secured for them. In fact, a reaction of popularity had set in; and the defeat of the previous Administration, which at first seemed an untoward circumstance to have occurred so near the close of his government, proved the most fortunate event for Lord Elgin's own reputation, for it gave unanswerable evidence to the constitutionality of his conduct, which had always been impugned. I cannot do better than quote his own words on this subject:—

"I have brought into office the gentlemen who made themselves for years most conspicuous and obnoxious for personal hostility to myself, thus giving the most complete negative to the allegation that I am swayed by personal motives in the selection of my advisers; and these gentlemen have accepted office on the understanding that they will carry out in all particulars the policy which I sketched out while my former Administration was in office, thus proving that the policy in question is the only one suited to the country—the only one which an Administration can adopt. I do not see how the blindest can fail to draw this inference from these facts. The first thing which my new Administration have had to do is to adopt and carry through the House the address responsive to my speech from the Throne. This is, certainly for me, and I hope for the country, the most fortunate wind-up of my connection with Canada which could have been imagined." [1]

It was indeed a fortunate wind-up, and we determined to celebrate it as such. For the last three months of our residence at Quebec we lived in a perfect whirl of gaiety. Balls, dinner and garden parties, and picnics, were the order of the day. Society took the cue from Government House, and I found, under the temptation of more congenial pursuits, my parliamentary attendance getting slack. The delights of a Canadian winter, with its sleighing and tobogganing parties, have become proverbial. Unfortunately we only enjoyed one month of them, as Sir Edmund Head, Lord Elgin's successor, had arrived, and we merely remained a few weeks to facilitate the transfer of the Government. Sir Edmund was so kind as to urge me to remain with him in the office I was now filling; but the promise which Lord Clarendon had previously made to find me employment in the East, where the stirring nature of the events which were transpiring, offered the strongest attraction, induced me to decline this offer and to return to England with Lord Elgin, and Lord Bury became my successor in Canada. When I left home I had not expected to be absent above eight weeks, but

[1] Extracts from the Letters of James, Earl of Elgin, to Mary Louisa, Countess of Elgin, 1847-1862. Privately printed.

the same number of months would now nearly have elapsed before our return to British soil. It was nevertheless with a heavy heart that on a bitter morning towards the end of December, with the thermometer 26° below zero, I left Quebec; the streets were for the last time lined with troops as we drove down to our place of embarkation, and the greater part of the society was collected on the bank of the St Lawrence, as, after taking an affectionate farewell of the friends with whom I had formed ties of warmer friendship than is usual after so short a residence, we stretched ourselves at the bottom of the bark-canoes in which we were to be ferried across the broad bosom of the river, at this time encumbered with huge ice-floes and enshrouded in a dense fog. The traject is not without danger, and is exciting in proportion. Our muscular boatmen paddle us rapidly across the narrow lanes of swift open water, haul us up on the ragged floes, and running on the ice by the side of the canoes, rush us rapidly across them, to plunge us into the river again on the other side, until, after more than an hour's battling with the ice, we find ourselves safely hauled up under the bank at Point Levi. A few days afterwards I watched the outline of the American continent fading on the horizon, and little imagined as I did so that this was only the second of twenty-two passages I was destined to make across the Atlantic in the course of the ensuing seven-and-twenty years.

CHAPTER V.

CRIMEAN AND CIRCASSIAN EXPERIENCES.

Owing to the events related in the last chapter, nearly a year had elapsed before I was again in a position to offer my services to the Government for employment at the seat of war, but Sebastopol was still holding out bravely, and the public were getting impatient at a siege so protracted and so barren of definite results. I was emboldened thereby to publish a pamphlet, in which I suggested the expediency of a campaign in the Caucasus, a part of the world to which it was difficult to attract attention, until the siege of Kars forced its strategic value upon public notice. Feeling strongly the importance of a diversion in this direction, and the use which might be made of the Circassians, who were in a chronic state of guerilla warfare with Russia, but with whom, during the year that our own hostilities with that empire had lasted, we had opened no relations, with the view of inviting their co-operation and alliance, I proposed to Lord Clarendon that I should undertake a mission to Schamyl, for the purpose, if possible, of concerting some scheme with that chieftain by which combined operations could be carried on, either with the Turkish contingent which was then just organised by General Vivian, or with the Turkish regular army. It had always seemed to me that to ignore the existence of a race of brave and warlike mountaineers, who were fanatic Moslems, fighting in the heart of Russia for their independence, and yet most easily accessible by sea, was wilfully to cast aside a most powerful weapon for attack which the fortune of war had placed in our hands: we had only to land a strong Moslem force at Sujak Kaleh, on the Black Sea coast, whether of Beatson's Bashi-Bazouks, or Vivian's contingent, or Turkish regulars, provided they were Moslems, to have the whole male population of Circassia, every one a trained warrior, flock to our standard. Such a force would have the friendly mountains on its right flank to retreat to in case of necessity, the river Kuban to protect its left flank, and the rich plains which lie between the Kuban and the mountains to march across.

The objective points of such an expedition would have been the passes of Dariel and Derbend. These two mountain defiles closed by an allied army of Circassians and Turkish or irregular Moslem troops, all access into Transcaucasia would have been barred to Russia except by way of the Caspian Sea from Astrakhan—a most difficult and tedious operation, for in those days the steam-transport upon it was too limited for the conveyance of an army except in minute dribblets. The Russian army in the Caucasus, at that time under General Mouravieff, only amounted to 60,000 men. The Transcaucasian Provinces of Abkhasia, Mingrelia, Imeritia, Georgia, and Gouriel were all of them disaffected to Russia,—as I afterwards had an opportunity of knowing when I campaigned through them,—and being almost exclusively Christian, would have welcomed with delight a Christian army come to release them from the Muscovite yoke. This army would only have had to contend with that under Mouravieff, and would have operated in combination not only with the force on the Kuban, holding the northern passes, but with a Turkish army advancing from the direction of Kars. Mouravieff and his force would thus have infallibly been caught in a trap, from which there was positively no escape. Not only would Kars never have fallen, but Russia would have lost all her Transcaucasian provinces to boot. At that time the allied armies, French, English, and Italian, round Sebastopol numbered 150,000 men; but even supposing none of these could be spared, Turkey could have furnished a force of 50,000 men under Omer Pasha, exclusive of the Kars troops, which, with 25,000 of Vivian's and Beatson's, would have sufficed for the operation.

These considerations I urged so strongly on Lord Clarendon, that he determined to send me to Constantinople with a letter to Lord Stratford de Redcliffe, authorising him to send me to Daghestan, in the Eastern Caucasus, where Schamyl had his stronghold, for the purpose of making certain overtures to him, at his lordship's own discretion. Lord Stratford listened most sympathetically to my proposal; indeed he had been for months urging on the Government that a campaign should be undertaken without delay for the relief of Kars—and of the rival plans proposed, was by no means opposed to the operation being undertaken by way of the Caucasus, as a diver-

F

sion to compel Mouravieff to raise the siege. He had also sent Mr Longworth to the coast of Circassia to communicate with the Naib, Schamyl's lieutenant in the Western Caucasus; but he declined to commit himself to sanctioning my proposed expedition to Schamyl, on account of the great personal risk which attached to such an enterprise. Of the Naib's own messengers, which he despatched from time to time from the Western to the Eastern Caucasus, it was calculated that not more than one in three ever reached his destination; to do so, it was necessary to cross a district in Russian hands, called the Two Kabardas. The only way to do this was to ride all night, and lie concealed in some hiding-place all day; but, as I understood, neither woods nor caves abounded, and to play a game of hide-and-seek in an open country, with a scattered hostile population, and Cossack guerillas continually scouring it in every direction for the express purpose of intercepting such messengers, was one which experience had proved had more often than not cost those who had engaged in it their lives. Lord Stratford's hesitation, therefore, to despatch me at once, proceeded from motives for which I could not feel otherwise than grateful, though I was much disappointed at his objections, which I did my best to overcome. Finally he gave me a sort of qualified promise, and in the meantime proposed to me as a consolation that I should accompany him to the Crimea on the occasion of his proceeding to the seat of war to confer medals and decorations on the gallant officers who had so well earned them. Until the day appointed for our departure arrived, he was so kind as to extend the hospitality of the Embassy to me, and here I came in contact with probably a more brilliant group of men, so far as talent was concerned, than could be found in any diplomatic circle in Europe.

Lord Napier, then Secretary of Embassy; Odo Russell, afterwards Lord Ampthill; Percy Smythe, afterwards Lord Strangford; Charles Alison, afterwards Minister in Persia,—were all men of quite remarkable ability, and the last two of exceptional oriental attainments; while, if Lord Pevensey, Lionel Moore, and Brodie, the three juniors, never made a mark in the world, it was from no lack of capacity of a truly high order, which they each severally possessed. The days passed in such society are not to be forgotten; and I have never since been thrown with so many men where the stories were so racy, the repartee so quick, the flow of wit so constant, or the conversation generally so brilliant, as among those by whom Lord Stratford was surrounded at the time of the Crimean war. If anything could reconcile me to delay in the realisation of my projects, it was life on the lovely shores of the Bosporus, under these conditions, with all the excitement attendant upon a residence at the Embassy, when any hour might bring stirring intelligence from the seat of war, and almost every day brought arrivals of officers fresh from it, with graphic details of personal adventure. The little quay at Therapia swarmed with uniforms, faded and war-worn, or spick and span, betraying the veteran or the new-comer, as the case might be; while a constant succession of transports and steam-vessels of all kinds, varied now and then by a man-of-war and *caïques* darting to and fro, imparted an air of animation to a scene which is at all times one of the most beautiful in Europe, but which was then invested with a thrilling interest.

At last the day fixed for our departure arrived, and on the 24th August 1855 we embarked on H.M. despatch-vessel Telegraph,—the party consisting of the Ambassador, Lord Napier, General Mansfield (afterwards Lord Sandhurst), Count Pisani—whose name must ever be identified with the British Embassy at Constantinople, as one of the oldest and most trusted members—Messrs Alison, Moore, Brodie, and myself. Owing to a fog, it was dark the following evening before we approached our destination, and we only knew of our proximity to land by the distant flashes of the guns through the darkness, and the sullen reverberation which followed them. When day broke, I found that we were at anchor at the entrance to Kamiesch Bay, which was crowded with the British fleet. Weighing, we steamed slowly through them, amid the thunder of salutes, the manning of yards, and the strains of the National Anthem, to our anchorage; then followed the official visits, and long discussions on the affairs of the nations, between Lord Stratford and Admirals Lyons and Bruat, during which I watched the progress of the bombardment through a telescope, being able distinctly to see the shells from the Russian batteries exploding in the French trenches, and the scurry which followed each such event. We spent the whole day in Kamiesch Bay, dining at night at a banquet given to the Ambassador on board the Royal Albert, at which the two English and two French admirals were present, besides a great many distinguished officers. I could not but feel the contrast as we sat on deck and sipped our coffee after dinner, listening to the incessant roar of the cannonade, and watching shell after shell explode in the darkness—between our own condition of luxurious and festive enjoyment, and the agonies which hundreds of poor fellows were at that very moment enduring.

The next morning we rode up to camp, where I was so fortunate as to find my old friend Captain Valentine Baker, then of the 12th Lancers (now Baker Pasha), in command of the headquarter escort, established in a capacious Indian hut, which he kindly invited me to share with him during my stay in the Crimea, and where, owing to its proximity to headquarters, I was in the best position to be informed as to the events which were transpiring. The Ambassador, less fortunate, as I considered, than I was, slept every night during his stay with the army on board the Telegraph, the labour of riding to camp and back each day adding not a little to the fatigue of the functions he was called upon to perform. First, there was a grand breakfast given in his honour by Sir James Simpson, who had succeeded Lord Raglan as Commander-in-Chief, the solemn dignity of which I was glad to escape, and take a more lively mid-day meal with Captain (now Admiral Sir Harry) Keppel, and some of the Naval Brigade. I had also many friends among the Engineers and Artillery, with one of whom I made an exciting expedition to the most advanced trench, which, as it was only a few weeks prior to the surrender of Sebastopol, had been pushed to an unpleasantly close proximity to the fortress, and the shelter of which, to my unprofessional mind and unaccustomed nerves, was meagre to a degree, and by no means dispensed with the constant exercise of watchfulness and agility, as the enemy's shells came lobbing into it, and exploding in all sorts of unexpected quarters. To go to the furthest extreme point, to pop one's head over the trench for a moment and take a hurried glance over the narrow space intervening between it and the nearest embrasures, to see them belch forth their smoke almost in one's face, to hear the ping of the rifle bullets aimed at too curious observers of this description, and suddenly to pop down again—was to achieve an experience which one felt it totally unnecessary to repeat, more especially as the main object of undergoing it at all seemed to be to be able afterwards to say you had done it. It was in the Engineers' camp that I first made the acquaintance of General Gordon—a fact which we had both forgotten, until, on comparing notes in Palestine in December 1883, only a month before he left London for Khartoum, we recalled the circumstances of our first meeting eight-and-twenty years before.

Scrambling about the camp before Sebastopol was attended with extreme difficulty for a visitor; the distances were so great, and the disposition of the army to a stranger seemed so complicated, that endless inquiries often landed you at last at a wrong destination. Then the walking was so detestable, that a horse, which had on each occasion to be borrowed, was an almost absolute necessity. I could scarcely recognise, as I wandered through the maze of tents and huts, that three years before I had driven across the same country from Balaclava into Sebastopol, without, so far as I can recollect, meeting a soul; and that the frowning batteries which held at bay the English, French, Italian, and Turkish armies had all been erected since then. It was a strange coincidence that, on leaving Sebastopol on that occasion, the wheel of the waggon I was in should have given way,[1] and afforded me an opportunity of sketching the identical slopes of Inkermann, with the stream meandering at their base, upon which, about eighteen months afterwards, the celebrated battle was destined to be fought.

Finding myself next to Sir John Burgoyne at dinner one night at headquarters, I reminded him of our meeting in London, and I asked him whether the information I had given him on that occasion, as to the defenceless condition of Sebastopol, was correct. He admitted that it was, and that after the battle of the Alma it would have been perfectly possible to have taken the town by assault; but he said it would have involved a great loss of men, as the fire from the houses in which the enemy were ensconced would have been very destructive, a loss which he calculated would be avoided by awaiting the arrival of the siege-train. He further had the frankness to admit, however, that he had not taken the genius of a Todleben into his calculations, and that they had been completely upset by the remarkable engineering skill, in the matter of earthworks, of that celebrated officer.

On the third day after our arrival in the Crimea, the grand function took place which had been the special object of Lord Stratford's visit to the seat of war. The weather was lovely. About 2000 men were formed into

---

[1] See The Russian Shores of the Black Sea in the Autumn of 1852; with a Voyage down the Volga, and a Tour through the Country of the Don Cossacks. By Laurence Oliphant. William Blackwood & Sons, Edinburgh and London: 1854.

a square, which was decorated with numerous flags floating in the breeze. A sort of raised dais had been constructed for the Ambassador, who, seated upon it, invested Sir Edmund Lyons and Sir Colin Campbell with the insignia of G.C.B., and several other officers with the lower grades of the same order. It was a striking moment as the guns thundered forth a royal salute, to hear it broken in upon by the boom of the cannon sending forth their defiant response, and to see now and then a shell bursting in the air, to remind one that these gallant soldiers, like the knights of old, were being decorated upon the field of battle, and amid the din of actual warfare.

Meantime I was getting anxious about my own fate. The Ambassador had been so much occupied with receptions, entertainments, and grand functions—among them a great display which M. Soyer gave us of camp cookery —that I had shrunk from troubling him with my personal affairs, and yet the prospect of going back with him to Constantinople did not smile upon me. The Duke of Newcastle, who was then in the Crimea, having resigned his seat in the Cabinet, projected a trip to the Caucasus, and was kind enough to invite me to accompany him; but I clung rather to the idea of a special mission to Schamyl in Daghestan, the necessity for which, it seemed to me, was every day more pressing. It had become evident that Sebastopol could not hold out much longer; but there was no reason to suppose that we were going to be dragged into a peace by the French, by which the results of the war would be in a great measure sacrificed. On the contrary, it seemed likely that the scene of operations would be transferred to another quarter, and that the Government would at last open its eyes to the fact that the most vulnerable spot in the Russian empire was the Caucasian provinces. I did not then know, what I discovered afterwards, as may be proved by official documents, that it entered into the policy of our Allies to sacrifice our Eastern interests to their own immediate necessities, though, as it afterwards turned out, at the period of my visit to the Crimea, General Pélissier was pursuing a course which could bear no other construction. At that very moment Lord Stratford was receiving from General Williams news of the straits to which the garrison of Kars was being rapidly reduced by the besieging army under General Mouravieff, and of the necessity of immediate relief being sent to prevent its capture; and was urging on the British Government the expediency of sending the Turkish army, then lying idle in the Crimea under Omer Pasha, to its relief. Six weeks before our visit, Omer Pasha had met the generals of the Allied armies in conference, had explained to them the useless inactivity to which he, with his whole army, was condemned, and had implored them to let him at once undertake an Asiatic campaign for the relief of Kars; but his arguments had failed to move them—General Pélissier being most emphatic in his objection to it, and General Simpson being a passive tool in the hands of his French colleague. Lord Stratford, however, took a very different view of the situation, and so strongly advocated the measure urged by Omer Pasha, that he had extracted the consent of the British Government to it, qualified, however, by the proviso, "that the Government of the Emperor will concur in it." The Emperor only concurred in it subject to the approval of General Pélissier, who flatly refused. It was at this juncture that we were in the Crimea,—the battle of the Tchernaya had been fought, the fall of Sebastopol had become a matter of days. There were 150,000 allied English, French, and Italian troops awaiting its surrender, and not exposed to the slightest danger; and yet, in General Pélissier's opinion, the safety of these three European armies depended upon the presence by their side of 30,000 Turkish troops. Had this force been allowed to leave the Crimea while we were there, the event proved that they would have been in plenty of time to have saved Kars, which did not capitulate for three months after this. A month later, the Turkish army was still kicking its heels in front of Sebastopol, to the great discomfort of the other three armies, who had difficulty enough in finding camping-grounds and supplies. Sebastopol had fallen a fortnight before. General Pélissier had been deprived of his last excuse, and yet we read in a despatch from Colonel (now General) Sir Lintorn Simmons, the English commissioner with the Turkish army, dated the 21st September: "General Simpson has informed me that he sees no objection to their [the Turkish troops] departure. The only obstacle seems to be that the assent of General Pélissier and the French Government has not been given." At last, a week later, this consent was reluctantly extracted. And the record of the campaign of the Turkish army in the Caucasus, in which I took part, proved that it was given three weeks too late. Had the Turkish army been released even the day after Sebastopol fell, it would have been in Tiflis before Kars surrendered, and Mouravieff would have been compelled to raise the siege of that fortress. As it was, we had arrived at a point 130 miles from Tiflis, or ten days' easy marching, with nothing to oppose our advance but a Russian force scarce a third of our own number, which had already suffered one serious defeat at our hands, and was in full retreat before us, when the news reached us of General Williams's surrender.

It was a story which has since almost found its parallel in the failure of the expedition to relieve General Gordon at Khartoum; but the circumstances which attended the fatal delay were not so well known, for at that moment the *entente cordiale* with France was supposed to be a consideration of paramount importance in our policy, and it might have been seriously imperilled had the British public thoroughly understood at the time that the fall of Kars, which was being defended by British officers, was directly due to the refusal of the French Government to allow a force which was doing nothing in the Crimea, to proceed to its relief.

It was doubtless the increased prominence which the exposed territories of Russia on the eastern shores of the Black Sea were likely to assume so soon as Sebastopol fell, which induced Lord Stratford to send Mr Alison from the Crimea at this time on a special mission to Circassia, with instructions to confer with Mr Longworth in anticipation of future contingencies, the more especially as the conduct of the Turkish officials who had been placed in the forts captured by us from the Russians on the coast of Circassia, and their treatment of the natives, had not been such as to give unqualified satisfaction. In Mr Alison's instructions he was directed to confer with Mr

Longworth in regard to my project of going as an emissary of the British Government to Daghestan, and I was informed that I was to accompany him.

It was therefore in high spirits that, on the evening of the last day of August, I embarked with Mr Alison on board H.M.S. Highflyer, Captain Moore, which was detached from the squadron in order to take us to Circassia. At Kertch I found the 71st Highlanders, whom I had known well the previous year at Quebec, and after spending a pleasant day with them, went on to Anapa, the first or most northerly Circassian fort which we had taken from the Russians. Here we transferred ourselves to H.M.S. Cyclops, which had been placed at the disposal of Mr Longworth; and in that comfortable and roomy old tub—of a type now obsolete—had a most enjoyable cruise along the Circassian coast, landing repeatedly at the dismantled Russian forts occupied by Circassians, who received us everywhere most cordially, for they had formed a most exalted idea of British prowess when they found that the forts which had always resisted their efforts had either been abandoned or surrendered at once to the guns of the British fleet. I had earnestly wished to proceed on my mission to Daghestan from Anapa, which I thought the most eligible starting-point; but both Alison and Longworth were of opinion that it would be desirable first to communicate with the Naib, Schamyl's lieutenant in the Western Caucasus, and procure, if possible, an escort.

We hoped to find that chief within reaching distance from the coast; but in this we were disappointed, and it was deemed undesirable to incur the delay of trying to reach him in the mountains, as it was considered important that a conference should first be held with Omer Pasha, who had just arrived at Trebizond, to decide upon the best strategical measures to be taken for the relief of Kars. To my mind the enjoyment of a yachting cruise in a comfortable man-of-war, at the loveliest season of the year, along the most exquisite coast-scenery to be found anywhere, and in most agreeable company, scarcely compensated for the uncertainty and delay which thus attended the realisation of my own project. Our party consisted of Messrs Alison and Longworth; Mr (now Sir Alfred) Sandison, the nephew and at that time the private secretary of the latter; Captain Ballard, who commanded the Cyclops; and myself. At Trebizond we found the Turkish Commander-in-Chief perfectly furious at the delay to which he had been subjected by the generals in the Crimea, unable to form any definite plan of campaign until he knew what the strength of his army was to be, and when it was to be at his disposal; a position of matters which was aggravated by the fact that while here we heard of the fall of Sebastopol, but received no intelligence that the Turkish army had left the Crimea in consequence.

The strategic question at issue was, whether it would be best to attempt the relief of Kars direct from Trebizond by way of Erzeroum—the objection to which plan was, that there was no harbour at Trebizond, and the disembarkation of troops might be attended with great danger, delay, and difficulty; or from Batoum, which possessed an excellent harbour, but the roads from which place, across the country to Kars, were almost impracticable for artillery; or whether it would not be best to land at Sukhum Kaleh, and march directly on Tiflis, thus threatening the whole of Russian Transcaucasia, and creating a diversion in favour of Kars by compelling Mouravieff to raise the siege of that fortress. On visiting Batoum, I was much struck with its great strategic value as a port—a value which the Russians recognise so fully, that they succeeded in acquiring it by the Treaty of Berlin, and are now fortifying it in direct defiance of a clause in that treaty prohibiting them doing so. The American code of commercial morality is, that it is perfectly legitimate to break a solemn contract if the advantages to be gained more than compensate for the damages which you will have to pay for so doing under a legal judgment. The modern code of international morality seems to be, that it is perfectly legitimate to break a treaty if you can do so without incurring the risks of war; and it is in accordance with that code that the Russians are now acting in the matter of Batoum.

The delays consequent upon the departure of his army from the Crimea, finally decided Omer Pasha to undertake a campaign in the Transcaucasus, with Tiflis as an objective point. Meantime Mr Alison left us at Trebizond, to go back to Constantinople; and we returned in the Cyclops to Sukhum Kaleh, to start upon an expedition from that point into the interior, which had been decided upon, with the object of distributing proclamations, calling upon the inhabitants to rise and co-operate with their Mohammedan brethren, who were coming to free them from the Muscovite yoke. As, however, there were reasons why we could not start upon this mission until Omer Pasha arrived, and as the Commander-in-Chief lingered so long at Batoum that our patience was becoming exhausted, Mr Longworth sent me back to that place in the Cyclops to discover the cause of the delay. In answer to my urgent representations that we were anxious before the season for crossing the mountains closed, to start on our expedition, Omer Pasha insisted that there was no cause for hurry; that he intended to summon a great meeting of Circassian chiefs at Sukhum Kaleh, and that he would then make arrangements for us all to start from Sujak Kaleh and go into the interior together, by way of the plains to the north of the range. I represented that we should thus be exposed to Russian attack; but he maintained that we could always retreat in case of necessity into the mountains on our right flank, and that he would arrange that the force should be large enough to resist any Cossack irregulars we were likely to meet. Meantime he desired me to return to Sukhum Kaleh and request Mr Longworth to come back to Batoum, and to stop on the way at a small place called Shefkatil, to meet there the Prince of Georgia's brother, and endeavour to make terms with him, which should induce the Prince to declare himself in favour of the Allies. On our way back we took provisions to the Turkish garrison at Redoute Kaleh, which, I verily believe, would have starved to death had it not been for our opportune arrival. Mr Longworth at once responded to Omer Pasha's appeal; but no Georgian prince was forthcoming at Shefkatil according to appointment, though an extremely picturesque emissary arrived at Batoum shortly after we got there, and had a long and secret conference with Omer Pasha. I suspect, however, that his master the Prince was not inclined to commit himself definitely to the desertion of the Russians; and as it afterwards turned out, it was fortunate for him that he contented himself with temporising. At last we succeeded in dragging Omer Pasha out of Batoum, and took him with us to Sukhum on board the Cyclops.

I had now performed the voyage between Sukhum and Batoum six times, hammering away in a futile manner on the rim of the country I so ardently desired to penetrate, unable to get any positive decision arrived at in regard to my mission, which was all the more aggravating, as it was constantly being talked of as a thing which, sooner or later, under some circumstances or other, either in company with Mr Longworth or alone, or with a strong force or a small escort, or by the mountains or by the plains, was to come off; but as week after week passed, it seemed further from being accomplished than ever. At last, three days after our arrival at Sukhum Kaleh, Omer Pasha informed me that he wished to send me on a special mission from himself to the Naib. As, when its purport was explained to Mr Longworth, it received that gentleman's full concurrence, my spirits rose as they had never done before. I had made all my preparations, received my instructions, and on the morning of my start was only waiting the arrival of the Turkish officer who was to accompany me, when he appeared with the depressing intelligence that Omer Pasha had changed his mind, and had given up the idea of sending the proposed mission, as news had reached him that the Naib was on his way from the interior to pay his respects in person to the Turkish generalissimo. I thought the Fates were certainly against me, as I sadly ordered my horse back to the stable, and resigned myself to the chapter of accidents. Omer Pasha had not been misinformed. The Naib arrived a few days after, and at the same time the Highflyer appeared, having on board the Duke of Newcastle and Mr (now Lord) Calthorpe. Transports also came pouring in from the Crimea, disgorging the army for which we had been so long waiting; and the picturesque harbour of Sukhum, with its fort and village—which had been abandoned by its Russian occupants when I first saw them, and was a spot of silent and deserted loveliness—was now a scene of life and bustle, and for those whose fate obliged them to live on shore, of no little discomfort.

Omer Pasha received the Naib with every mark of respect and consideration. He was evidently a personage of great authority among the mountaineers, and was very proud of an expedition he had just made against the Russians in the province of Karachai, which he declared was a great success, but which some Karachai men, whom I afterwards saw, pronounced a failure. He was invested by the Commander-in-Chief with Turkish official rank as Governor of the Western Caucasus, and in that capacity could, I thought, have easily forwarded me in safety to Schamyl. Whether as a bigoted Moslem he had a prejudice against allowing me to penetrate where no foreigner had ever been before, or was jealous of any direct communication with Schamyl, between whom and the outside world he was at that time the sole intermediary, I know not; but he made objections to my proposed journey on the ground of the lateness of the season and the insecurity of the country, which neither Omer Pasha nor Mr Longworth used any arguments to overcome. Had

G

they done so, I do not think he would have persisted in his opposition; indeed I have a strong suspicion that Omer Pasha looked upon the mission with disfavour, believing, as did Mr Longworth, that it would be rendered unnecessary by a successful advance on Tiflis, from which point Daghestan and its celebrated chieftain could be visited without difficulty by Mr Longworth himself, as well as by Turkish emissaries, none of whom were anxious to undertake the risks of a mission under present conditions. I was therefore finally compelled to reconcile myself to the disappointment, and gladly accepted an invitation from the Duke of Newcastle to accompany him on a short trip into the interior. Our party was a large one, and consisted of his Grace, Mr Calthorpe, Captain Moore, Mr Simpson (the well-known and popular artist of the 'Illustrated London News'), Mr Longworth, Mr Sandison, and myself. A small abandoned Russian post on the coast, called Vardan, was our starting-point, and the utterly unknown and unexplored Circassian province of Ubooch the scene of our wanderings. These lasted for a little more than a week, and led us high into the mountains, through the most romantic scenery, and among a people as new and interesting to us as we must have been to them. As, however, I published a record of our adventures and observations on that occasion,[1] I will not allude to them further now. On our return to Sukhum Kaleh, we became the guests of Prince Michael of Abkhasia—of which province Sukhum is the capital—who organised a grand shooting-party at one of his country residences in

---

[1] Patriots and Filibusters. By Laurence Oliphant. William Blackwood & Sons, Edinburgh and London: 1860.

honour of the Duke, who afterwards returned to England, whilst I, finding all chance of diplomatic work of the kind I ambitioned at an end, for the present at all events, attached myself to the Turkish army, with which there were then five English officers, and especially to Colonel Ballard of the East India Company's Service, who commanded two battalions of Rifles, and was an officer of signal capacity and merit. Under him I did some amateur soldiering, and devoted myself to chronicling the events of the campaign in the columns of the 'Times,' afterwards republished,[1]—a duty which seemed to me the more necessary, as there was no correspondent of any paper with the army throughout, and no public record would otherwise have existed of a military episode in the highest degree interesting at the time, and which, had it been successful, would have been pregnant with the most important political results. On my return to Constantinople I received a reprimand from Lord Stratford for having imposed this task upon myself while engaged in a *quasi* diplomatic capacity; but I represented that I considered this to have come to an end as soon as the diplomatic object which had brought me to Circassia had become unattainable, and that as I was receiving no pay at the time, my pen was at my own disposal: at the same time, I declined an offer which he kindly made me that I should remain at Constantinople as his private secretary.

The chief incidents of the campaign were the battle of the Ingour; the long and unaccountable delay at Sugdidi,

[1] The Transcaucasian Campaign of the Turkish Army under Omer Pasha: A Personal Narrative. By Laurence Oliphant. With Maps and Illustrations. William Blackwood & Sons, Edinburgh and London: 1856.

the capital of Mingrelia, which followed it; and the disastrous retreat when the winter rains set in, and the news reached us of the fall of Kars. In regard to the first, the ease with which we overcame the Russian army sent to oppose us, proved the facility with which we might have advanced on Tiflis, and rendered it all the more difficult to explain the delay of a fortnight which had occurred.

The ostensible reason for our inaction after the battle of the Ingour, was the necessity which had arisen for changing our base from Sukhum to Redoute Kaleh for commissariat and other transport. It was to this latter point that we ultimately retreated—not before the enemy, but the weather—losing a very large proportion of our force from fever and starvation, harassed night and day by Cossack irregulars, drenched to the skin by flooded rivers and unceasing torrents of rain, and compelled to endure privations which, in my own case, brought on an illness that I thought at one time would abruptly terminate my record of them. As it was, I was barely able, on the 22d of December—just four months after I had landed in the Crimea—to scramble on board a steamer bound for Trebizond; and about the same day, between our rear-guard and some Cossack skirmishers, the last shot of the war was fired.

I would say one word finally in regard to the peace which followed, and which, by its premature conclusion, prevented the scene of our late campaign again becoming the theatre of hostile operations—this time to be undertaken by an English army, supported by the Turkish contingent and Bashi-Bazouks which we had organised, and by a Turkish force of regulars co-operating with us on the

Kuban. This plan was abruptly put an end to by a peace which practically did nothing towards checking Russia's Asiatic policy. But even then she would have been powerless to resist the insertion of a clause which would have changed the whole course of events in the East since that period, and this was simply for England to refuse to consent to the reoccupation by Russia of the nine or ten forts which we had taken from her, and which had been dismantled on the Eastern or Circassian shore of the Black Sea.

When we consider that even when, by the Russian occupation of the coast and the erection of these forts, the Caucasus had become a besieged mountain, its brave defenders, unable to obtain arms or ammunition from without except with the greatest difficulty, had successfully held Russia at bay for thirty years, it is evident that the final conquest of the country and its annexation to the empire would have been a work of enormously increased cost and labour—if, indeed, it could ever have been achieved—had the whole of its coast remained in the hands of the Circassians, and traffic with the outside world been thus unimpeded. With the Russians deprived of a Black Sea fleet, and their access to Circassia barred from the coast, which would thus have been open to all comers to supply the population with arms, volunteers, and material aid, the absorption of this wild and inaccessible mountain-range into the empire would have been a matter almost of impossibility; it would have remained a barrier permanently separating Russia from her Transcaucasian provinces, and have protected Turkey from that campaign in 1878 which resulted in the annexation of

Kars and Batoum, and is about shortly to culminate in the acquisition of Armenia and the ultimate extension of the Russian frontier to the shores of the Mediterranean.

The neglect of this simple precaution has entailed consequences which have had a predominant influence on recent events in the East. The Russian Government, perceiving the narrow escape they had made from a termination of the war which would have checkmated their policy in Asiatic Turkey, took the most stringent measures, as soon as peace was concluded, to repair the weak spot in their armour of national defence and aggression, by concentrating their whole energies upon the final subjugation of the Circassians. This, after some years of severe fighting, they succeeded in achieving; and the Moslem highlanders, refusing to part with an independence for which they had struggled so long and so bravely, emigrated *en masse* into the dominions of the Sultan.

The influx of about 200,000 destitute strangers, of all ages and both sexes, was a severe strain upon a crippled treasury; and large numbers were settled in colonies in Bulgaria and other parts of the empire, there to shift for themselves as best they could. Lawless by nature, cattle-lifters by training and instinct, brave and inured to wars, they found themselves planted in a fertile country, surrounded by a race in close affinity with the one they most detested, speaking almost the same language, and professing the same abhorred religion. The Bulgarian atrocities followed, as a matter of course. One might as well have transplanted a penniless clan of Highlanders in the middle of the last century into Kent, and expected them to live peaceably with their neighbours, as have colonised Circassians in the midst of Bulgarians and have expected fraternisation.

The philanthropic British public, who a few years previously had held meetings of sympathy and collected funds for the relief of the poor expelled Circassians, now demanded vengeance against Turkey for the atrocities committed by them upon the Bulgarians; and the Russian army crossed the Danube to execute it, while the British public calmly looked on, and saw every object, to attain which they had expended so much blood and treasure in the Crimea twenty-four years before, ruthlessly sacrificed, and the treaty of 1856, which had resulted from it, torn up and scattered to the winds. We had already yielded the important clause prohibiting Russia from having a fleet on the Black Sea: we then, by the Treaty of Berlin, gave her back Bessarabia, permitted her to annex Kars, with the harbour of Batoum, and consented to the unlimited extension of her influence across the Danube. All this was due, in the first instance, to our having concluded the Crimean war without finishing the work to which we had set our hand, by means of a Transcaucasian campaign with a British army, with the Circassians as our allies; and in the second, to our having utterly ignored the strategical value and importance of the country they occupied, and to our having taken no steps at the conclusion of peace to secure its independence.

How little apprehended at the time were the circumstances connected with the fall of Kars,—which an ignorant public attributed chiefly to neglect on the part of Lord Stratford,—and the effect which our Circassian policy was destined to produce upon subsequent events in the East, may be gathered from the following letter from the Ambassador himself, dated 30th April 1856, to whom I had sent a copy of my narrative of the campaign in which I had just been engaged, and who was as much disappointed at the sudden and inept conclusion of the war, as was everybody else who had the interest of their country at heart, and understood the position of affairs at the time.

"I am greatly obliged to you," he writes, "for thinking of me in the distribution of your Circassian volume. I accept the copy you have kindly sent me as a valuable testimony of your regard. I have been assailed with so much reckless self-seeking malignity, that the discernment of any disinterested witness having a just hold on public confidence is doubly precious to me. Many a false notion respecting the fate of Kars and its neighbourhood remains still to be dispelled; but I rely with confidence on that sense of justice and love of truth which seldom fail our countrymen after allowing themselves the indulgence of a little temporary riot. We shall be delighted to see you again whenever you are tempted to explore these regions in a more complete manner. The restoration of peace gives so much uncertainty to our plans, that I can hardly venture to look forward beyond a month.—Yours very sincerely, STRATFORD DE R."

The misfortune is, that whatever may be "the sense of

justice and love of truth of our countrymen," their ignorance of political conditions abroad, especially in the East, and their effect upon British interests, remains unchanged. They were unable then to perceive that the sure way to prevent a Russian advance upon India was to wrest from her her Transcaucasian provinces, and that we could attack her far more easily and effectively in Circassia than in Afghanistan. Although we have allowed the golden opportunity to escape us, strategically this proposition still holds good—should we unfortunately ever find ourselves forced into hostilities with the Power which is ever the disturbing element in Eastern affairs, we should act, not on the defensive at Herat, but on the offensive at Batoum and Sukhum Kaleh, and endeavour to occupy the country between the Black Sea and Caspian—thus cutting her line of communication to the East, and forcing her to concentrate her attention on her own frontiers instead of upon ours. To do this effectively, however, it would be necessary to come to an understanding with Turkey, both in regard to our passage into the Black Sea, which it would be better to arrange peaceably than by force, and in regard to a Turkish military contingent, which, with the thousands of Circassians who would flock to our standard at the prospect of returning to their own country, would form a most valuable auxiliary force; while the restoration to Turkey of the Asiatic provinces recently annexed by Russia, with possibly a further extension of territory towards the Caspian, would in some measure repay her for the sacrifices to which she is being now subjected in Europe. It was universally admitted at the close of the

Crimean war, by those who were engaged in it and had studied the subject, that the true theatre of operations from the first should have been the Transcaucasus. The proof of it was that we were making preparations to convey an army there when peace was made. Is it possible that the lesson we learnt then should be so soon forgotten?

CHAPTER VI.

ADVENTURES IN CENTRAL AMERICA.

I HAD not been many months back from Circassia, and, Micawber-like, was waiting for something to turn up—not anxiously, however, for the London season of 1856 was not without its attractions—when, towards the close of it, I found myself once more starting for Liverpool on another trip across the Atlantic, my fellow-traveller on this occasion being my much-valued and lamented friend Mr Delane of the 'Times,' to whom I was able to act as cicerone on our arrival at New York, where we underwent a round of festivities and enjoyed an amount of hospitality which, I used to think afterwards on perusing the columns of the Thunderer, had not been altogether without their effect. The pressure of my companion's editorial duties unfortunately obliged us to part all too soon—he to return to England, and I to visit each one of the British North American colonies in turn, on some business with which I had been intrusted; but I cannot neglect this opportunity of paying the tribute of a grateful memory to one of the best and truest men I have ever known.

My intimacy with Delane extended over nearly twenty years, during which I had frequent business as well as uninterrupted private relations with him. I had thus abundant opportunities of testing alike the power of his intellect and the warmth of his affections, and found in him a man who, with everything to spoil him, was never spoilt—who never allowed his social or public position to paralyse in the slightest degree that generosity of nature which was constantly prompting him to extend his strong arm to help those in trouble, and to perform acts of kindness which were never known except to the recipients of them. As an instance, I remember on one occasion bringing to his notice the case of a widow whose husband, an officer who had been severely wounded in the Crimea, was refused her pension because, although it was not denied that he died of his wound, he lingered a day or two beyond the allotted time within which he ought to have succumbed, the plea of the War Office being that an awkward question might be asked in the House of Commons if an exception were made in his favour. On my showing him the correspondence, Delane immediately took up the cudgels for the widow, and a leading article appeared in the old slashing style, which concluded with the following stinging epigram, in allusion to the possibility of an objection being taken in Parliament: "The House of Commons is never stingy, except when it suspects a job; the War Office is always stingy, except when it commits one." But the question was never allowed to come before the House; for two days after the appearance of this article, the widow got her pension.

We made at New York the acquaintance of all the leading members of the press of that city at an entertainment given by them to Mr Delane; and the occasion was doubly interesting, because the Presidential election was going on at the time, which resulted in Buchanan being sent to the White House at Washington. How little did any of us, in the political discussions in which we took part, foresee how pregnant with disastrous results that Presidentship was destined to be,—that it would involve the most bloody civil war of modern times, and that nearly thirty years would elapse before a Democratic administration would again be formed in the United States! Among the eminent men whose acquaintance we made, and whom it is interesting to recall to memory—for they have all, I think, passed away—were General Scott, then Commander-in-Chief of the army; Commodore Perry; Mr Grinnell, who fitted out the first-American Arctic expedition; and Bancroft, the historian. We fraternised much with a most agreeable group of Southerners, from whom I was glad to accept invitations to visit them on their plantations,—an experience I the less regret, as I was thus able to form an independent judgment of the practical working of the "peculiar institution" which was destined so soon to be abolished; to see the South in the palmy days of its prosperity, under conditions which can never recur again; and to enjoy a hospitality which possessed a charm of its own, however much one might regret the surroundings amid which it was exercised, or condemn the abuses to which the system of slavery gave rise. I put the result of my observations on record at the time in an article in 'Blackwood's Magazine'; and from what I saw and heard, it was not difficult to predict in it the cataclysm which took place four years later, though the idea of the South resorting to violence was scouted in the North; and when, upon more than one occasion, I ventured to suggest the possibility to Republicans, I was invariably met by the reply that I had not been long enough in the country to understand the temper of the people, and attached an importance it did not deserve to Southern "bounce." When, three months after the close of the war, I again traversed the same States which I was now visiting during a period of peace and plenty, the contrast was heartrending. Homesteads which then were rich and flourishing, were now masses of charred ruins; whole towns had been swept away. This, I remember, was conspicuously the case at Atlanta, where only a few wooden shanties—where I found it very difficult to get accommodation for the night—indicated the site of the former town. It is now again a flourishing city. Ruin and devastation marked the track of invading armies over vast tracts of country, and testified alike to the severity of the struggle and the obstinacy of the resistance. In this respect the country exhibited a very striking contrast to France after the German campaign. As it was my fortune to accompany the German armies through a great part of the war, and to march with them through several provinces of France, I could compare the conditions of the theatre of military operations with that of the Southern States immediately after the war, and judge of the nature of the conflict by the traces which it left. In the latter case, one may say that, except immediately round Paris and in one or two isolated localities like Châteaudun, it left no traces at all, and enabled one to estimate at its proper value, even if one had not been present at the battles, the flimsy nature of the resistance which had been offered.

Perhaps one of the best evidences of the different character of the fighting which took place between the Northern and Southern armies in America, and that which occurred in France, is to be found in the fact that the Franco-German battles were essentially artillery combats; and that, with the exception of one or two of the earlier battles, such as Spicheren and Gravelotte, the opposing forces never came to close quarters at all. In fact, during the Loire campaign, which I made with the Grand Duke of Mecklenburg, both sides played at such long bowls that it was very difficult, even with the aid of a field-glass, to see a Frenchman; whereas, towards the close of the American war, both sides almost abandoned artillery as a useless arm, and a source of weakness rather than of strength, when men, not to be deterred by noise, rushed in on the guns. Modern inventions and machine-guns may make this more difficult, but certainly the artillery of even fifteen years ago, mitrailleuse included, required an amount of protection when opposed by a resolute foe, which scarcely compensated for the relatively small extent of injury it could inflict; and I have often thought that if the German armies had found themselves confronted with the comparatively raw and untrained levies of the American rebellion, they would have discovered that there is another art of war altogether from that in which they have perfected themselves—of which they have had as yet no experience—and which consists in an invincible determination to get at close quarters with the enemy as quickly as possible, and, if necessary, to die there rather than come away.

In no Southern city, perhaps, was the stress of war

more severely felt than in New Orleans, though it was never devastated by shot and shell. At the time of my first visit in the winter of 1856-57, it was socially the most delightful city in the Union; and as I was fortunate in the possession of many friends, and of an age to appreciate gaiety, my stay there was one of unqualified enjoyment. In the autumn of 1865 it was the saddest place I ever entered,—sadder to me, perhaps, from the contrast as I had known it in happier days. Some of my friends had been killed, others were totally ruined, others in self-imposed exile. A new and not a pleasant class had taken their place, trade was at a stand-still, enterprise of all sorts was languishing, and a feeling of gloom and despondency reigned supreme. My last visit there was made during the last days of 1881, when it seemed like a city rising from the dead: hope and joy beamed from every countenance; and though, after the lapse of so many years, I scarcely found a soul I knew, there was a life and animation which augured well for the recovery of the place from its long torpor. Still it has undergone a change which will prevent it ever becoming the New Orleans I first remember. Then its charm lay in its French-Creole society—an element which has given way to the inroad from the North—and, if I may venture to confess it, in a certain lawlessness, which made it what, in local parlance, was called the "jumping-off place" for harebrained expeditions of a filibustering character to Cuba, Central America, or any other tempting locality. Among the most hospitable houses on the occasion of my first visit, was that of Mr Pierre Soulé, formerly United States Minister to Madrid, and whose son—at whose wedding I assisted—fought a duel with the Duke of Alva, which made some noise at the time. At this juncture Walker was endeavouring to establish himself as President of Nicaragua, and engaged in a war with the Costa Ricans, who were being aided in their resistance to his attempt by money and men supplied by Commodore Vanderbilt, with whom Walker had foolishly quarrelled upon the subject of the transit route through Nicaragua, of which the American capitalist desired to retain the control. Mr Soulé was acting in New Orleans as Walker's agent, and he explained to me that Walker's intention was not, as erroneously supposed by the British Government, to conquer the small republics of Central America, with the view of annexing them to the United States, but for the purpose of welding them into a new Anglo-Saxon republic—a project which it seemed to me, though it was undertaken by a single man, was not more immoral than similar enterprises are when undertaken by governments, and one which was calculated to benefit not only the Central American States themselves, but the cause of civilisation generally. Subsequent observation confirmed me in this view, which has been further illustrated by the history of the country during the thirty years which have elapsed since this time, when it has been the prey to constant revolutions, while it has made absolutely no advance in the arts of peace. I therefore listened with a favourable ear to Mr Soulé's offer of a free passage to Nicaragua in a ship conveying a reinforcement of 300 men to Walker's army, and of carrying strong personal recommendations to that noted filibuster, who was requested by Mr Soulé to explain the political situation to me, in the hope that on my return to England I might induce the British Government to regard his operations with a more favourable eye than they had hitherto done. The fact that if I succeeded I was to be allowed to take my pick out of a list of confiscated *haciendas*, or estates, certainly did not influence my decision to go, though it may possibly have acted as a gentle stimulant; but I remember at the time having some doubts on the subject from a moral point of view. Had I been brought up in the city, or been familiar with the processes of promoting joint-stock companies, these probably would not have occurred to me. As it was, I remember spending Christmas-day in high spirits at the novelty of the adventure upon which I was entering. And here I may remark, as an illustration of the rapidity with which, in my capacity of a moss-gathering stone, I was rolling about the world, that my Christmas-days during these years were passed in very varied localities.

On Christmas-day 1854 I was in Quebec; on the same day 1855 I was in Trebizond; in 1856 at New Orleans; and in 1857 in the Canton river.

It was on the last day of the year that the good ship Texas cleared out of New Orleans with 300 emigrants on board. At least we called ourselves emigrants—a misnomer which did not prevent the civic authorities, with the city marshal at their head, trying to stop us; but we had the sympathies of the populace with us, and under their ægis laughed the law to scorn. It would have been quite clear to the most simple-minded observer what kind of emigrants we were the day after we got out to sea, and the men were put through their squad-drill on deck.

There were Englishmen who had been private soldiers in the Crimea, Poles who had fought in the last Polish insurrection, Hungarians who had fought under Kossuth, Italians who had struggled through the revolutions of '48, Western "boys" who had just had six months' fighting in Kansas, while of the "balance" the majority had been in one or other of the Lopez expeditions to Cuba. Many could exhibit bullet-wounds and sword-cuts, and scars from manacles, which they considered no less honourable —notwithstanding all which, the strictest order prevailed. No arms were allowed to be carried. There were always two officers of the day who walked about with swords buckled over their shooting-jackets, and sixteen men told off as a guard to maintain discipline. Alas! the good behaviour and fine fighting qualities of these amiable emigrants were destined to be of no avail; for on our arrival at the mouth of the San Juan river we found a British squadron lying at anchor to keep the peace, and the steamer by which we hoped to ascend the river in the hands of our enemies, the Costa Ricans. Our first feeling was that we were not to be deterred by such trifles. The men were all drawn up below, each had received his rifle, revolver, and bowie, with the necessary ammunition, and all the arrangements were made for cutting out our prize, which was lying about 300 yards off, in the night. As a compliment, which I could not refuse but did not appreciate, I was given command of a boat (I think it was the dingy), and I costumed myself accordingly. Just before sunset we observed to our dismay a British man-of-war's boat pulling towards us; and a moment later, Captain Cockburn, of H.M.S. Cossack, was in the captain's cabin, making most indiscreet inquiries as to the kind of emigrants we were. It did not require long to satisfy him; and as I incautiously hazarded a remark which betrayed my nationality, I was incontinently ordered into his boat as a British subject, being where a British subject had no right to be. As he further announced that he was about to moor his ship in such a position as would enable him, should fighting occur in the course of the night, to fire into both combatants with entire impartiality, I the less regretted this abrupt parting from my late companions, the more especially as, on asking him who commanded the squadron, I found it was a distant cousin. This announcement on my part was received with some incredulity, and I was taken on board the Orion, an 80-gun ship, carrying the flag of Admiral Erskine, to test its veracity, while Captain Cockburn made his report of the Texas and her passengers. As soon as the Admiral recovered from his amazement at my appearance, he most kindly made me his guest; and I spent a very agreeable time for some days, watching the "emigrants" disconsolately pacing the deck, for the Costa Ricans gave them the slip in the night and went up the river, and their opponents found their occupation gone. The question they now had to consider was how to get to Walker. Few ever succeeded in doing so; and the non-arrival of this reinforcement was the immediate cause of the disaster which obliged "the blue-eyed man of destiny," as his friends called him, not long after to escape from the country. Poor Walker! he owed all his misfortunes, and finally his own untimely end, to British interference; for on his return to Central America, where he intended to make

Honduras the base of his operations, he was captured at Truxillo by Captain (now Sir Nowell) Salmon, and handed over to the Honduras Government, who incontinently hung him. This was the usual fate which followed failure in this country; and those who fought in it knew they were doing so with a rope round their necks—which doubtless improved their fighting qualities. I did not know, however, until my return to England, that rumour had accredited me with so tragic an end, when at the first party I went to, my partner, a very charming young person, whom I was very glad to see again after my various adventures, put out two fingers by way of greeting, raised her eyebrows with an air of mild surprise, and said in the most silvery and unmoved voice, "Oh, how d'ye do? I thought you were hung!" I think it was rather a disappointment to her that I was not. There is a novelty in the sensation of an old and esteemed dancing partner being hanged, and it forms a pleasing topic of conversation with the other ones. Eight years after this escapade, Admiral Erskine and I used to meet under very different circumstances: he was member for the county of Stirling, and I for the Stirling burghs, and he used laughingly to maintain that he had rescued me from a gang of desperadoes, and restored me to respectable society—a view which I attribute to narrow prejudice; for if you come to sheer respectability, there can be no doubt in the mind of any one who has tried both, that the life of a filibuster is infinitely superior in its aims and methods to that of a politician: a conclusion which was forcibly impressed upon my mind by one of my earliest experiences in the House of Commons, when a Reform Bill was passed by the Conservatives, which they would vehemently have opposed had it been brought in by the Liberals, and which the latter, in defiance of their political convictions, opposed because it was brought in by the Conservatives—a piece of political filibustering on the one side, as immoral to my unsophisticated mind as the tactics by which it was met on the other, but which, by voting steadily against the party to which I had the honour to belong, I contributed my mite to thwart. It did not take me long after this to discover that I was not cut out for a party man, and I entered into the repose of the Chiltern Hundreds.

To return to the purer atmosphere of Greytown: there was no inducement to go ashore, as there was absolutely nothing to see in the sleepy little *mestizo* town; so I took leave of my hospitable naval entertainers, and embarked in a passing steamer for Aspinwall, and crossed the Isthmus to Panama, where I found a mild revolution in progress, which had for the time handed over the town to the tender mercies of the negro part of its population.

It had always occurred to me that if one wanted to connect the two seas by a ship canal, the first part of the Isthmus to examine was the narrowest. Yet so far as I am aware, this route has never, even to this day, been surveyed. While at Panama, I thought I would make the attempt, and indeed reached a point by the Bayanos river within seventeen miles of the Gulf of Mexico. It is true that I was confronted by a high range of hills, which the hostility of Darien Indians—who obstruct the progress of the explorer by shooting little poisoned arrows at him through blow-pipes—prevented my traversing; but I heard that at one place there was a low pass, across which the Indians were in the habit of dragging their canoes; and I still think Monsieur Lesseps, before deciding to make the canal by the side of the railway, and thus encountering the almost insuperable obstacle of the Chagres river—which it may be predicted with tolerable certainty will prevent the work from ever being completed—would have done well to examine the country between the Bayanos river and Manzanilla bay. I argued these considerations in an account of my expedition which I published in 'Blackwood's Magazine' at the time. Upon returning from it, I recrossed the Isthmus, and proceeded to Carthagena, meeting on the steamer an interesting priest, who, on discovering my filibustering propensities, proposed to me to enter into a conspiracy for making a revolution in Honduras and upsetting the Government. This was to be done in the interest of the Church to which he belonged, the president for the time being having so far emancipated himself from spiritual guidance as—in the opinion of the highest ecclesiastical authorities—to render a change desirable. My informant assured me, under a solemn pledge of secrecy, that the whole matter was arranged; that the revolution would probably be bloodless or nearly so; that he was on his way to Europe in search of funds —for just in proportion as you had money, could you save the shedding of blood; but that, in order to be prepared for all contingencies, a few resolute men were required. These he would prefer to obtain, if possible, from England, —the importation of Americans for such purposes not having proved satisfactory — witness Walker, who was invited to help in a revolution, and who, when he had gained the day for the presidential candidate he came to assist, deliberately ousted him, and put himself in his place.

I expressed my sense of the compliment paid to the more disinterested character of my countrymen, and asked the holy father how many of them he wanted. To my astonishment he said twenty would be enough. They were only required as leaders when fighting was to be done; and if there were more, it would be difficult to provide for them afterwards. In fact I was to bring out from England twenty of the biggest dare-devils I could find, land them at a time and place which would be appointed, and obey orders, which I should receive from a bishop! My spiritual tempter was rather disappointed to learn that I was not a Romanist, as then I should have been supported by the high moral consciousness that I was fighting in the cause of the Church; and was obliged to rest satisfied with my assurances that I was free from theological bigotry of any kind. Men, he said, derived great spiritual benefit by fighting on the right side, even though, to begin with, the motives by which they were actuated were low ones. This naturally suggested the question, What temporal advantage was to accrue to me for the service I was rendering the Church? He was not in a position, he replied, to make me any definite promises in this respect; but I might count on high office, probably the head of the War Department, if I developed strong clerical sympathies. What a vista of conquest and greatness did this suggestion open to my youthful and ardent imagination! To be War Minister of Honduras at seven or eight and twenty, with Costa Rica, Guatemala, San Salvador, and Nicaragua, all waiting to be gobbled up. I would out-Walker Walker. Of course we did not get to this climax till after several days of secret confabulation, for I had to inspire the holy father with confidence. Meantime my moral sense was getting more and more confused. Decidedly there was something in the atmosphere of Central America which had a tendency to mix things up. Possibly it is still haunted by the shades of Pizarro and Kidd and Morgan, and freebooting and buccaneering influences hang round the lovely land to tempt the lonely wanderer disgusted with the prosaic tendencies of modern civilisation. I went so far as to learn a secret sign from this pious conspirator, so that on my return with my twenty men I should know how to find a friend in case of need. After all, he was only proposing to me to do on a small scale in Honduras what a clerical deputation five years afterwards proposed to the brother of the Emperor of Austria to do in Mexico on a larger one, and which that unhappy prince accepted as a religious duty.

I had a long talk with the Emperor Maximilian at Trieste just before he started for Mexico, and gave him the benefit of some of my Central American experiences; for when I heard the noble and lofty ambitions by which his soul was fired, I foresaw the bitter disappointment in store for him, though I could not anticipate his tragic end.

"It is the paradise of adventurers, sir," I remember saying, "but not a country for any man to go to who has a position to lose or a conscience to obey." In my small way I felt, after I had escaped from the influence of my ghostly tempter, that I had both, and dismissed him and his proposals from my mind. I watched, however, the fortunes of Honduras in the papers; and sure enough, not many months elapsed before the Government was overthrown by a peaceful revolution, as the father had predicted, and a new president and administration were installed in its place, where the name of the priest himself figured more than once as an important character in the politics of the country.

Almost immediately on my arrival in England, a dissolution of Parliament, followed by a general election, took place, and I was actively engaged for a fortnight endeavouring to filibuster a constituency. I failed in the attempt; but I was more than consoled by the fact that during the contest a special embassy to China was decided upon, with Lord Elgin as ambassador, who offered, if I did not get into Parliament, to take me out with him as his secretary. As special embassies to China are rarer events than general elections, I accepted my defeat with a light heart, more especially as I knew I had made the seat sure for next time, and a month afterwards was steaming down the Bay of Biscay on my way to far Cathay, with my dreams of empire in Central America relegated to the limbo of the past.

At Singapore we transferred ourselves from the P. & O. Company's steamer in which we had made the journey thus far, to H.M.S. Shannon, a 50-gun frigate commanded by Sir William Peel. She was a magnificent specimen of the naval architecture of those days; and her captain, who was justly proud of her, was, I think, not altogether satisfied with the prospect, during war-time, of the peaceful duty of carrying about an ambassador which had been allotted to him. Poor fellow! his fighting propensities were destined all too soon to be gratified, and the brilliant professional career which seemed in store for him to be abruptly and fatally terminated. I have never met a naval officer who so completely realised one's *beau idéal* of a sailor, or in whom a thorough knowledge of and devotion to his profession was combined with such a sound judgment, such gentle and amiable qualities, and such chivalrous daring. In some points there was a marked similarity in his character to that of General Gordon. There was the same high principle, stern sense of duty, lofty aspiration of aim, unbounded self-reliance, and intolerance of what seemed unworthy or ignoble, whether in governments or individuals.

It was at Galle that we had heard the first news of the outbreak of the Indian Mutiny; but the appalling details reached us at Singapore, and determined Lord Elgin, on his own responsibility, to divert the destination of the China expeditionary force from Hong Kong to Calcutta. Meantime we proceeded ourselves to the former place; and after staying there a few weeks to transact some necessary business, Lord Elgin determined to go himself to Calcutta, with the view of affording Lord Canning all the moral support in his power. On our return to Singapore in company with H.M.S. Pearl, commanded by Captain Sotheby, we found the 90th Regiment, together with some other troops, waiting for transport to Calcutta. These were embarked in the two ships, and we proceeded with them to India.

The transport which had conveyed the 90th Regiment had been wrecked in the Straits of Sunda, and one young officer had particularly distinguished himself in the confusion attendant upon getting the men safely ashore and putting them under canvas. This was the junior captain; and as he took passage with us in the Shannon, I was so fortunate as to make his acquaintance. I little suspected, however, when we parted at Calcutta, that the next time I was destined to meet him it would be as Lord Wolseley.

CHAPTER VII.

CALCUTTA DURING THE MUTINY, AND CHINA DURING
THE WAR 1857-1859.

THE extraordinary sensation produced by our arrival at Calcutta, and the relief which the appearance of a large body of British troops at so critical a juncture afforded the foreign population, I alluded to in a book published two years later;[1] but as this narrative had reference more especially to war and diplomacy in China, I may be permitted to recall the impressions which Calcutta made upon me at the time, and which are omitted in it. Certainly at the moment of our arrival the prevailing sentiment was panic. Each day witnessed the appearance of refugees from up country, with tales of fresh horrors. The whole country seemed slipping from our grasp: Delhi and Agra were in the hands of the mutineers; an English garrison, with a numerous party of civilians, with ladies and children, were besieged in Lucknow, which Havelock had not yet succeeded in relieving; the solitary survivor of the Cawnpore massacre had only arrived two or three days before. He was pointed out to me one

[1] Narrative of Lord Elgin's Embassy to China and Japan.

afternoon in awe-stricken tones by a friend. Almost every private house was an asylum for refugees. I was the guest of my old friend, the late Sir Arthur Buller, and shared his hospitality, with two ladies who had both been obliged to fly for their lives. One of them in particular had a very narrow escape. She left the station at which she was staying at nine P.M., fearing an outbreak, but scarcely anticipating it so soon. By six o'clock the next morning every man, woman, and child in the place had been murdered. For two nights and a day she rode or drove with a double-barrelled gun across her knees. Although she was robbed of this and of all the money she possessed, her life was spared by the natives she encountered; but during these thirty-six hours she tasted no food, and I remember being deeply impressed by the narrative of her adventures, though these are all the particulars I can recall. As everybody one met had lost some dear relative or friend, or was in feverish anxiety as to the fate of those from whom no news had been received, a fearful gloom pervaded the community; and this was heightened by the suspense attaching to Lucknow, where so many officials in both branches of the service, with delicate women and children, were collected. Every day we expected to hear the news of its fall; and with the experience of Cawnpore fresh in our memories, we knew that this meant the massacre, under the most revolting conditions, of every soul. It was no wonder, under these circumstances, that every soldier we brought was hurried up to Havelock, and that a naval brigade formed from the Shannon and Pearl, and placed under the command of Sir William Peel, was organised without delay. The whole force was drawn up on the morning of its despatch to the front, and addressed in a stirring speech by Lord Elgin, when we parted from our shipmates, many of whom we should never see again. There can be little doubt that these reinforcements, arriving when they did, enabled Havelock to relieve Lucknow, and that the salvation of that place by the English was the turning-point of the Mutiny. The China force thus diverted by Lord Elgin without waiting for instructions from home, thereby indefinitely postponing his own mission, amounted to 5000 men; and these just turned the scale at the critical moment. As a testimony to this, I cannot do better than quote a letter addressed by Sir Henry Ward, whose position as Governor of Ceylon enabled him to judge of the situation as well as any man, to Lord Elgin :—

"You may think me impertinent," he says, "in volunteering an opinion upon what, in the first instance, only concerns you and the Queen and Lord Canning. But having seen something of public life during a great part of my own, which is now fast verging into the 'sear and yellow leaf,' I may venture to say that I never knew a nobler thing than that which you have done, in preferring the safety of India to the success of your Chinese negotiations. If I know anything of English public opinion, this single act will place you higher in general estimation as a statesman than your whole past career, honourable and fortunate as it has been. For it is not every man who would venture to alter the destination of a force upon the despatch of which a Parliament has been dissolved, and a Government might have been superseded. It is not every man who would consign himself for many months to political inaction in order simply to serve the interests of his country. You have set a bright example at a moment of darkness and calamity; and if India can be saved, it is to you that we shall owe its redemption, for nothing short of the Chinese expedition would have supplied the means of holding our ground until further reinforcements are received."[1]

I have ventured to introduce this quotation because I do not think that either in public estimation, or in the accounts of the Indian Mutiny which have been published, the important bearing of this act on the part of Lord Elgin upon the destiny of our Indian empire has ever been sufficiently recognised and appreciated. The ambassador was at this time staying as the guest of Lord and Lady Canning, with his brother Sir Frederick Bruce, and Mr (now Sir Henry) Loch, at Government House. Here I used constantly to dine, and here I remember meeting Lord Clyde on the evening of his arrival in India to take the command of the army. It gave one a curious sensation to pass the native sentries at the gates and in the corridors of the Governor-General's residence, and see them all keeping guard with ramrods in their hands, instead of the muskets of which they had been deprived; and I was much struck, amid the universal exasperation, mingled with panic and gloom, which prevailed, at the perfectly calm and even unemotional attitude both of Lord and Lady Canning. For not only was the Governor-General overwhelmed with the cares and anxieties arising out of the formidable progress which the Mutiny was making, but he was exposed to the severest censure on the part of the English community at Calcutta, by whom he was nicknamed Clemency Canning, and who accused him of a forbearance in his conduct of affairs and treatment of the natives which had brought matters to their present pass,

[1] Extracts from Letters of Lord Elgin. Privately printed.

and which they believed imperilled not only the Indian empire, but their own lives. As nothing has a tendency to destroy the faculty of calm judgment so completely as panic, the violence of the language employed was usually in proportion to the degree of alarm that was felt—a sentiment no doubt exaggerated by the fact that it was mingled with contempt for the race from whose cruelty so much was feared.

"I have seldom," says Lord Elgin, in his diary during this episode, "from man or woman since I came to the East, heard a sentence which was reconcilable with the hypothesis that Christianity had ever come into the world. Detestation, contempt, ferocity, vengeance, whether Chinamen or Indians be the object. There are some three or four hundred servants in this house (Government House). When one first passes by their salaaming, one feels a little awkward. But the feeling soon wears off, and one moves among them with perfect indifference, treating them not as dogs, because in that case one would whistle to them and pat them, but as machines with which one can have no communion or sympathy. Of course those who can speak the language are somewhat more *en rapport* with the natives; but very slightly so, I take it. When the passions of fear and hatred are grafted on this indifference, the result is frightful, an absolute callousness as to the sufferings of those passions, which must be witnessed to be understood or believed."

I remember meeting one clergyman who contrasted, in my mind, very unfavourably with the filibustering friends with whom I had lately been associating, in the ferocious vindictiveness of his language, and the fury with which he expressed his indignation with Lord Canning because the latter had removed some commissioners who, not content with hanging all the rebels they could lay their hands on, had been insulting them by destroying their caste, and thus interfering, in their belief, with their prospects in a future state of existence. Alluding to this conversation, Lord Elgin remarks: "The reverend gentleman could not understand the conduct of the Government; could not see that there was any impropriety in torturing men's souls; seemed to think that a good deal might be said in favour of bodily torture as well. These are your teachers, O Israel! Imagine what the pupils become under such a leading!" The poor man was evidently utterly demoralised by fear. The holy father who offered to make me War Minister of Honduras was, I think, a better specimen of the Church militant here upon earth than he. Perhaps if, during my early experiences, I had not met such a singular variety of ecclesiastical specimens in different parts of the world, instead of remaining a rolling-stone to this day, they might have builded me into one of their temples.

At the same time, I must admit that the treatment of such a rebellion as that with which Lord Canning had to deal, involves very difficult and complicated considerations, as well from a moral as from an expediency point of view. I think there can be little doubt that if, when the first regiment mutinied at Barrackpore, the Governor-General had ordered them to be blown from the guns, instead of treating them with the leniency he did, the Mutiny would have been nipped in the bud, while he would have been handed down to posterity as a butcher of the most ferocious description, and his name branded with universal execration. No one would have known what thousands of lives and untold horrors might thus have been spared, and how merciful this act would have been, judged by the light of events which only transpired because it was not consummated; for had the Mutiny been thus checked, there would have been no apparent justification for an act of such barbarity. An illustration of an opposite kind occurred some years later in the case of the late Governor Eyre of Jamaica. It is impossible to say, now, what massacres by the negroes his timely severity may not have prevented: it is easy for those ensconced comfortably by their own firesides to sit in judgment upon men who have this tremendous responsibility to bear, and who feel that the lives of thousands of their countrymen and women depend upon the promptitude and vigour of their action; and it would be well that these arm-chair humanitarians should remember that the very spirit which prompts them to show no mercy to an unfortunate governor who may, under this terrific pressure, commit an error of judgment, is just the tendency which would lead them, if they were put in the place of their victim, to act as he did. Another very interesting instance of the same kind was brought under my immediate notice in Ceylon. I was in that island when a native rising occurred in the Kandyan province in the year 1849. Lord Torrington was Governor at the time, and my father was the Chief-Justice. It was soon apparent that the movement was not dangerous; not a European life was taken, and beyond the gathering on one or two occasions of some hundreds of natives, and the robbing of one or two planters' bungalows, nothing of importance occurred. Nevertheless, martial law was proclaimed, continued over a long period —I forget how long—but from first to last some two hundred natives were shot or hung. The sentiments of the English community became divided; so strong a current of public opinion set in condemnatory of the acts of the Government, that it was thought best at last to invoke the action of the civil tribunals, and a few acres were exempted from the operation of martial law in Kandy, in order that my father might try some of the leading rebels who had been captured, for high treason. This was a manifest blunder on the part of the Governor; either the country was too disturbed for the civil courts to sit, or it was sufficiently peaceable to render the action of the courts-martial unnecessary. As it was, while sitting in court listening to the tedious formalities of the ordinary legal processes, I actually on one occasion heard the distant reverberation of the volley which was terminating the existence of a man who had been tried the same day for the same crime by a drum-head court-martial. This was an insult alike to the majesty of the law and the common-sense of the community, and excited so strong a feeling of resentment on the part of the latter, that it ultimately led to Lord Torrington's recall. At the same time I have always felt that if Lord Torrington committed an error in judgment, which he undoubtedly did, it was one for which he was not to be judged too hardly, considering the pressure which at the first moment of panic was brought to bear upon him from certain quarters, though it was difficult to realise the state of mind which, after the insignificant character of the movement became evident, led him to prolong the state of martial law, and intrust the lives of men to the judgment of two or three young military officers, when there was no reason why they should not have the advantage of a trial in a legally constituted court. It may generally be assumed that when the British community cease to feel that danger exists, it has passed away some time before. A governor may often have to resist their demand for severity; he is safe in acceding to their appeal for clemency—and this was made by the majority of the Europeans in Ceylon for some time before the pressure of public opinion became so strong as finally to put an end to summary executions. Under no circumstances have the public in England any right to work themselves up to a state of excitement upon a subject upon which their remoteness from the scene of action, and ignorance of local conditions, absolutely disqualify them from passing a judgment. By so doing they run the risk of committing grave injustice and of blasting the career of conscientious and painstaking public servants, who, if they have blundered, are certainly not likely to have done so wilfully, and whose action, which they so loudly condemn, may have averted a very grave catastrophe.

The only excitement during our month's stay in Calcutta, beyond that attendant upon the arrival of news and refugees from the interior, was the anticipation of a riot—happily falsified—during the great Mohammedan festival of the Mohurrum. Some of the more timid residents adopted all sorts of precautions for escape in case of a general massacre; indeed there was a universal sense of living on a volcano, which imparted some piquancy to an existence that during the heats of August would otherwise have been decidedly dull.

By this time we had felt enough of what India during the Mutiny was like, not to care to prolong our experience, especially as there was no possibility of active cooperation; so we were not sorry to hear that a P. & O. steamer, which had been expressly chartered and fitted up for the accommodation of the embassy, was ready; and in it we bade adieu to Calcutta on the 3d of September, and shortly after found ourselves once more at anchor in the harbour of Hong Kong, within two months after we had left it.

The incidents of our war with China, and of our embassy to that country and Japan, which extended over two years, were so fully recorded in the history of it which I published shortly after our return to England, that it leaves me little to relate here. The experience was one pregnant alike with excitement and instruction. The excitement consisted in the novelty of some of our methods of warfare and the incidents attendant upon it, and the instruction in the new regions we visited. It was strange, for instance, in this nineteenth century, to find one's self adopting the contrivances of a by-gone age, and scaling walls by means of ladders in the face of the enemy. I do not know when I have felt a keener thrill of emotion than when we raced for the ladders at the taking of Canton, and clustered up them like bees, holding on to one another's legs, and nearly pulling each other down in the eager scramble. It was on this occasion that I saw Lord Gilford (now Admiral the Earl of Clanwilliam) shot in the arm. Then came the rush into the city, with its million of inhabitants, all crouching in terror, to capture Yeh, an achievement which was performed by Sir Astley Cooper Key, who seized him by the neck as he was in the act of scrambling over a wall in his back-garden, and held him down till assistance came. I came up a moment later with General Crealock, who made an admirable sketch of the truculent mandarin, while he was still trembling with alarm and uncertainty as to his fate. The other most memorable incidents, so far as they affected me personally, were the capture of the Peiho Forts, the scaling of the walls of Tientsin, and the bombardment of Nankin. On the first occasion, I had obtained permission from Lord Elgin to accompany the attacking squadron, and accepted the invitation of the late Captain Roderick Dew to go on board the Nimrod, the ship told off to lead the attack. When I saw the rows of batteries bristling with cannon on each side of the narrow river, between which we were to run the gauntlet, I somewhat repented of my warlike enthusiasm, and suggested to my kind host that I thought I should be safer in the maintop than on deck. He recommended me, however, to wait and see how the shot went; and it was fortunate I took his advice, for one of the first carried away the whole maintop. The Chinese had trained their guns, making sure we should attack on a high tide. As we attacked at low water, nearly all their shot passed over the attacking gunboats, and we escaped with but few casualties, the whole number not amounting to thirty. A year later, when the same forts were attacked, the Chinese had profited by experience, and repulsed the British force under Admiral Hope with a loss of over 400 men out of 700.

The scaling of the walls of Tientsin was a very absurd affair. Some English officers in the town having been insulted, and redress refused, a column of marines was sent down to exact it, upon which the gates were closed, and they were denied admittance. These gates were so massive that nothing short of artillery or battering-rams would have forced them. It occurred to Captains Sherard Osborn and Dew, with whom I happened to be, and who were accompanied by a boat's crew, to scale the walls and come upon the enemy in rear. This was no sooner said than done. By means of a pent roof of a house under the walls, and the crevices in the wall itself, we scrambled up unobserved, and, drawing our revolvers, suddenly dashed with loud yells upon the dense mass of people holding the gate on the inside. These, too panic-stricken to think of counting our numbers, and not knowing how many were behind us, fled in all directions, and we had quietly unbarred the gates and let in the troops before they had time to recover themselves. In this amusing operation not a shot was fired or a drop of blood spilt. It was different at the bombardment of Nankin, when the Taiping rebels opened upon us very unexpectedly as we were steaming past their batteries in the Furious, accompanied by four other ships of the squadron. Lord Elgin and I were standing with Captain Osborn on the bridge, and the first shot cut through a rope a couple of feet above his lordship's head. Osborn immediately ordered us both below, and the ambassador went down into his cabin to find another round-shot which had just entered it through the ship's side—so he did not seem much safer there. I was leaning over the bulwarks watching the batteries when another round-shot came through them close under my arm, one of the splinters tearing out my watch-chain. The ball then passed across the crowded deck without touching a soul, and through the opposite bulwark.

For interest, however, nothing equalled our entry into the bay of Yedo, and our fortnight's residence in that city, which until then had been hermetically sealed to foreigners. The suddenness with which Japanese civilisation burst upon our surprised senses, and its extreme novelty, can scarcely be realised now; but to have been the first Europeans who ever invaded the exclusive precincts of that great city was an experience never to be forgotten. So also was our memorable cruise for 600 miles up the unknown waters of the Yang-tse-Kiang, with its cities desolated by civil war, its majestic reaches, fine scenery, and the wondering population on its banks, as we steamed silently past them or wriggled for hours, and sometimes days, on some treacherous shoal. This kind of work, varied by one or two special missions upon which I was sent—one to Soochow, a large and at that time rarely visited city in the interior, where I had an interview with the governor-general of the province, and another to the head of the Taiping rebellion at Nankin, was pleasanter than that which afterwards fell to my lot as commissioner for the settlement of the trade and tariff, which used to involve a daily ride in chairs to the Chinese officials appointed for the purpose in Shanghai, numerous unwholesome Chinese repasts, and incessant wranglings over export and import duties. In June 1858 Sir Frederick Bruce returned to England with the Treaty of Tientsin, and I became acting secretary to the Embassy.

At last it all came to an end, winding up with an interesting four days' march with a column of 1200 men to a town near Canton, where it was considered desirable to make a display of force, on which occasion the French contingent, consisting of 150 men, who did not fire a shot, were afterwards reported in the French papers to have performed prodigies of valour. My companion on this march was the late Sir Harry Parkes, with whom, as well as with Sir Thomas Wade, I had been constantly associated, and whose unflinching nerve, knowledge of the language and of the character of the people, enabled him to render inestimable service. In his premature death in the midst of a brilliant career, the country has lost one of its most conscientious and gifted servants. In April 1859 the Embassy, having successfully accomplished its labours, often in the face of difficulties which seemed at the time almost insurmountable, returned to England.

CHAPTER VIII.

SOME SPORTING REMINISCENCES.

JUST four-and-thirty years have elapsed since I wrote my first article in 'Blackwood's Magazine.' It was entitled "A Sporting Settler in Ceylon," and was a review of Mr (now Sir Samuel) Baker's most graphic and entertaining book, 'The Rifle and the Hound in Ceylon.' I ventured to suggest to my friend the late Mr John Blackwood that, as I had taken part in many of the incidents that are there described, and had participated in some of those striking episodes of sport, I might be allowed to try my 'prentice hand at reviewing the book. Till then I had been more familiar with the use of the gun than of the pen; but the former has been long since laid aside in favour of the latter, and, on the whole, I think more sport can be got out of society than out of any herd of elephants, provided that you know where the weak spots lie, and your aim be accurate. Whether the effects which result to the literary sportsman in search of social quarry, are comparable from a moral and physical point of view with those which are involved in the pursuit of *feræ naturæ*, is a very different question; and when I look back to the years '49 and '50, and remember the keen unmitigated delight with which I anticipated a day in the jungle with the dogs, I doubt whether any more healthy or innocent form of enjoyment exists than the chase in wild tropical mountains of the grand animals with which they abound.

For this purpose there is no spot more delightfully situated than Newera Ellia, the sanatorium of Ceylon. It is a small plain, now partially converted by artificial means into a lake, surrounded by mountains, the highest rising to a height of nearly 9000 feet above the sea, and 2000 above the plain. Six-and-thirty years ago these highlands were all heavily timbered, as their elevation was too great for coffee-planting. I believe, however, that since they have been found adapted to the cultivation of tea and cinchona, plantations have taken the place of the thick jungle, which in those days were abundantly stocked with elephants, cheetahs, elk, wild boar, and many other descriptions of game. So numerous and daring were these animals, that the footprints of elephants which had been paying a nocturnal visit to the kitchen-garden were often to be seen among the cabbages; the loud bark of the elk was constantly audible from the house; and on more than one occasion cheetahs were killed making depredations upon the live stock. Upon one of these the bold forager came down and carried off a calf from the lawn at mid-day—not, however, without being observed. We followed him up so closely that he was obliged to drop his prey not many hundred yards after entering the jungle; and set three spring-guns, covering the carcass, feeling assured that the cheetah would return. We were not disappointed: an hour had scarcely elapsed before we heard the guns go off, and on rushing to the spot found the traces of blood, which we followed until we reached the animal breathing his last gasp. He was a fine specimen, but not so large as another which we captured alive in a trap, which we had baited with a kid. Although at this distance of time I have forgotten his exact dimensions, he was the largest I ever saw, and I preserved his skin for many years.

In those days there were generally two and sometimes three packs of hounds at Newera Ellia, each consisting of eight or ten couple; and at certain seasons I went out elk-hunting on foot—for the jungle was too thick to ride through—almost every morning, sometimes being in at the death of two of these noble animals before mid-day. The sambre, or elk, as he is popularly called, usually stands about thirteen hands high, and has magnificent antlers. When brought to bay he makes a gallant fight for it; and as it was not considered orthodox to carry any other weapon than a long hunting-knife, the final struggle was generally exciting, and by no means devoid of risk. The sport was rendered doubly enjoyable by the contrast it presented to the life in the plains. One left Colombo with a thermometer ranging perhaps from 90° to 95°, and in twenty-four hours was enjoying the blaze of a crackling wood-fire, glad to turn into bed under a thick blanket, and in the early morning to turn out again and find the edges of the puddles on the road fringed with a thin coating of ice. The reaction from the enervating heats that had been escaped, produced a delightful feeling of exhilaration, which was increased by the pleasures of anticipation, as one followed the experienced master of the pack and his dog-boy into the jungle, with the certainty, whichever beat one tried, of a scramble through splendid scenery, and the chance of some wild adventure by "flood or fell." Down all these wooded valleys dashed mountain torrents, in one of which the instinct of the elk would most probably bring him to bay; while here and there the forest ended abruptly, and enclosed island-like patches of open land, of greater or less extent, covered with long coarse grass, to which the game would also be very apt to turn, trusting to his superior fleetness in the open as a means of escape. There were always two or three greyhounds, or Scotch deerhounds, with the pack, to provide for this contingency; and these were kept in a leash, to be slipped as soon as the game broke cover, or, in the event of a bay, to be despatched in aid of the less powerful hunting-dogs. These, as a rule, were not necessarily thoroughbred, it being found that well-bred dogs were apt to get too keen, and lose themselves in their ardent pursuit of their game—falling, probably, a prey to the cheetahs; while your cur would abandon the chase when he found himself too far from home, and prudently return to the bosom of his family.

One of the inconveniences—as it constituted also one of the excitements—of this sport was, that you were liable at any moment to come upon game that you were not looking for, and did not want to find. I remember upon one occasion, after listening to the music of the dogs in the distance as they were apparently crossing some patch of open, to judge from the pace they were going, and after making up my mind as to the direction the elk was taking, and the pool in which he was likely to come to bay—for

I knew the country well for miles round—making a rush by the only available path through the dense jungle, and coming suddenly upon the stern of an elephant taking his mid-day siesta; at least I presumed, from his motionless attitude, that he was dozing, and I was thankful for it. He was standing in the narrow path, and completely blocked it up. I was so near him that I could have pulled his tail, had I felt inclined to be impertinent; as it was, the only course open to me was a strategic movement to the rear. The jungle was so thick that it was impossible to turn him without attracting his attention; and, under the circumstances, it seemed a pity to disturb his noon-day dreams. As he was quite alone, he was probably a "rogue" or "must" elephant; and in that case my chances of escape, should he happen to detect me, would have been small. I felt compelled even to deny myself the pleasure of trying to get a glimpse of his head and face. His huge hind-quarters towered above me as fixed and motionless as though they had been carved in stone. After staring at them for a minute or two, and turning the situation over in my mind, I retired stealthily and on tiptoe; and the result was, that before I could strike another path in the desired direction, the sound of the chase had died away. However, I made steadily for my pool, and as I approached it, knew, from the changed notes of the hounds, that what I had anticipated had occurred. The elk was standing on the edge of a fall some twenty or thirty feet high, with a part of the pack squatting on their haunches in a semicircle, barking at him, but afraid to go in at him: one foolhardy young cur had apparently been rash enough to venture too near, and got an ugly gash for his pains, which he was now licking disconsolately. The rest of the pack, with the seizing hounds and their owner, had apparently gone off upon some other scent, for they were nowhere to be seen, so I had all the fun to myself. No sooner did I appear upon the scene, than the elk made a bound, and plunged over the cataract into the pool below. It was a dark, deep-looking hole, some twenty yards in diameter, and here he began to swim about, apparently uninjured. The pack, declining to follow him in his leap, ran round, and jumping in from below, were soon all swimming about him, giving tongue and snapping prudently at his stern. As he apparently shrank from the shallow water, and kept swimming about the centre, there was nothing for it but to go in after him. So, putting my knife between my teeth, I swam out to him. When one is young and excited, the idea that animals suffer pain does not seem to occur to one; at all events, I look back to my performance upon that occasion with a certain feeling of disgust. The picture of the fine animal, with his head and magnificent antlers thrown back, his eye-balls staring, and his tongue half out, rises before me as vividly as if it was yesterday; but I cannot remember the details of that horrible struggle. I know that it lasted a long time; that more than once I had to swim ashore and rest; that the waters of the pool were tinged with blood from the repeated stabs I gave the poor beast, for it was difficult, while swimming, to strike a vital spot with sufficient force for it to be fatal; that the dogs, in their excitement, were very apt to mistake me for the elk; that, finally, we all came tumbling into the shallow water together, and that there I despatched him — a splendid animal of unusual size. I have had several encounters with elk at bay, and more than once have seen dogs receive such severe wounds that they have died of them, so savagely has the elk fought; but none of them were so exciting as this—perhaps because I was alone.

One soon got to know, from the way they gave tongue, whether the dogs were on an elk or on some other animal. A steady barking for a long time in one place was sure to indicate either a wild boar or a cheetah. On one occasion when we came up, we found the whole pack sitting in a circle round a tree, with their noses in the air, barking frantically, and on looking up we saw in the fork of the branches, about twelve feet from the ground, a cheetah, with his back curved like a cat, and his long tail swaying to and fro, looking viciously down, as though making up his mind for a spring, and only hesitating which hound to choose. It was a difficult matter to get the dogs off, and not altogether a safe one, as one never felt sure that the brute would not spring upon a hound as he saw them retreating. However, in spite of the aggressive expression of his ugly countenance, he was only too happy to be left alone, and we parted with every token of mutual respect, if not of esteem. This was the only occasion on which I ever saw the dogs "tree" a cheetah, and it is a somewhat rare occurrence; but they often used to bring a boar to bay, to the great disgust of their owner, who knew that it possibly meant the loss of a dog or two, and would certainly involve some severe wounds.

Once I came upon the pack when they had got a porcine monster ensconced in a bush, out of which gleamed his great curved tusks, while a dog lying dead by his side showed to what effective use he had already put them. The pack were evidently demoralised at the sight, for they kept at a respectful distance, but barked frantically. One or two dogs bolder than the rest would occasionally make a rush in; and they were so far useful, that they distracted the brute's attention, and enabled my friend and myself to crawl behind, while the dog-boy was helping the dogs to make demonstrations in front. Our object was to hamstring the beast while his attention was otherwise engaged; and this we succeeded in doing in one leg, though the suddenness with which he turned upon us when he felt the cut made us jump back with remarkable alacrity. We had meant to do both legs at the same moment, but the half-squatting position of the boar made it difficult, and I failed in mine; so we had to wait for another opportunity, for the boar was now on his guard. I did not note the time it took us to despatch this animal, but I do not think I exaggerate when I say that our struggle lasted half an hour, so wary was he, and so difficult was it to approach him near enough to stab him without getting gored. On the chance of having to deal with boars, it is as well to let the dog-boy carry a short spear.

In India, when out shooting from an elephant, I once shot a boar, paralysing his hind-quarters without killing him. I had been having good sport, and had only two or three bullets left. With the prospect of still needing these, I did not like to waste a ball on an animal unable to move, and thought of getting down to despatch him with my knife.

"Stop," said the mahout, when he learnt my intention;

"that is quite unnecessary. I will tell the elephant to kill him."

The mahout accordingly communicated his instructions to the elephant, who evidently did not relish them. The more the mahout urged him to advance on the boar, the more the latter showed his angry tusks, and the more the elephant backed away from him. Suddenly, as the result of repeated goading, the latter seemed to make up his great mind. He wheeled sharply round, backed upon the boar, got him between his hind legs, and fairly ground him up, —I heard all his bones cracking.

A very different kind of sport from that I have been describing at Newera Ellia, is to be had in the flat country in the northern province of Ceylon. One of the pleasantest shooting-trips I ever made, was in company with a friend—now the governor of a West India island—in this part of the country. We took a tent, a first-rate cook, and a train of a dozen or more men to carry our baggage, bedding, drinkables, and condiments, trusting entirely to our guns for the staple of existence for the whole party. As the game is most abundant in a region almost totally uninhabited, we could not rely upon the resources of the natives. We were then in the dry season, when the only water-supply is contained in ponds, or tanks, as they are called. Many of these dry up, and those that contain water, being far apart, become the resort of the wild animals inhabiting a wide range of country. The pleasantest time to shoot is at night: in the first place, because it is so fearfully hot, that it is almost impossible to be out during the day between nine in the morning and five in the afternoon; and in the second, because one is certain to see a much greater variety of game, and to have a much better chance at them.

Our plan of operations was to pitch our tent in the shadiest grove we could find near a tank. We then had two circular holes dug in the ground at a convenient distance apart on the edge of the tank—each hole four or five feet in diameter and about two feet deep. Round these we piled brushwood a foot high. This gave us a screen about three feet high, and in these holes we lay in ambush. A brilliant moon is of course indispensable for this kind of sport; and to assist our aim we whitened the sights of our rifles. Then, after a good dinner, we sallied forth, each accompanied by a native, who carried a bottle of strong cold tea, some sandwiches, and some dry elephant's droppings, to serve as tinder and keep a spark in all night for our pipes. I have counted the following different specimens of game come down to drink in the course of the night: elephants—a herd of sixteen—several buffaloes, a cheetah, two bears, some elk and wild boar, and a large herd of spotted deer, besides hog-deer, porcupines, and smaller animals. The latter always came early in the night; and in order not to disturb the larger game, which generally came after midnight, we usually refrained from firing at them. The deer were so numerous that it was always easy to kill two or three by daylight, so we reserved the moonlight hours for nobler sport. Even when the elephants came down it was more interesting to watch them than to shoot them. There would be the fine old patriarch with his harem, and the young ones performing the most fantastic aquatic gambols:

the clumsy disportings of a baby elephant, at a loss to know how to give full vent to the exuberance of his spirits, is one of the most grotesque sights imaginable, and one only to be witnessed under such exceptional conditions as I have described. Looking through a peep-hole in the brushwood screen, one could watch them at one's leisure. On one occasion, on their return from the water, in which they had been paddling and splashing themselves, to the jungle, the whole herd would have walked straight into the hole in which I was squatting had I not shown myself. I had already marked the father of the flock as the one I intended to kill, and he was not ten paces from me when I fired. He stopped, while the herd scattered, and fearing he would charge, I gave him the second barrel, and he sank ponderously to the earth. In my excitement I did not stop to reload, but making sure he was dead rushed out to secure my trophy. I had just got out my knife, and was stretching out my hand to lay hold of his tail to cut it off, when to my disgust he slowly rose and walked off after the ladies, leaving me amazed and confounded, and the subject of a good deal of chaff on the part of my companions. I was more lucky with a wild boar an hour or two afterwards. He, too, was approaching me in a direct line, coming from the jungle, when I fired at him, upon which he made a rush straight at me. The impetus was so great that, though he received the second barrel full in the forehead, he actually rolled dead into the hole. So close was my rifle to his head the second shot that his hair was all singed where the ball had entered. I have killed several wild-boar at different times in my life, but his were the largest tusks I ever got.

Feathered game were no less abundant and varied. There were pea-fowl, jungle-fowl—which is more like the domestic fowl than any other wild bird I know—and various kinds of water-fowl, from which it may be inferred that we fared sumptuously every day. Our cook, who was really an artist, and had served an apprenticeship under a French *chef* at Government House, found ample scope for his talents, and did full justice to his training. He had been careful before starting to lay in a good supply of sauces and flavourings. This was the kind of *menu* he used to place before us: wild-boar's head, venison-pasty, salmi of wild duck, roast peacock with buffalo-tongue, and curry of jungle-fowl. Our camp-followers rioted in good living; and though, including servants and horse-keepers, they numbered sixteen or eighteen, it was impossible for them to consume all the game we killed, and this in spite of neither of us being remarkably good shots.

The most singular shot I ever made was under rather peculiar conditions. It was a blazing hot day—I should think the thermometer must have been over a hundred in the tent—and I was lying panting on my bed, in a state of entire nudity, vainly trying to get a wink of sleep, in anticipation of the night-watch in store for me, when my servant stealthily crept into the tent with the intelligence that there was a flock of pea-fowl just outside. He held the flap of the tent back, and there they were strutting about within a hundred yards of it. As I looked they seemed to be taking alarm, and, afraid of losing them, I seized my rifle and rushed out with nothing else on. It was useless to attempt to stalk them—the plain upon which they were was a hard surface of baked cracked clay, with scarcely a shrub upon it. The only plan was to get as near them as possible—not an easy matter, for they took to running too, and pea-fowl can run faster than one has any idea of. At all events they seemed to me to do so, as, with bare head and body exposed to the scorching rays of the mid-day sun, I hurried on in pursuit, cutting my bare feet terribly on the sharp angles of the cracked clay. At last they took to wing, and I brought down to my surprise a splendid bird—at least he was splendid to look at, but proved rather tough to eat, for he was an old cock. I thought of clothing myself with his feathers so as to be able to return to the camp with some decency, but it might have looked vainglorious, considering the wonderful shot I had made. Indeed I took some credit for it at the time, for it is not everybody who has knocked over a peacock on the wing at a hundred yards with a rifle, especially with nothing on; but I am free to admit, after this lapse of time, that it was a pure fluke. I was so out of breath and blinded by perspiration at the moment, that I fired without being able to take any kind of aim. In India, where pea-fowl are sacred, they are perpetually offering the most tantalising shots to the sportsman, who is unable to take advantage of them; but no such prejudice exists in Ceylon, and they form a most valuable addition to the larder.

I remember once, when campaigning with the Turkish army in the provinces of the Transcaucasus, arriving at Sugdidi, the capital of Mingrelia, the day after the battle of the Ingour, only to find it deserted, and provisions scarce. Going out on a foraging expedition, and thinking that, as the palace had only just been abandoned by the Princess Dadiani, I might find something in the larder, I directed my steps in that direction, but found Turkish sentries at every ingress. Suddenly I heard the scream of a peacock, and my Ceylon experience recurred vividly to my mind. What a contribution to our mess he would be, I thought, if I could only get hold of him! Shooting him in the gardens of the palace was out of the question; indeed, I found that the one he was in was enclosed with a high wall. Scrambling to the top of it by the aid of the branches of a tree, I saw several members of his family strutting about. Now, it so happened I had provided myself with a hook and line with the view of also trying my luck in the river, and as I had a piece of bread also in my pocket, the notion occurred to me of fishing for one of these majestic birds from the top of the garden wall. This idea I immediately put into practice, and in a few moments my efforts were rewarded, and I was gingerly hauling up a tender young hen, in an agony lest her weight and struggles should break the line before I got her safely landed. A night or two afterwards I was dining with Omer Pasha, and recommended him to try one of the Princess's pea-fowl, a hint which resulted in my partaking of one at his table shortly afterwards.

In Ceylon, as a rule, the game is so abundant that one is never reduced to experimenting on strange diet. I once dined off young monkey, which is something like rabbit, but immeasurably superior to it. Travelling in the wilds of America, I lived for some time on bear-meat, which is excellent; and once the entire rations for the day for four of us consisted of a jay, a magpie, and a woodpecker. During the last days of the siege of Paris I tried the dainties which were then in vogue; but they were so far disguised by the exercise of culinary skill, that they all tasted very good. It requires a little practice to recognise at once the difference between dog, cat, and rat, if they are all prepared with equal care and delicacy. One of my sporting friends in Ceylon, camping out with his pack, and depending solely upon their exertions, succeeded, thanks to the talent and ingenuity of his cook, in giving some British tourists who paid him a visit a most varied *menu*. There was *ris de veau, filet de bœuf, côtelettes en papillotes, poulet sauté*, and I don't know what else besides. It was some time before his guests discovered that, under these high-sounding names, they were eating various preparations of elk. If it is the tailor who makes the man, it is the cook who makes the beast. In China and Japan diet is proverbially attended with the greatest uncertainty, and I never dined with a native of either of these countries without suffering for it the next day. On one occasion I was given a soup in which was floating what appeared to be pieces of vermicelli, chopped in lengths of about an inch. On inquiring what these little string-like substances were, I was informed they were rock-leeches!

But to return to our camp by the tank-side. I never in any part of the world saw so many deer as there were in its neighbourhood. The country was flat and park-like, the difference being that there was only a little burnt-up grass, and that the trees were for the most part represented by thorny bushes, from ten to fifteen feet high, dotted about it. Among these, large herds of deer were constantly feeding; and they had been so little molested, that it was no difficult matter to stalk them.

The tanks abounded in alligators, who came ashore to bask in the sun, all their heads turned towards the water except the watcher, whose face was turned landwards. When he gave the signal of danger, there was a general stampede into the tank. They were so numerous that we did not think them worth powder and ball, and their horny hides made it more trouble to kill them than they were worth. Once, when we were walking home, I saw my friend, who was walking parallel to myself on the other side of the tank, which was about fifty yards broad, take a shot at an alligator right in front of him; an instant afterwards I heard the ball crash into the branches of a tree under which I was walking. It had been deflected at right angles from the reptile's back, and I had a narrow escape in consequence. There is a method of catching alligators which I once saw practised in the southern part of the island, which affords some sport to those who are indifferent to the suffering it entails. You take a live puppy, and strap him on to a raft, formed of two pieces of tough wood lashed in the form of a cross. You sharpen all the four points of this cross, and fasten to it a hank of twine a yard long; to this you attach a rope. You then float your puppy, who is calling attention to his unhappy predicament by yelping loudly, on a still pool or backwater of the stream, and tie the end of the rope to a tree. You then see that your revolver is handy, and, with half-a-dozen or more natives, you sit under the tree and watch. In a few moments a pair of enormous jaws appear above the surface of the water, the puppy disappears into them, but they do not close with the facility with which they opened, for the cross has stuck in the brute's throat, and the strands of the hank of twine have got between his teeth. You now lay on to the rope with a will, and slowly draw the reluctant monster to shore, while he lashes the water with his tail in impotent rage. When you have got him on shore, you keep at a respectful distance, and make ball-practice with your revolver at his eye. If you keep on doing this long enough, you finally kill him. The alligators in some of the rivers of Ceylon are so voracious and numerous, that the natives, who are very fond of bathing, stake off their bathing-places. From these strongholds you can safely taunt an alligator, should he come and poke his nose between the bars, and sniff your tempting flavour—even jobbing at it with a knife. Near the mouths of the rivers, I have had places pointed out to me by the natives where they said it was safe to bathe, as the water was too salt for the alligators and too fresh for the sharks. My impression is, had I made the experiment, that I should have found them both there.

I once made rather an interesting shooting excursion to a rarely visited island, called Karative, on the western coast of Ceylon. It was evidently once a mere sandbank, and though it is fifteen miles in length, it narrows in places to a width of fifteen or twenty yards, the sea in rough weather making a clean breach over it. In parts it is more than a mile wide, and is covered with a low thick jungle, with patches of open. It is inhabited only by a few fishermen. It is well stocked with deer, buffalo, and wild black cattle. These latter are doubtless the descendants of cattle that were originally tame, but it must have been very long ago, for their fine delicate limbs and active motions, and uniformly black colour, present marked characteristics of difference from tame cattle; while their great shyness renders them an extremely difficult animal to shoot. I only managed to bag one, which I stalked after rather an original fashion. The herd were grazing in the open, so far from any jungle that it seemed impossible to get near them. It was a perfectly still day; the sea was like glass, as it generally was on the lee side of the island; and they were not above fifty yards from its edge; so I determined to stalk them from the sea. It was a nice sandy bottom, which did not deepen too abruptly, and when I had waded in about fifty yards I found myself up to the armpits. I had to wade for nearly a quarter of a mile, always keeping nothing but my head and shoulders visible, before I found myself opposite the herd, tormented the while by the fear that some sporting shark might consider me as good game as I thought the black cattle. Then crawling carefully shorewards, I got an easy shot at about eighty yards, and knocked over a fine young bull. We also stalked successfully, in the course of two days' shooting here, a couple of wild buffalo. The natives made a very novel suggestion: they were great fishers of porpoises, which they captured for the sake of the oil, and possessed in consequence a quantity of strong porpoise-nets. These they proposed to stretch across a narrow isthmus, from sea to sea, and staking them firmly, to drive the deer into them. As, when thus stretched and staked, they would be about eight feet high, there would be no chance of escape for the deer. At each end of the net men were stationed, who concealed themselves, as we did ourselves, while the drive was in progress, so as to prevent the deer, when they saw their danger, making a rush for the sea. It was a moment of great excitement, as we heard the crackling of the jungle in advance of the beaters betoken the presence of game; then out rushed half-a-dozen noble animals. We sprang to our feet as they crossed the narrow patch of open at full speed, and turning neither to the right nor left, dashed headlong into the net. In a moment all was confusion; there was a heap of deer entangling themselves more and more in their frantic struggles to break loose and escape, while the men ran up with ropes to bind them and make them captive: this was no easy matter, as their sharp hoofs and antlers inflict nasty wounds; however, it was at last successfully accomplished. I shall never forget the appearance which that struggling mass of men and deer presented, but I cannot now call to mind how many we captured—the stag with the finest antlers, I know, escaped.

Buffalo are very dangerous animals to shoot, I think more so than elephants, as it is more difficult to get away from them when they charge. I was once charged by one when riding peacefully on horseback and entirely unarmed, and he gave me an unpleasantly severe chase across country before I could shake him off.

The easiest way to shoot bears is to smoke them out of the holes or caves which they use as sleeping-places, and which the natives always know, and to lie in wait for them at the mouth; or to watch for them by tanks— though probably the commonest method is to drive them. This is the plan adopted in Turkey. Seven years ago, while staying at Constantinople, I was invited to join a bear-shooting expedition. News had arrived that they were numerous on the peninsula of Guemlik, in the Sea of Marmora, and good sport was promised us as a certainty. Nearly twenty years had elapsed since I had fired off a gun. I had never used a breech-loader in my life, for they had come into fashion after my day, and I had lost all kind of sporting enthusiasm; but the trip promised to be enjoyable so far as climate, new country, and fine scenery were concerned, and I was tempted by the society of four agreeable companions to make one of the party, rather as a spectator than as an active participator in the sport, which was the more reasonable as I was the only one of the party who had ever shot a bear. We landed at Guemlik, where H.M.S. Fawn, then surveying the Sea of Marmora, was lying at anchor, and adding two or three of the officers to our party, made a night sail in a native boat to the small fishing-village from which we were to strike inland. From this point we advanced in the early morning through lovely scenery some three or four miles into the interior, and found ourselves in the midst of a beautifully wooded, rolling, upland country, with open grassy valleys, rich soil, and abundance of water, almost totally uninhabited, and only thirty miles as the crow flies from Constantinople. It is one of the anomalies of Turkey that a region twenty miles in length by about ten broad, comprising fine forests and splendid agricultural land, should be lying waste within so short a distance of the capital of the empire and of the market which it affords. However, had it not been so, we should have had to go farther afield for our bears. As it was, with a good gang of beaters, we toiled all day without any result except a few false alarms. *En revanche* we had splendid appetites and sound slumbers on leaf-beds under the blue canopy of heaven, for we had brought no tents with us. Meantime I had so far caught the infection that I had accepted the offer of his second gun from a friend, and had occupied the post assigned to me at each beat with the most sportsmanlike conscientiousness. Next day we tried some new country. I had expressly asked the master of the hounds to post the others in the best stations, and was occupying the least likely place in one of the drives, my thoughts at the time far away from bear-shooting, when the sudden clamour of the dogs right in front of me roused my attention. There was no doubt about it this time. I was standing on the slope of a valley, bare except for a few bushes, near a path which led across a little stream into a wood on the opposite slope, which was now resounding with the shouts of beaters and the yelping of dogs. As I fixed my eyes on the point where the path entered the wood, I saw Bruin emerge. Slowly and deliberately he trotted up the path straight towards me; slowly and deliberately I retired behind a bush about six yards from the path, so as to screen myself from his observation and have a shot, which, even after twenty years without practice, it would be impossible to miss. The bear did not quicken his pace, and he was exactly abreast of me. I fired—at least I pulled the trigger. The first barrel responded with a gentle tick; the second followed suit. I almost fancied I could see the bear wink. At all events, he did not quicken his pace, and I had almost time to put a couple of cartridges into my gun—which, I need not say, did not go off for the simple reason that there was nothing in it—before he disappeared into some brushwood. Thus my first and only experience of breech-loaders has not been encouraging. But how was I, who had never been out with a party of breech-loading sportsmen, to suppose that, after I had loaded my own gun, and leant it against a tree during luncheon, somebody else's servant would come and abstract the cartridges and put them in his pocket, and then after luncheon hand me the gun without saying a word about it? I had been accustomed to consider that when I had loaded a gun myself it remained loaded unless I fired it off. The idea that any one else would consider himself entitled to draw the charge and pocket the cartridges never entered my head; but it seems it is the custom, for on my remonstrating with the man, who was an Englishman, he replied—

"Well, sir, I thought you would ha' looked to see whether the gun was loaded before you undertook to fire it off."

So I had to accept the situation, and the chaff by which it was accompanied; and as we none of us had another chance, I established my reputation as a "duffer," and we returned to Constantinople empty-handed.

The most magnificent country for sport, because the game is both larger and of a rarer description than in Ceylon, is in the Nepaulese Terai. Here, besides elephants, of which there are great numbers, there are tigers and rhinoceroses, and many other kinds of large game. In one of our beats here, which were organised on a large scale by the late Jung Bahadoor, whose guest I was at the time, we came upon traces of a rhinoceros, and were in great hopes that we should enclose him in the huge net of beaters that had been spread to surround the game, and which consisted of 400 elephants and two regiments of soldiers; but to my great disappointment he managed to break through and get away. We got, however, in the course of this beat, a couple of tigers, and several deer and wild boar. This is the only country in which the singular sport can be obtained of hunting wild elephants with tame ones, and capturing them alive,—an experience of which the Prince of Wales partook, also under the auspices of Jung Bahadoor, on the occasion of his visit to India. His Royal Highness, however, witnessed it as a spectator on horseback, which is exciting enough, but nothing to be compared to participating in it as an active combatant on the back of one of the elephants engaged in the *mêlée*. When I proposed that I should be allowed to make this experiment when I was with Jung Bahadoor in the winter of 1851, he at first absolutely refused, on the ground that it would be too dangerous for a novice—and was at last only induced to consent on my acquitting myself creditably at a rehearsal, when I was sent among the trees on the bare back of an elephant, with nothing but a rope to hold on by, and made to dodge the branches, as he was sent through them at his full speed. But this was nothing to the difficulty of arriving sound in wind and limb at the end of the chase on the following day, when the elephant I bestrode, or rather upon which I squatted monkey-fashion, formed one of a band of 150, tearing at a clumsy run through the jungle after the wild herd, which it finally overtook, and

L

with which it engaged in a pitched battle. I shall never forget the uproar and excitement of that singular conflict; the trumpeting of the elephants—the screams of the mahouts—the firing by the soldiers of blank-cartridge—the crashing of the branches as the huge monsters, with their trunks curled up, butted into one another like rams, and their riders deftly threw lassoes of rope over their unwieldy heads,—formed a combination of sounds and of sights calculated to leave a lasting impression. It is so difficult to take prisoners under these conditions, that we thought we did well in capturing four out of a herd of twelve. The mahout of the elephant I was on had particularly distinguished himself in one encounter, and presented me with the splintered tusk of an elephant that had been broken off in a charge upon us, as a trophy. I came home utterly exhausted by the violent exertion which had been necessary to escape being smashed to pieces by overhanging branches, or crushed by the mob of jostling elephants, which must have inevitably been my fate had I lost my grip of the loop of rope which was all there was to hold on by. In order the better to cling on, I had taken off my shoes, and my bleeding hands and feet bore testimony to the violence of the struggle it had cost me to retain my precarious position; but so great was my excitement at the time, that I only discovered afterwards how much my skin was the worse for wear.

All other sport in India of which I have partaken pales by comparison with this experience, though I know of nothing in its way to compare with a good day's pig-sticking, nor anything more disagreeably agitating than tiger-shooting on foot. Not being utterly reckless of existence, I was only once induced to share in this pastime; and as I felt that the chances were all in favour of the tiger, I was infinitely relieved to find that a rustling in the bushes within ten yards of me proceeded from a hyena, into which I did the unsportsmanlike thing of firing promptly, thus causing the tiger, which, I afterwards discovered, was just behind him, to head back upon the beaters, and break through them, to the great disgust of my poor host, a most daring sportsman and infallible shot, who afterwards fell a victim in the Mutiny under the most painful circumstances. It was under his auspices that I shot my first and only blue bull or nylgau, an animal the flesh of which is capital eating.

One of the most interesting countries I ever visited, in so far as large game is concerned, is the Malay Peninsula. I once took advantage of the kind invitation of the Tumangong, now the Sultan of Johore, to cross over from Singapore into his territory, and found on my arrival at a village, situated on a river a short distance in the interior, which had been recently settled by Chinamen engaged in the cultivation of gambier, that the whole population was panic-stricken by the depredations of tigers. No fewer than fifty men had been carried off by these ferocious beasts during the preceding three weeks while out at work. On one day alone five had disappeared, and the graveyard was full of umbrellas, the sign that the bones below them had been picked by tigers. Twenty plantations in the immediate vicinity were deserted in consequence; and as I had brought my rifle with me, I proposed going to one of these with a live bait, and watching for a marauder. The Chinamen would not hear of beating the jungle, as they felt convinced that they would simply fall a prey to the tigers, with which it was literally swarming. They eagerly accepted the other proposition, however, and soon secured a couple of dogs, who were doomed for bait. With these we started for a night-watch. Unfortunately, we had scarcely reached the deserted plantation, from which three men had been taken a day or two previously, when the sky became suddenly overcast, and the rain came down in a tropical torrent, putting all hope of sport out of the question. I much regretted I had not time to prolong my visit to this village, as, by killing tigers here, one would have been rendering a real service to the people; besides this, the surrounding country was full of other and in some respects more interesting game.

On the banks of these muddy rivers the sportsman, if he is also a naturalist, will find a double interest in bagging a saladang or wild water-ox, a species peculiar to the Malay Peninsula. In the recesses of these magnificent but gloomy forests he may surprise the wary tapir; while rhinoceroses are abundant, and elephants and nearly all the animals known in Southern India and Ceylon are to be found besides. I do not know how it may be now, but twenty-nine years ago, when I was there, these jungles were untrodden by the sportsman, and I feel convinced that any enterprising Nimrod who should go there now would find a happy hunting-ground.

CHAPTER IX.

AN EPISODE WITH GARIBALDI, AND AN EXPERIENCE
IN MONTENEGRO.

THE political attention of Europe was chiefly occupied during the early part of the year 1860 by negotiations of a mysterious character, which were taking place between the Emperor Napoleon and Count Cavour, which were consummated at Plombiéres, and which resulted in an arrangement by which, in return for the services France had rendered Italy during the war with Austria, and no doubt with a view to further favours to come, it was arranged on the part of Italy that Savoy and Nice should be given to France, provided that the populations of those provinces expressed their willingness to be thus transferred from one crown to another. The operation was one which I thought it would be interesting to witness, as I felt decidedly sceptical as to the readiness of a population thus to transfer their allegiance from one sovereign to another, and exchange a nationality to which, by tradition and association, they were attached, for one which they had been in the habit of regarding hitherto rather in the light of an enemy and a rival than as a friend. I therefore went in the first instance to Savoy, satisfied myself that my suspicions were well founded, and that the people in voting for annexation to France were doing so under the most distinct pressure on the part of the Italian Government and its officials on the spot, and that the popular sentiment was decidedly opposed to the contemplated transfer; and then proceeded to Turin, with the intention of going on in time to be present at the voting at Nice, after having conferred with certain Nizzards to whom I had letters of introduction at Turin, where the Chambers were then sitting, It was a self-imposed mission from first to last, undertaken partly to gratify curiosity, partly in the hope that I might be able to aid those who desired to resist annexation to France, and with whom I felt a strong sympathy, and partly to obtain "copy" wherewith to enlighten the British public as to the true state of the case. This I did to the best of my ability at the time;[1] but it was not possible then to narrate those more private incidents which, after the lapse of seven-and-twenty years, as most of the actors are dead, and the whole affair has passed into history, there is no longer any indiscretion in referring to.

At Turin I presented my letters of introduction to one of the Deputies from Nice, by whom I was most kindly received. Finding how strongly my sympathies were enlisted in the cause of his countrymen, he introduced me to several Nizzards, then staying in Turin for the purpose if possible of thwarting the policy of Count Cavour in so far as the transfer of their province to France was con-

---

[1] Universal Suffrage and Napoleon the Third. By Laurence Oliphant. William Blackwood & Sons, Edinburgh and London.

cerned. It is due to the great Italian minister and patriot to say that no one regretted more deeply than he did the necessity of parting with Nice, and of forcing from the inhabitants of that province their consent to their separation from Italy. It was, in his view, one of the sacrifices he was compelled to make for the unification of Italy—or rather the price which the Emperor demanded for abstention from active opposition to the creation of a United Italy; and even then, Napoleon never anticipated that it would ultimately include the Papal States and the kingdom of Naples. But inasmuch as it had been agreed that this annexation should only take place with the free consent of the populations concerned, and that, provided the Italian Government abstained from influencing them in an opposite sense, France could not claim the provinces if the plebiscite went against annexation—the Nizzards maintained that the unity of Italy would not be imperilled by allowing the people freedom of choice, and that it was not fair of the Government to throw all its influence into the scale, and to coerce them in the direction opposed to their wishes. It was probably a question upon which no one was really competent to form an opinion but Cavour himself. In all likelihood the understanding between that astute Italian and the French Emperor was, that the provinces must be given to France by fair means or foul, and that it was Cavour's business to make them appear fair. No one knew better than the Emperor how plebiscites might be arranged. However, this is only a conjecture: what is certain is, that the Nizzards whom I met at Turin were as patriotic as any other Italians, and did not wish to imperil Italian unity for the sake of Nice. They only wanted the terms of the convention with the French Emperor fairly carried out, and the people of Nice to be allowed to vote in entire freedom.

I confess I felt somewhat of a conspirator when, on the second night after my arrival at Turin, in response to an invitation to meet the Nizzard Committee, I was shown up a long dark stair to a large upper chamber, somewhere near the top of the house, where some fourteen or sixteen men were seated at a table. At its head was a red-bearded, slightly bald man, in a poncho, to whom my conductor introduced me. This was General Garibaldi, who, as a native of Nice himself, was the most active and energetic member of the Committee, and most intolerant of the political *escamotage*, as he called it, by which his birthplace was to be handed over to France. The point which the Committee was discussing when I entered was, whether it was worth while attempting any parliamentary opposition, or whether it would not be better to organise an *émeute* at Nice, which would at all events have the effect of postponing the vote, and of proving a strong feeling of opposition on the part of the people. Garibaldi was decidedly in favour of this latter course. Though a member of the Chamber himself, he had no belief, he said, in being able to persuade it to take any view that the Government would oppose; nor, in fact, did he see any form of parliamentary opposition open to him. His dislike and contempt for all constitutional methods of proceeding, and strong preference for the rough-and-ready way of solving the question which he advocated, were very amusing. The strongest argument in favour of the course he proposed lay in the fact that on the Sunday week, or in ten days from the night of our meeting, the vote was to take place at Nice, and if peaceable measures were persisted in much longer, there would be no time to organise violent ones. I had remained silent during the whole discussion, when Garibaldi suddenly turned to me and asked me my opinion. I ventured to say that I thought constitutional methods should be exhausted before violent ones were resorted to.

"Oh," he said, impatiently, "*interpellatione, sempre interpellatione!* I suppose a question in the Chamber is what you propose: what is the use of questions? what do they ever come to?"

"There is one question," I said, "which I think you should ask before you take the law into your own hands, and if you are beaten on that, you will be able to feel a clearer conscience in taking stronger measures, for the Chamber will, from our English constitutional standpoint, have put themselves in the wrong."

The fact of my being an Englishman made me an authority in a small way in the matter of parliamentary proceedings, and I was eagerly asked to formulate the motion which I proposed should be laid before the Chamber. I do not at this distance of time remember the exact wording, but the gist of it was that the Franco-Italian Convention, which provided for a plebiscite to be taken at Nice, should be submitted to the Chamber before the vote was taken, as it seemed contrary to all constitutional practice that a Government should make an arrangement with a foreign Power by which two valuable provinces were to be transferred to that Power, without the Chambers of the country thus to be deprived of them ever having an opportunity of seeing the document so disposing of them. It took Garibaldi some time to get this point into his head, and when he did, he only gave it a very qualified approval. However, it commended itself to the majority of those present, was put into proper shape, and, finally, Garibaldi consented to speak to it, but in such a half-hearted way that I did not feel much confidence in the result.

The next night I dined with Cavour, but avoided all allusion to the Nice question; indeed, when I thought of the magnificent services he had rendered to Italy, of the extraordinary genius he had displayed in the conduct of affairs, and of his disinterested patriotism, my conscience smote me even for the small share I was taking in an intrigue against his policy. But then his policy was one of intrigue from first to last—of splendid intrigue it is true, in which the Emperor of the French was to a great extent caught in his own toils—and one intrigue more or less would not matter, provided we could succeed without injuring the cause we all had at heart. Indeed I am convinced that Cavour in his secret soul would have been pleased at the success of a conspiracy which would have saved Nice to Italy, if it could have been made plain that he had no complicity in it; though he would probably have found a great difficulty in making the French Emperor believe this, and it might have involved him in serious complications. However, the game was too interesting not to take a hand in it, even if it was a very insignificant one; and the sympathy that I felt for my host, which his charming manner and which his subtle but great ability was ever sure to win for him, in no way conflicted with the regard I was already beginning to conceive for blunt, honest Garibaldi, with his hatred of the tortuous methods and diplomatic wiles of the great minister. Two days after, I went to the Chamber to hear Garibaldi speak to his interpellation. I had spent an hour or two with him in the interval talking it over. But certainly politics were not his strong point. He would not make a note or prepare his ideas; he told me several times what he intended to say, but never said twice the same thing, and always seemed to miss the principal points. I was not surprised, therefore, at a speech which brought down the House with cheers from its patriotic sentiments and glowing enthusiasm, which abounded in illogical attack upon Cavour, but which never really touched the point of his motion. Members who had cheered his references to United Italy could quite logically vote against his motion, for practically he had never spoken to it; and when we met later, after an ignominious defeat, he shrugged his shoulders and said—

"There, I told you so; that is what your fine interpellations and parliamentary methods always come to. I knew it would be all a waste of time and breath."

"Not so," I said; "at any rate, you have put yourself in the right; you have asked the Government to let you see the treaty under which Italy is to be despoiled of two of its fairest provinces, and they have refused. They have decided to hand them over to a foreign Power, without giving the country a chance of expressing an opinion upon the bargain which has been made, or of knowing what it is to get in return. I think, in default of this information, you can now, with a clear conscience, take any measures which seem to you desirable to prevent this act of arbitrary spoliation."

"Meet us to-night," he said, "and we will talk matters over."

So we had another conference in the upper room, and all were united in the opinion that the time had come for preventing the plebiscite from being taken on the following Sunday.

The plan proposed was a simple one, and did not involve any serious disturbance. It was alleged by the Nizzards present that the local officials had instructions to mislead the people, by telling them that the Government ordered them to vote "Yes"; and that, in fact, the Prefect and all the subordinate *employés* were engaged in an active canvass among the peasantry, who did not understand enough of the question, which had never been explained to them, to take a line of their own and vote "No" against the wish of the authorities. It was maintained that a fortnight of active canvassing by Garibaldi and the Nice Committee, with other patriots—who, when they understood it, would eagerly embrace the cause—would suffice not only to enlighten public opinion, but completely to change it; and that, if the day of the plebiscite could be postponed to the Sunday fortnight, the plebiscite might safely be taken on that day, with a tolerable certainty that the popular vote would be given against the annexation. The French troops were at this juncture on their return, after the peace which had been concluded between Austria and France at Solferino, to France, *viâ* the Riviera, and a large body of them were actually at Nice. It had been arranged, however, that, to avoid all appearance of compulsion, the town should be entirely denuded of troops on the day of the plebiscite, and that the Italian as well as the French soldiers should evacuate it for the day. The coast would therefore be comparatively clear for a popular movement, which, after all, would be on a very small scale—for all that it was intended to accomplish was to wait until the vote was taken, and then, before the contents could be counted, to smash the ballot-boxes, thus rendering a new ballot necessary. The friends of Nice at Turin would then negotiate with the Government to have the plebiscite taken a fortnight later; and they trusted to the effect which this disturbance would produce, and to the attention that would thus be called throughout the country to the attempt which had been frustrated, to force a premature vote to obtain this concession.

It was finally decided that on the following Saturday Garibaldi should leave Genoa, in a steamer to be chartered for the purpose, with two hundred men, and choosing his own time for landing, should enter the town, and break the ballot-boxes before the authorities had time to take the necessary precautions. I forget now the details of the plan; indeed I am not sure that they were discussed, as the affair was naturally one which was to be kept secret, and the execution of which was entirely to be intrusted to Garibaldi. The General now asked me whether I wished to join in the expedition, and on my expressing my readiness to do so, invited me to accompany him to Genoa a day or two afterwards. We made the journey in a carriage which had been reserved for him, and in which there was nobody but the General, his aide-de-camp, and myself. We had scarcely any conversation on the way, for he had brought a packet, containing apparently his morning's mail, and he was engaged in reading letters nearly the whole way. These for the most part he tore up into small fragments as soon as he had made himself acquainted with their contents; and by the time we reached Genoa, the floor of the carriage was thickly strewn with the litter, and looked like a gigantic waste-paper basket. My curiosity was much exercised to imagine what this enormous correspondence could be; but I have since had reason to believe that they were responses to a call for volunteers, but not for the Nice expedition. "And now," he said at last, after tearing up the last letter, as though his mind had been occupied with some other matter, and turning to me, "Let us consider what part you are to play in this Nice affair." I assured him I was ready for any part in which I could be useful. It was then arranged that immediately on my arrival at Genoa I should go to the diligence office, and try and engage at once an extra diligence to start the same evening for Nice. When I had secured the diligence, and arranged the hour for the start, I was to report to Garibaldi, who gave me the address at which he was to be found; he would then instruct eight or ten of his friends to wait for me at the outskirts of the town. These I was to pick up, and they were to prepare matters for his arrival on the following Sunday morning with 200 men. He also wrote a note in pencil to a confidential friend in Nice, introducing me to him, informing him that I was in his confidence, that I would explain to him so much of the plan as I knew, and be ready to offer any assistance in my power. By the time all these arrangements were discussed and the note written, we reached Genoa. In order to lose no time, as it was now getting late in the afternoon, after hurriedly taking some refreshment, I went off to the diligence office. Here I did not find my mission so easy of accomplishment as I expected. I asked whether it was possible to get an extra diligence to Nice.

"Yes," said the clerk; "by paying for it."

"All right," I replied; "tell me what it costs."

"How many passengers?" he asked.

Now Garibaldi had impressed upon me great reserve in this respect.

"I do not wish," he had said, "the people at the office to know who are going, or how many; you must engage the diligence, if possible, for yourself, and answer no questions."

Now that it came to the point, I found this an extremely difficult matter to do. The only plan was to fall back upon the proverbial eccentricity of the Milord Anglais.

"Oh, I have a friend or two; we meant to go by the diligence this morning, but were detained at Turin. It is my habit whenever I am too late for a diligence to take another. I like having a whole diligence to myself, then I can change about from one seat to another, and am sure not to be crowded."

"And you are ready to pay for sixteen places and six horses for that pleasure?" said the clerk.

"If I like to spend my money that way, what does it matter to anybody else?"

"What baggage have you?"

"A portmanteau each."

"It is very irregular," persisted the clerk; "such a thing has never happened to me before as for a man to want to engage a whole extra diligence to carry himself and his friend and a couple of portmanteaus, and I cannot take the responsibility of giving you one without consulting my superiors, which it is difficult for me to do at this late hour. If you like, I will give you a large carriage which holds six,—that ought to satisfy you."

Finally it was arranged that if I came back in an hour, the clerk would in the interval find out whether I could have the diligence, and I would then give him my answer in regard to the carriage, in the event of the diligence being refused.

I now repaired to the hotel which Garibaldi had indicated as his address, and which was a rough, old-fashioned, second-rate-looking place upon the quay. There was no doubt about the General being there, for there was a great hurrying in and out, and a buzzing of young men about the door, as though something of importance was going on inside. Before being admitted to the General, I was made to wait until my name was taken in to him: it was evident that precautions were being taken in regard to admissions into his presence. After a few moments I was shown into a large room, in which twenty or thirty men were at supper, and at the head of the table sat Garibaldi. He immediately made room for me next him; and before I had time to tell him the result of my mission at the diligence office, accosted me with—

"*Amico mio*, I am very sorry, but we must abandon all idea of carrying out our Nice programme. Behold these gentlemen from Sicily. All from Sicily! All come here to meet me, to say that the moment is ripe, that delay would be fatal to their hopes; that if we are to relieve their country from the oppression of Bomba, we must act at once. I had hoped to be able to carry out this little Nice affair first, for it is only a matter of a few days; but much as I regret it, the general opinion is, that we shall lose all if we try for too much; and fond as I am of my native province, I cannot sacrifice these greater hopes of Italy to it."

I will not vouch for these being the very words he used, but this was their exact sense.

I suppose my face showed my disappointment, for, as I remained silent, he continued—

"But if you desire to fight in a good cause, join us. I know you are not a soldier, but I will keep you with me, and find work for you."

I have never ceased regretting since I did not accept this offer. I should have been the only one of the 800 *prodi* that left Genoa a fortnight later who was not an Italian. I afterwards saw these 800 decorated at Naples. It is true many followers joined Garibaldi almost immediately on his landing; but those who embarked with him from Genoa were to a man Italians. While I was hesitating, the General explained to the Sicilians present the circumstances under which I was among them, and the offers he had made me, in which they all cordially joined. I had, however, just left England, expecting to be absent about a month, and had made engagements there which necessitated my return. Moreover, I had become so interested in this Nice question, and knew so little of what the chances of success were in Sicily, that I scarcely felt disposed to embark in an enterprise which, at the first glance, seemed rash and foolhardy in the highest degree. I wavered in my resolution, however, a good deal during supper, under the influence of the enthusiasm by which I was surrounded; and finally bidding Garibaldi a cordial farewell, and wishing him and his companions all success, beat a retreat, fearing that I should be unable otherwise to resist the temptation, which was every moment getting stronger, of joining them.

I went next morning to the office in time to catch the diligence, and my friend the clerk received me with a compassionate smile.

"So you have given up the idea of having a diligence to yourself," he remarked.

I fear he thought me not merely a very eccentric but a very weak-minded Englishman. I humbly crawled up into the *banquette* with a nod of assent, disappointed and dejected, and more and more a prey to vain regrets that I had not cast in my lot with the Sicilians.

At Nice I delivered the letter of introduction I had received from Garibaldi, now become useless, and told the gentleman to whom it was addressed the whole story. What I heard from him, combined with what fell under my own observation, made me feel still more regret at the abandonment of the enterprise; for it was the general opinion that the Nice episode would not have delayed the Sicilian expedition. Half an hour would have sufficed to break the ballot-boxes and scatter the votes; and Garibaldi could have been back in Genoa, and left the further details to those interested in carrying them out. I asked why it was necessary for Garibaldi to be present at all at so simple an operation, and whether there was not any one in the town who could collect a few determined men and carry it out. But the idea was scouted as impossible. There was only one man in all Italy, the magic of whose name and the prestige of whose presence was sufficient for these things. In Nice itself there was no one either with the faculty to organise, the courage to execute, or the authority to control, a movement of this sort; and I therefore consoled myself by taking the only revenge I could upon a population so weak and so easily misled by their authorities, by voting myself for their annexation to France. Of course I had no right whatever to vote; but that made no difference, provided you voted the right way. As for voting "No," that was almost impossible. The "No" tickets were very difficult to procure, while the "Yeses" were thrust into your hands from every direction. If ever ballot-boxes deserved to be smashed, and their contents scattered to the winds, those did which contained the popular vote under which Nice now forms part of the French Republic; and the operation of breaking them was one which a dozen resolute men, who were prepared to stand the consequences, might have performed with the greatest ease.

At the same time I am bound to say that, looked at by the light of subsequent events, and the prosperity which has attended Nice since its incorporation with France, the inhabitants have had no reason to regret the *escamotage* of which at the time they seemed the victims.

Two or three months after my return to England, in my quality of a rolling stone, I began rolling again. I rolled very pleasantly through Hungary, gathering moss of various sorts at divers hospitable Magyar country-houses. I rolled on to Belgrade, reaching it the day before Prince Milosch's death, an event which it was expected would produce a revolution—which, however, proved a mere flash in the pan—and witnessed the very singular funeral of that remarkably able and wicked old man. Here I made the acquaintance of his son and successor Prince Michael, destined to meet a violent death by assassination, and while staying with my old friend Mr Longworth, with whom I had been associated five years before in Circassia, and who was now Consul-General in Servia, was joined by the late Lord Edward St Maur; with him I rolled on through Bosnia and the Herzegovina, wilder and more turbulent in those days than they are now, abounding in brigand bands, enchanting scenery, and fleas, and in a chronic state of guerilla warfare with the Turkish Government, which invested travelling through the country with the pleasing charm of perpetual risk to life and limb. We sailed down the Narenta in an open boat, cruising delightfully through the archipelago of islands which fringe the Dalmatian coast to Ragusa. We rolled on by way of Cattaro into Montenegro, where I made the acquaintance of the Prince, then just married; and here I gathered a piece of moss which was so characteristic of the scale upon which the administration of the Principality was conducted, that it is worth narrating. The little town of Cettinje, which is its capital, did not then contain any hotel, properly so called, but the rare stranger who visited it was accommodated in a sort of lodging-house, in which there were one or two spare bedrooms; or, if they were not actually spare, their occupants turned out, I suppose for a consideration, on the arrival of a guest. The chamber assigned to me had apparently been thus vacated. Its former occupant had evidently been a man of modest requirements, for the entire furniture consisted of a bed, a huge chest, and a chair. I much wondered at the absence of a table and the presence of the chest, but the latter was better than nothing; and when a boiled chicken was brought to me as my evening repast, I spread one of my own towels upon it, in the absence of a tablecloth, and squatting uncomfortably on the solitary chair, proceeded to make the best of existing conditions. I was in the act of dissecting an extremely tough wing, when the door suddenly opened, and a stalwart Montenegrin, looking magnificent in his national costume, stalked in. He addressed me with great politeness in his native tongue—at least I gathered from his manner that he was polite, for I could not understand a word of what he said. As he was evidently a man of some position, in other words, as he seemed to be a gentleman of Montenegro, I rose and bowed with much ceremony, addressing him fluently in the English language; upon which he drew an immense key from his pocket, and pointed to the lock of the chest, thus giving me to understand that he wished to open it. In order for him to accomplish this, it was necessary for me to remove my dinner, an operation which was speedily performed. As he seemed a frank and engaging sort of person without any secrets, and as I was possessed with the natural curiosity of a stone gathering moss, I looked over him while he opened the chest, to see what was in it. To my astonishment it was full to the brim of bags of money. Not only this, but my strange visitor opened one of them, and poured out a handful of gold. They were evidently all full of gold. When he had counted out what he wanted—which, as well as my memory serves me, was over a hundred pounds—he tied up the bag again, replaced it, locked up the chest, helped me with many Sclavonic expressions, which I have no doubt were apologies, to lay my cloth and spread my banquet again; and with a final polite salutation vanished, leaving me alone, and in perfect confidence with the untold treasure which he had thus revealed to me. There was something almost uncanny in dining and sleeping alone with so much money. At night the chest seemed to assume gigantic proportions, and I felt as if I had been put into a haunted room. The absolute confidence placed in me, an utter stranger, for I had not been in the place a couple of hours, and had not yet presented my letter of introduction to the Prince, appalled me; and I went to sleep vainly trying to unravel a mystery so unlike any I had expected to find in the barren wilds of Montenegro. It was not solved until next day, when, dining with the Prince, I met my visitor of the previous evening. I then acquired the information, through a Russian gentleman present who spoke French, that the chest upon which I had dined contained the entire finances of the Principality; and that the Montenegrin who had unlocked it, and vacated his chamber in my behalf, was its Chancellor of the Exchequer!

From Montenegro we rolled down to Corfu, where Mr Herbert, then attached to the Legation at Athens, joined us, and we spent some very pleasant days together. I little thought when I parted from my friends, to embark on board the steamer for Ancona, how tragically their young lives were destined to be terminated—Lord Edward to fall a victim to a bear while shooting in India, and Herbert to be held for a ransom by brigands, and finally murdered by them near the plains of Marathon. At Ancona I found the hospitals full of wounded from the battle of Castel Fidardo, which had just been fought; thence I rolled through Italy in a diligence for three days and two nights, in company with sundry Papal *sbirri* as fellow-passengers, who were escaping to the shelter of Rome from the provinces which the Pope was rapidly losing, in terror of their lives lest their identity should be recognised by the inhabitants of the villages at which we stopped to change horses; and so into the sacred city, where all was suppressed excitement at the changes which were transpiring in the Italian Peninsula.

But I did not linger there, for I was anxious to see Garibaldi once more, now administering at Naples the kingdom which he had conquered since we had parted a few months before. He received me with affectionate cordiality, and listened with interest to my account of the taking of the vote at Nice, but insisted that he could not regret the decision he had arrived at, as he felt convinced that his Sicilian expedition would have been marred had he involved himself in political difficulties with his own Government at such a crisis, in which he was very possibly right. Then I rolled out to see a little fighting near Capua, but all the serious work had been accomplished, and I lodged a few days with my friend the late General Eber, who had made his headquarters in the royal palace at Caserta; lodged sumptuously, for every room and every bed in the palace was occupied except the royal bedroom and the royal bed, which the General himself had been too modest to appropriate, and which, as it was the only one vacant, he assigned to me—a bed so gorgeous, with its gold and lace and satin, that I doubted whether the king himself did not keep it for show. However, it turned out a very good one to sleep in.

At last the day came when Victor Emmanuel arrived to receive a kingdom from the hands of the Nice sailor; and as I saw them both appear on the balcony of the palace from the square below, I was reminded of a certain day twelve years before, when I formed one of a mob in that same square, at the moment that, by Bomba's order, it was fired upon by the troops, and I was able to identify the very *port cochère* into which I had fled for refuge on that occasion. Now I was listening to the voice of the deliverer, standing with bared head, and in red shirt, presenting a kingdom to his sovereign, and to the ringing cheers of the liberated multitude, as, with enthusiastic demonstrations of joy, they welcomed their new ruler. Thus did United Italy owe its existence to a combination of the most opposite qualities in the persons of its two greatest patriots, who would not work together; for it is certain that Cavour could never have created it without Garibaldi, or Garibaldi have achieved success without Cavour.

CHAPTER X.

THE ATTACK ON THE BRITISH LEGATION IN JAPAN
IN 1861.

IN October 1860, Mr de Norman, First Secretary of Legation in Japan, who was temporarily attached to Lord Elgin's second special embassy to China, was barbarously tortured and murdered at Pekin; and early in the following year I was sent out to succeed him. Sir Rutherford Alcock, who had been appointed Minister to Japan under the treaty which we made with that country in 1858, when I was acting-secretary to the special mission, had applied for two years' leave; and thus the prospect was opened to me of acting as *chargé d'affaires* at Yedo for that period. It was one which my former brief experience in that interesting and comparatively unknown country rendered extremely tempting; and early in June I reached Shanghai, on my way to Yokohama. I was extremely sorry to find that I had just missed Sir Rutherford, who had left Shanghai, only a fortnight before, for Nagasaki, from which town he intended to travel overland to Yedo—a most interesting journey of at least a month, through an entirely unknown country;

an experience which, in view of my future residence in it, would have been valuable in many ways. There was nothing left for it but to go, on the first opportunity, by sea; and towards the end of the month I reached Yokohama, from which port I lost no time in pushing on to Yedo. Here I found the Legation established in a temple at the entrance to the city, in one of its principal suburbs, called Sinagawa. It was separated from the sea by a highroad, and on entering the large gateway, an avenue, about three hundred yards long, led to a second gateway behind which stood the temple buildings. In the outside court were the servants' offices and stables, in which stood always, saddled and bridled, like those of the knights of Branksome Hall, the horses of our mounted Japanese bodyguard, without whose escort no member of the Legation could at that time take a ride abroad. Besides these, there was a foot-guard, partly composed of soldiers of the Tycoon, or Temporal Emperor, as he was then called, and partly by retainers of the Daimios, or feudatory chiefs of the country—the whole amounting to 150 men. These guards were placed here by the Government for our protection, although some of us at the time thought that the precaution was altogether exaggerated and unnecessary, and that their constant presence was intended rather as a measure of surveillance over our movements. To what extent this latter motive operated it is impossible to conjecture, but the sequel showed that the apprehensions of the Government for our safety were by no means unfounded. I had been accompanied from England by Mr Reginald Russell, who had been appointed *attaché*, and it was with no little curiosity that we rode up the avenue to what was to be our future home.

Two or three members of the Legation were waiting to receive us, and showed us over the quaint construction which had been appropriated by the Japanese Government to the use of the first foreign Minister who had ever resided in their capital. Part of the building was still used for ecclesiastical purposes, and haunted by priests; but our quarters were roomy and comfortable, the interior economy being susceptible of modification in the number, size, and arrangement of the rooms, by the simple expedient of moving the partition-walls, which consisted of paper-screens running in grooves. The ease with which these could be burst through, as it afterwards proved, afforded equal facilities of escape and attack. One felt rather as if one was living in a bandbox; and there was an air of flimsiness about the whole construction by no means calculated to inspire a sense of security in a capital of over two millions of people, a large proportion of whom, we were given to understand, were thirsting for our lives. Fortunately for our peace of mind, we did not realise this at the time, and were taken up rather by the quaintness and novelty of our new abode, and the picturesqueness of its surroundings. We congratulated ourselves upon the charming garden and grounds, comprising probably two or three acres, abundantly furnished with magnificent wide-spreading trees, and innumerable shrubs and plants which were new to us; while small ponds and tiny islands contributed a feature which is generally to be found in the landscape-gardening in which the Japanese are so proficient. Sir Rutherford Alcock was not expected to arrive for a week, and I occupied the time in establishing myself in my new quarters, and in exploring the neighbourhood on horseback.

On these occasions we were always accompanied by an escort of twenty or thirty horsemen, or *yaconins*, as they are called, mounted on wiry ponies, shod with straw shoes, and with a marked tendency to being vicious and unmanageable. These exploratory rides were a great source of delight and interest to me, for although I had been in the country before, my visit had only lasted a fortnight; and my time had been exclusively devoted to official work, and the examination of the city of Yedo itself, so that I had seen nothing whatever of the surrounding country. Now we scampered across it, to the great consternation of our escort, who found great difficulty in keeping up with us— so much so, that upon more than one occasion only two or three of the original number succeeded in reaching home with us. I had determined, moreover, upon making an entomological collection for the British Museum, and set the juvenile part of the population of the villages through which I passed to collecting insects, in the hope that on subsequent visits I might find something worth having. I was successful in almost my first ride in finding a common-looking but very rare beetle; and in this pursuit my English servant—who had spent his youth in the house of a naturalist and ornithologist, and was skilled in the use of the blow-pipe, and in the cleaning and stuffing of birds —took an eager interest.

After I had been at Yedo about a week, we received news of the approach of Sir Rutherford Alcock and his party, and rode out ten miles to meet them. We were delighted to see them arrive safe and sound after a land-journey of thirty-two days, as we had not been without anxiety on their behalf—for Japan at that period was a region in which sinister rumours were rife, and we never knew how much or how little to believe of them; but now the great experiment of traversing the country for the first time by Europeans had been safely and successfully accomplished, and perhaps contributed to lull us into a security, the fallacy of which was destined so shortly to be proved to us.

On the night of the 5th of July a comet was visible, a circumstance to which some of us possibly owed our lives, for we sat up till an unusually late hour looking at it. As one of the party was gifted with a good voice and an extensive repertory of songs, and the evening was warm and still, we protracted our vigil in the open air until past midnight. At our mid-day halt on my ride from Yokohama to Yedo, I had acquired the affections of a stray dog, by feeding him with our luncheon-scraps; and this animal had permanently attached himself to me, and was lying across the threshold of the door of my room when I went to bed. I had scarcely blown out my candle and settled myself to a grateful repose, when this dog broke into a sudden and furious barking, and at the same moment I heard the sounds of a watchman's rattle. We had two of these functionaries, whose business it was to perambulate the garden alternately throughout the night, and to show that they were on the alert by springing from time to time a rattle made of bamboo which they carried. Roused by these noises, I listened attentively, and distinctly heard the sounds of what seemed a scuffle at the front door. My room was on the other side of the house, and opened on to the garden, from which quarter it was entirely unprotected. It was connected with the front of the house by a narrow passage, the walls of which, if I remember right, were of lath-and-plaster, or at all events of some firmer material than the usual paper-screens. Thinking that the disturbance was probably caused by some quarrel among the servants, I jumped out of bed, intending to arm myself with my revolver, which was lying in its case on the table. Unfortunately my servant had that day been cleaning it, and after replacing it and locking the case, had put the key where I could not lay my hand upon it. A box which contained a sword and a coat of mail, which had been laughingly presented to me before leaving England by an anxious friend, had not been opened; so, although well supplied with means both of offence and defence, I was forced in the hurry of the moment to content myself with a hunting-crop, the handle of which was so heavily weighted, that I considered it a sufficiently formidable weapon with which to meet anybody belonging to our own household that I was likely to encounter. Meantime the dog continued to bark violently, and to exhibit unmistakable signs of alarm. Stepping past him, I proceeded along the passage leading to the front of the house, which was only dimly lighted by an oil-lamp that was standing in the dining-room; the first room on my left was that occupied by Russell, whom I hurriedly roused, and then hearing the noise increasing, rushed out towards it. I had scarcely taken two steps, when I dimly perceived the advancing figure of a Japanese, with uplifted arms and sword; and now commenced a struggle of which it is difficult to render an account. I remember feeling most unaccountably hampered in my efforts to bring the heavy butt-end of my hunting-whip to bear upon him, and to be aware that he was aiming blow after blow at me, and no less unaccountably missing me, and feeling ready to cry with vexation at being without my revolver, and being aware that it was a life-and-death struggle, which could only end one way, when suddenly I was blinded by the flash of a shot, and my left arm, which I was instinctively holding up to shield my head, dropped disabled. I naturally thought I had been shot, but it turned out that this shot saved my life.

Among those who had accompanied Sir Rutherford Alcock from Nagasaki was Mr Morrison, then consul at that port. His servant seems to have encountered one of our assailants, masked and in chain-armour, in his first rush into the building, about which he fortunately did not know his way, and the servant, escaping from him, succeeded in safely reaching his master's room, and in arousing him. Seizing his revolver, Morrison sallied forth, and, attracted by the noise of my struggle, approached from behind me, and placing his revolver over my shoulder, shot my antagonist at the very moment that he had inflicted a severe cut with his long two-handed sword on my left arm, a little above the wrist. A moment after, Morrison received a cut over the forehead and across the eyebrow from another Japanese, at whom he emptied the second barrel of his pistol. An instant lull succeeded these shots. It was too dark to see what their effect had been, but the narrow passage was no longer blocked by the forms of our assailants. My impression is that one was on the ground. We were both bleeding so profusely, and felt so disabled, that there was nothing left for us but to retreat, and this we instinctively did to the room which contained the light. This was placed in a part of the dining-room which had been screened off so as to make an office for Sir Rutherford Alcock, with whose bedroom it communicated. The screen reached about three-fourths across the dining-room. In this office we found Sir Rutherford, who had just been roused, and were joined in the next minute or two by three other members of the Legation, Mr Russell, and my servant B., all hurriedly escaping from a noise and confusion which increased in intensity every moment. B., on the first alarm, had begun to load his double-barrelled gun, and had finished with the exception of putting on the caps—this was before the days of breech-loaders—when two Japanese jumped in at his window. Fortunately, spread out before it on a table were two open insect-cases, with the spoils of the week impaled on pins. On these the assailants jumped with their bare feet, and upsetting the table, came sprawling into the room, thus giving B., who had lost the caps in the start he received, time to spring through the paper wall of his room, like a harlequin, and reach us in safety. At this juncture the position of affairs was not reassuring. We numbered eight behind the screen, of whom two were *hors de combat*. Our available means of defence consisted of three revolvers and a double-barrelled gun. Of the European inmates of the Legation three were missing; one of these was Mr Wirgman, the artist of the 'Illustrated London News,' who had accompanied Sir Rutherford in his journey from Nagasaki; and of the two others, one lived in a cottage somewhat detached from the temple. Meantime Sir Rutherford, who fortunately possessed some surgical skill, was engaged in binding up my arm. The gash was to the bone, cutting through three of the extensor tendons, so that to this day I am unable to hold erect three fingers of my left hand. I should undoubtedly have bled to death had it not been for the efficient measures thus kindly and promptly adopted to stop the hæmorrhage. As it was, I was becoming very faint from loss of blood, as I now discovered that I had also received another and very serious wound over the right collar-bone, and unpleasantly near the jugular vein, of which, in the excitement of the struggle, I had been totally unconscious. Also a very slight tip from the sword high up on the right arm, the mark of which, however, is still visible; and a blow which I did not discover till next day, which broke several of the metacarpal bones of the left hand. I never could imagine how or when I received this blow; but it was an evidence that we must have been at one moment of the struggle at very close quarters.

Meantime the noise of cutting and slashing resounded through the house; and while it drew nearer every moment, we were at a loss to conceive who our assailants could be, and why the guard had not come to our rescue —unless, indeed, they were in the plot to murder us. At last we heard all the glass crash on the sideboard in the dining-room, and we knew that our moment had come. My companions had made up their minds to sell their lives dearly; and every man who was fortunate enough to possess one, was standing with his finger on the trigger of his revolver, while this time the caps were safely on B.'s double-barrelled gun. I suggested to one of the party—I forget which now—that they would have a chance for their lives by escaping into the garden and hiding among the bushes, which they could easily have done; but the answer was that they could not take me with them, and they had determined not to desert me, but to stand or fall together—for which I felt at the time intensely grateful, and do still, though I had at that moment given up all hope of escape. I was overcome by a feeling of faintness, which made me regard the prospect of immediate death with complete indifference, until B., while he was giving me some water to drink, murmured in my ear, "Do you think they will torture us, sir, before they kill us?" This horrible suggestion brought out a cold perspiration; and I trust I may never again experience the sensation of dread with which it inspired me, and which I was too weak to fight against. It did not last long, however, for almost at the same moment there was an immense increase of noise, and the clashing of swords, intermingled with sharp cries and ejaculations, resounded from the other side of the screen, and our curiosity and hope were excited in the highest degree, for we thought it indicated a possible rescue. In a few moments it subsided, and all was still; and Sir Rutherford, followed by Mr Lowder, went cautiously out on a reconnoitring expedition, to find the dining-room looking like a shambles, and to discover some Japanese retreating down the passage, at whom Mr Lowder fired a shot from his revolver. Shortly after they returned, Mr Macdonald, one of the gentlemen whose room was situated out of the line of attack, appeared disguised in a Japanese dress, accompanied by some of the guard, excited and blood-bespattered, and we knew that we were saved by them, though not a second too soon. Had our assailants not been attacked in rear by the guard at the moment they were in the dining-room, they must inevitably in a few seconds more have discovered us behind the screen, and this account of that eventful night's proceedings would never have been written. We were now informed that some of our assailants had been killed, that the guard were searching for others in the grounds, and that reinforcements had been sent for. These appeared soon after; and I have never seen a more dramatic and picturesque sight than these men, all clad in chain-armour, with their steel head-pieces, long two-handed swords, and Japanese lanterns, filing through the house, and out into the starlight. It was like a scene from the "Huguenots," and as I watched them from the arm-chair in which I was still lying, swathed and bandaged, was one of the most vivid impressions produced upon my mind on that night of lively sensations.

About this time Mr Wirgman, the artist of the 'Illustrated London News,' turned up, coated with a thick breastplate of mud. He had taken refuge under the house, which was raised about eighteen inches from the ground, and crawling in on his stomach, had remained in profound but somewhat dirty security under the flooring. With the true spirit of his calling, he immediately set about portraying the most striking features of the episode, for the benefit of the British public. Mr Gower, another gentleman who lived in a little cottage apart, also appeared safe and sound, having been throughout removed from the scene of the strife.

It was about three o'clock in the morning that I determined to struggle back to bed; and even then the soldiers were hunting about the garden for concealed members of the gang that had attacked us, prodding the bushes with their swords, and searching into hidden recesses. As, supported by friendly arms, I tottered round the screen into the dining-room, a ghastly sight met my gaze. Under the sideboard, completely severed from the body, was a man's head. The body was lying in the middle of the room. I had in the first instance rushed out of my bedroom barefooted, and in my night-dress. I now found myself slipping about in blood,—for butchers' work had been done here,—and feeling something like an oyster under my bare foot, I perceived it was a human eye. One of the bodies was terribly disfigured; the whole of the front part of the head had been sliced off as though with an adze, leaving only the back of the brain visible. Early in the morning I was roused from a troubled doze by six or eight solemn-looking elderly Japanese, who announced that they were the Imperial physicians come to inquire after my health. I positively refused to allow them to remove the bandages and examine the wounds; so they contented themselves with looking very wise, examining my tongue, and placing their ears over my heart. As the day advanced, and I recovered somewhat from the excitement and the exhaustion, I was surprised at finding that I suffered so little pain, and felt so well, considering the amount of blood that I had lost. So I scrambled out to look at the scene of the conflict—for it was difficult under the circumstances to remain quietly in bed. I naturally first visited the spot where I had met my Japanese opponent, and discovered that the reason we had so much difficulty in getting at each other was owing to a small beam, or rather rafter, which spanned the narrow passage, about seven feet from the ground. Its edge was as full of deep sword-cuts as a crimped herring, any one of which would have been sufficient to split open my skull, which my antagonist must have thought unusually hard. I evidently owed my life to the fact that I had remained stationary under this beam, which had acted as a permanent and most effective guard—the cuts I received being merely the tips from the sword as it glanced off. There was a plentiful bespattering of blood on the wall at the side, in which was also indented the shape of the handle of my hunting-whip. The blow must have been given with considerable force to make it; but I feel convinced that under such circumstances one is for the moment endowed with an altogether exceptional strength. I now pursued my investigations into some of the other rooms, which all bore marks of the ferocious nature of the attack. The assailants appear to have slashed about recklessly in the dark, in the hope of striking a victim. Some of the mattresses were prodded through and through; one bedpost was completely severed by a single sword-cut; and a Bible lying on a table was cut three-quarters through. We were now in a position to add up the list of killed and wounded, and estimate results generally, while we also had to calculate how they might affect our own future position and policy.

Although one of our assailants, a stalwart young fellow with a somewhat hang-dog countenance, was taken prisoner and afterwards executed, we had some difficulty in making out at the time of whom the gang was actually composed. That they were Lonins there was no doubt. Lonins are an outlaw class, the retainers or clansmen of Daimios who, having committed some offence, have left the service of their prince, and banding themselves together, form a society of desperadoes, who are employed often by their old chiefs, to whom they continue to owe a certain allegiance, for any daring enterprise, by which, if it fails, he is not compromised, while if they succeed in it, they have a chance of regaining their position. The question was, to which particular Daimio these Lonins belonged; and upon this point our guard was singularly reticent. Nor was any light thrown upon the matter by the following document, which was found on the body of one of the gang who was killed, and which ran as follows:—

"I, though I am a person of low standing, have not patience to stand by and see the sacred empire defiled by foreigners. This time I have determined in my heart to undertake to follow out my master's will. Though, being altogether humble myself, I cannot make the might of the country to shine on foreign nations, yet with a little faith, and a little warrior's power, I wish in my heart separately, though I am a person of low degree, to bestow upon my country one out of a great many benefits. If this thing from time to time may cause the foreigners to retire, and partly tranquillise the minds of the Mikado and the Government, I shall take to myself the highest praise. Regardless of my own life, I am determined to set out."
Here follow fourteen signatures.

This document, while it showed that the motive which

suggested the attack was the hope that it might frighten us out of the country, also proved that the number who had been engaged in it, on this occasion, was fourteen. Some years afterwards I met several Japanese in London, and had some opportunities of being of service to them. I happened one day to mention to one of them that I had been in the British Legation on the night of this attack. "You don't say so!" he replied. "How glad I am that you escaped safely! for I, to whom you have shown so much kindness, planned the whole affair, and was in Sinagawa, just outside the gates, all that night, though, not being a Lonin myself, I did not take an active part in it." He then told me that the Lonins belonged to Prince Mito, upon whom, from his known hostility to foreigners, our suspicion had rested from the first; and as a reminiscence of the event, in addition to the one I already carried on my arm, he presented me with his photograph. We now heard that three of the Lonins, to avoid being captured alive, had committed suicide by ripping themselves up, an example which was followed by two more a day or two afterwards, making the total list of killed and wounded twenty-eight, which was composed as follow:—

DEFENDERS.

Killed.

1 Tycoon's guard.   1 Porter.   1 Groom.

Severely wounded.

1 Secretary of Legation.   1 Porter.
1 Tycoon's guard.   2 Servants of the Legation.
1 Daimio's guard.

Slightly wounded.

1 Consul.
7 Tycoon's guard.
2 Daimio's guard.
1 Priest of the temple.

ASSAILANTS.

Killed.

2 on the spot.
3 tracked next day, committed suicide.
2 tracked later, committed suicide.
1 captured, wounded, and executed.

    Killed, . . . 11
    Wounded, . . . 17
    Total, . . 28

We heard afterwards that the six Lonins still unaccounted for were caught and executed at intervals later, but had no means of verifying the statement; but whether it was true or not, the whole forms a record of a tolerably bloody night's work. We were strongly recommended by the Government to place three of the heads of the Lonins over our gateway as a terror to evil-doers, but I cannot remember whether this advice was followed or not. We were now able to gather from our servants many incidents of the attack. It seems that our assailants first knocked at the outside gate, but being refused admittance, scaled the fence and killed the porter. In passing up the avenue in front of the stables, they came across a groom, whom they also killed. They then slew a dog, and severely wounded the cook, who seems to have heard a noise and gone out to see the cause of it. In like manner they captured a watchman, whom they tried to persuade to show them the way;

but he managed to escape, receiving, as he did so, two severe cuts on the back: however, he ultimately succeeded in concealing himself in a lotus-pond. This man's back presented the most ghastly appearance, and I did not think he could have lived. The Japanese have a treatment of their own for sword-cuts, derived from much experience in them. Instead of bringing the edges of the skin as closely together as possible, they plug the wound with chewed paper,—a method which, if it is efficacious, leaves the most hideous marks of the gash. The band now seems to have scattered, and to have broken into the temple in parties of three or four, coming across an unfortunate priest as they did so, who, however, was not very severely wounded; and then in the darkness they dashed into all the rooms, slashing recklessly about them, and plunging their swords through the mattresses in the hope of transfixing a sleeper. There can be little doubt that they would have succeeded in their purpose, had it not been for the lateness of the hour at which most of us had retired to rest.

Before daybreak Sir Rutherford Alcock had despatched an express messenger to Captain Craigie of H.M.S. Ringdove, then lying at Yokohama, twenty miles distant, describing the position of matters, and urgently requesting him to come at once to our assistance. Meantime the native guards had been increased to 500 men. At one o'clock in the afternoon we were cheered by the sight of twenty blue-jackets, led by their officers, tramping up the avenue, their faces beaming with the anticipation of a possible fight in store. Their arrival inspired a confidence which our previously defenceless condition probably exaggerated; for what could so few even well-armed men do against the hostile population by whom we were surrounded, had they chosen to renew the attack, which we considered highly probable? They were accompanied by Monsieur Duchesne de Bellecour, the French Minister, who, on learning of our adventure, instantly put himself on board the Ringdove, bringing with him a party of French sailors, "pour partager les dangers," as he chivalrously remarked. Our most welcome reinforcement instantly set to work improving our means of defence. The palisades all round were looked to and strengthened, and every conceivable measure of precaution taken, to prepare for another attack during the night, which seemed highly possible,— for we thought that the escaped Lonins might spend the day in recruiting their numbers, and assault us in much stronger force. We heard from various sources that the city was in the highest state of excitement, and we felt, therefore, that we had only as yet, perhaps, been actors in the first scene of a drama, the *dénouement* of which it was impossible to foresee. At the same time, we quite felt that the decision at which our Minister had arrived was the right one, and that we must hold our position at all hazards, as it would never do to allow either the Japanese Government or people to suppose that we could be frightened by isolated acts of violence into abandoning rights which had been solemnly assured to us by treaty. With the exception of the American, there was no other foreign Legation in Yedo at the time, and it had so far escaped molestation. In anticipation of a lively night, an elaborate system of sentries was organised upon a somewhat composite basis. At both the gates, and at various points in the grounds, was a mixed guard of Japanese and English or French, while at every bedroom-door a Japanese and a blue-jacket kept watch together. I don't think anybody slept much that night; and whenever I did fall into a doze, it was only to wake with a start from a dream in which I was being attacked. The bamboo rattle of the Japanese watchmen, associated as it was with my first alarm, produced a painful impression upon my weakened nervous system; and it was a relief to gaze at my two sentries stolidly facing each other from opposite sides of the doorway, both armed to the teeth according to the fashion of their respective civilisations, unable to interchange an intelligible word, but each, no doubt, entertaining some curious speculations in regard to the other.

All through that first night I fancied I heard the angry murmur of the dense population by which we were surrounded, who seemed to me as sleepless as ourselves; but this may only have been the effect of a fevered imagination. The night passed off without an alarm, but it was only the first of a series in which this unpleasant state of tension was in no degree relaxed. Nor did the days bring much relief. Sinister and unpleasant rumours were constantly reaching us through sources of information which, it is true, were not to be much relied upon, for they were Japanese, though in some cases more or less secret. It was not safe for a foreigner to show himself outside the gates, so that we felt more or less beleaguered, while official visits were paid and communications were being kept up between the Minister and the Japanese Government. Nobody thought of laying aside his revolver for a moment; and whether he was eating his meals or copying a despatch, it was always placed on the table beside him.

Under these circumstances I was only an encumbrance, for I was unable to use either arm, and my wounds needed more serious attention than it was possible to give them on shore. After the first two days, therefore, I was put on board the Ringdove, under the care of the assistant-surgeon. Captain Craigie, who was living on shore, most kindly placed his cabin at my disposal; and here I entered upon a series of experiences which, in their way, were the most disagreeable which it has ever been my lot to encounter.

After the wound on my right shoulder was sewn up, my right arm was bandaged to my side, so as not to open the sutures; my left arm was also firmly bandaged, so that I was deprived of the use of both, and had to be fed by my servant. Then, from loss or poverty of blood, I became covered with boils, which of course were worse just under the bandages. In addition to this, ophthalmia broke out among the crew, and I got it in both eyes. The thermometer was standing at 95°. I was as red as a lobster from prickly heat, which produced an incessant irritation, and the cabin buzzed with mosquitoes like a beehive. A bandage over both eyes kept me in total darkness; and it was as difficult to lie on my back on account of the boils, as on either side because of my arms. The monotony of this existence was only relieved by having myself constantly scratched; by indicating the localities of mosquitoes I wished killed; by having nitrate of silver poured into both eyes, which felt very much as if they were being extracted with corkscrews; by having my wounds cleaned, plastered, and attended to; by being fed, and smoking. It is for such emergencies that a beneficent Providence has especially provided tobacco.

As every available man was on shore, there was nobody to talk to except the assistant-surgeon and the second master. It was just when I was suffering the most acutely from this accumulation of miseries that we had another serious night-alarm. I was vainly trying to find the best position to doze in when I heard a great scrimmage on deck, and some sharp words of command given in an excited tone. Rousing B., who was sleeping near me, I told him to hurry on deck and see what was the matter. In a moment he came back in the highest state of excitement, with the pleasing intelligence that an armed Japanese junk was bearing down to board us, and that everybody was on deck with pikes and other weapons of defence. As all the combatant part of the crew had been landed for the defence of the Legation, leaving only the engineers, stokers, cook, steward, and one or two others on board—the Ringdove was only a gunboat—this information was not reassuring. It seemed that sooner or later I was destined to meet the fate of a rat in a trap. Listening anxiously, I heard the shouting increasing, evidently now proceeding from Japanese throats, and then felt a great bump. Apparently the climax had arrived, and I sent B. up again to assist in repelling the boarders. In two or three minutes the noise ceased, and he reappeared, accompanied this time by the doctor, who told me that the junk had sheered off. Whether the collision had been with hostile intent, and those on board had changed their minds on finding us prepared for them, and abandoned the idea of attempting to take us, or whether it was simply the result of clumsy navigation, remained a mystery, which the darkness of the night, and the suddenness of the whole episode, rendered it impossible to solve.

If my various tortures were severe while they lasted, the length of their duration was fortunately short. Owing to the fact that they were unaccompanied by any fever, and that I could eat well, I speedily began to regain strength, and in less than a week was able to go on deck. Here I began to revel in a delightful feeling of security, which had become quite a novel sensation; the ophthalmia was cured, and I could indulge in the full enjoyment of the novel aquatic life by which I was surrounded,—in watching the quaint-shaped junks passing to and fro, and the no less quaint-looking fishermen plying their vocation after their peculiar and original methods, in their no less peculiar and original costume, which often consisted of absolutely nothing except a bandage over their noses, the reason for which I never discovered. Their chief occupation seemed to be to prod the muddy bottom of the bay with long tridents for eels. Then there was historic Fusi-yama, with its beautiful conical summit towering over all, and the city of Yedo, with its extensive suburbs straggling for miles all round the margin of the bay.

A few days later I was glad to find myself able to obey a summons from Sir Rutherford Alcock to come on shore in order to be present at a conference with some of the chief Ministers of State on the subject of the recent attack. It was a blazing hot day, and when I reached the shore, exactly opposite the gate of the Legation, I found the intervening street occupied by the procession of an important Daimio. On the occasion of the progress of one of these great feudal princes, they used to be followed by a small army of *samurai* or clansmen, numbering sometimes as many as a thousand, all two-sworded swashbucklers, all ready to fight on the smallest provocation to uphold the dignity of their chief, and exceedingly sensitive on the point of honour. The natives, on meeting a procession of this kind, were expected either to move away from the road altogether, or humbly to prostrate themselves while it passed. Under no circumstances was anybody allowed to cross it. This was an insult which it was considered should be wiped out by the death of the rash man who should offer it. Since the great revolution which practically extinguished the Daimios, and which was one of the results of intercourse with foreign nations, I believe these dangerous processions have been abolished. At the time I had no idea of the extreme tenacity of the Japanese on this point of etiquette, or of the risk I should run if I attempted to cross the procession. I stood for some time watching the line, which seemed interminable, the men marching slowly in pairs. At last the heat of the mid-day sun became so overpowering that I feared I should faint. The gate of the Legation, only a dozen yards off, stood invitingly ajar, and, perceiving a wider gap in the line than usual, I made a dash through it. The *samurai* were so much taken by surprise, that before they could draw their swords I was past them, but not before I had time to perceive their murderous intent, and to slam the gate in the faces of two or three that rushed after me. After our conference with the Ministers was over, I was informed by Sir Rutherford that he had written to Sir James Hope, then admiral on the station, requesting his presence, and that nothing could be finally decided upon until after a consultation with him, but that he had determined to abandon his intention of going home on leave, and would remain at his post until he received instructions from home; that he had further decided on sending me back to England to furnish any information which might be required in addition to the full narrative of events contained in his despatch, and also to be the bearer of a personal letter from the Tycoon to the Queen, apologising for the occurrence. The question of indemnity, and the nature of the satisfaction to be required, were matters also to be discussed; while the trip was one by which, under the circumstances, my health could not fail to derive benefit. During the month which now elapsed before the admiral arrived, the only event of importance which occurred was the news that two Ministers of State who had been to see the Tycoon were attacked by Lonins: they were, however, bravely defended by their retainers, and, after a severe struggle, the Lonins were completely defeated, many being made prisoners. I now began to perceive how necessary it was, as a measure of self-protection, for Daimios always to be attended by a large escort.

At last, about the middle of August, Admiral Hope arrived, accompanied by Sir Hercules Robinson, then Governor of Hong-Kong, and it was determined that we should lose no time in paying an official visit in grand state to the Japanese Minister for Foreign Affairs. This involved passing through the most crowded and disaffected quarters of the town, for a distance of about two miles. I scarcely knew whether I was sufficiently recovered to make this effort on horseback, but the alternative was to be cooped up in a *norimon*,—a sort of palanquin, which, however, had the disadvantage of being square, and not oblong, like the latter, and thus obliged me to maintain a squatting position during the whole time. As I considered that the chances were rather in favour of our being attacked than otherwise, I preferred riding, although I had to be led, as I was unable to hold the reins. Still, with a sharp pair of spurs, I had always the chance that my steed, in a wild and headlong flight of his own, would carry me out of the *mêlée*.

The party consisted of the Minister, the Admiral, Sir Hercules Robinson, several naval officers, members of the Legation, and myself, escorted between two lines of marines and blue-jackets, who certainly looked as if they were prepared to give a good account of any Lonins who might be rash enough to attack us. The streets through which we passed were densely crowded with scowling multitudes, amongst whom the two-sworded gentry, whom we knew entertained towards us feelings of special animosity, were very numerous. Our progress was necessarily slow, so that it was an hour before we arrived at the building where the two Ministers for Foreign Affairs were waiting to receive us. We found them attended by many other officials, for it was the custom in Japan never to allow these audiences to assume a private character; and many of those who were present exercised the functions of *metsuke*—in other words, of Government spies or reporters.

After the first formal compliments had taken place, in

accordance with preconcerted arrangement all the English officers and gentlemen who had accompanied us withdrew, leaving only the Minister, the Admiral, and myself, and the interpreters. This was a signal for all the Japanese, except the two Ministers, to retire—an unprecedented event, so far, in the annals of Japanese diplomacy; but it was to be accounted for by the fact that the Ministers had a confidential communication to make to us affecting another European Power, which could not otherwise have been kept quiet: it was therefore in their own interest to break through their ordinary course of procedure.

After discussing this question, Sir Rutherford Alcock informed them that I was to be the bearer to England of the Imperial Missive to the Queen, and we talked over the possible chances of another attack, and the inconveniences which seemed to attend an official residence in the capital of Japan. The first Minister, Ando Tsusimano Kami, remarked, in the course of this conversation, that peril to life was an incident inseparable from high office in his country, and that everybody who filled it, whether foreign or Japanese, must, as a matter of course, run the risk of being murdered. I thought then that this was a mere complimentary way of reconciling us to what was intended to be sooner or later the invariable fate of foreign officials in Japan. But a very short time afterwards poor Ando Tsusimano Kami proved, in his own person, the unjustness of my suspicions; for he was attacked by a band of eight Lonins, dragged from his *norimon*, and so severely wounded that for some time his life was despaired of. So far as I was personally concerned, the most important result of this interview was the decision which was arrived at—

that before going to England I should proceed in H.M.S. Ringdove to the island of Tsusima, situated in the straits of the Corea, accompanied by Admiral Hope in his flagship, to investigate the truth of the report which we had received of the Russians having made a permanent settlement in that island, contrary to treaty, and to take measures accordingly. A few days afterwards I sailed from Yedo on this most interesting mission.

CHAPTER XI.

A VISIT TO TSUSIMA: AN INCIDENT OF RUSSIAN AGGRESSION.

THE circumstances under which my visit to Tsusima was made, as the result of my interview with the Japanese Ministers, described in the last chapter, derive additional interest from the fact that now, after an interval of twenty-six years, Russia is manifesting aggressive tendencies in the same direction. This is evident from the following paragraph, taken from the 'Times' of the 2d September 1885. It was, however, in 1861, and not in the previous year, as erroneously stated, that the incident occurred:—

"RUSSIA IN THE COREA.—German papers publish the following extract from the 'Vladivostok'—a journal published in the seaport of the same name at the extreme southern corner of the Russian Asiatic coast: 'The importance of Vladivostock as a seaport is seriously affected by the fact that it is frozen in winter. Hence the opinion has been gaining ground that either Port Lazarev, in Corea, or the island of Quelpaert (33° 11' N. lat.), or that of Tsusima (34° 40' N. lat.), should be substituted for Vladivostock. As to Port Lazarev, it is by no means certain that it is free from ice all the year round; and, what is of greater moment, it would be necessary to take possession of about the half of the Corean peninsula in order to secure undisturbed occupation of the port—a proceeding certain to provoke the enmity of Japan. The situation of Quelpaert is excellent, but unfortunately there is not a good haven in the island. The island of Tsusima was visited about 1860 by the Russian frigate Possadnik, and the Russian flag was hoisted but subsequently withdrawn. It is some 600 miles distant from our own territory, and so could not well be made a basis of operations. It would seem, therefore, unavoidable to preserve Vladivostock as the base of all serious operations; but to occupy and fortify Tsusima as a marine station well armed and provisioned. It would thus help to make good some of the drawbacks of Vladivostock.' In connection with this suggestion, it may be mentioned that the island of Tsusima is Japanese territory, and could not be occupied except with the consent of the Government of Japan."

It is to be remarked that the last sentence is the comment of the German paper, and does not form part of the quotation from the 'Vladivostok.'

I sailed from Japan in H.M.S. Ringdove in August, under instructions from Sir Rutherford Alcock; Admiral Hope proceeding thither at the same time in his flag-ship, to render such assistance and advice as might seem necessary. The timidity of the Japanese Government at the time was so great that they declined to give us any official assistance, for fear of becoming embroiled with Russia, and I was obliged to proceed to Nagasaki for the purpose of picking up an interpreter. It is about 150 miles from that port to Tsusima; and on the morning following our departure from Nagasaki, we found ourselves in sight of the island, its twin peaks rising to a height of from 1500 to 1800 feet, heavily timbered to their summits, with here and there a clearing and a wreath of smoke, indicating the presence of a scattered population. We were approaching the island from the south-east, and were in entire ignorance of its ports or centres of habitation. We knew that it was the territory of a prince or Daimio, and we presumed that it must have a capital, so we sent a boat on shore as we neared a fishing hamlet, to ask the way to it. In pursuance of the directions thus received, we continued steaming for a couple of hours along the south-eastern shores of the island, and were much struck by its evident fertility, its fine forests, and pretty scenery, as we opened up one wooded valley after another. Suddenly we came upon a small semicircular harbour, affording an admirable shelter for country craft, with a narrow entrance between projecting wooded bluffs. At the head of this little haven, and skirting its shore, was the town of Fatchio, a place containing possibly from 10,000 to 15,000 inhabitants, and the residence of the Daimio, whose palace, I was afterwards informed, was about four miles distant.

We did not go much beyond the mouth of the harbour, being entirely ignorant of its depth of water and the character of the anchorage; and I immediately went on shore to open up communication with the inhabitants. This, however, did not prove a very easy matter. First, some petty officials came down and warned us off. Finding that we paid no attention to their gesticulations, and insisted on landing, they retreated a few yards as we jumped on shore, forming, with the assistance of a crowd which now joined them, a semicircle at a distance of a few yards, without manifesting any signs of hostility, but with the apparent intention of amiably and good-naturedly barring our way, should we attempt to go into the town. Our interpreter now commenced a parley, the result of which was, that we were shown into a pretty little wooden erection like a summer-house, on the margin of the sea, at a distance of about a quarter of a mile from the town, and requested to wait there until our arrival and wishes were reported in the proper quarter. Here we were objects of interest to an admiring crowd, principally composed of small boys, for more than an hour, when a messenger returned with the information that the officials refused to receive me, and requested me to return on board the ship and leave them in peace. This I positively declined to do. As it was now getting on towards the afternoon, I said that, so far from complying with their wishes, I intended to send for my meals and sleeping arrangements, and live in the summer-house—which at that time of year formed delightfully cool quarters—if necessary, for a week. I explained that my patience was inexhaustible, that my time was unlimited, and that I had the less scruple in forcing myself upon their hospitality, as I should ask them for nothing, not even for protection, as I should make arrangements for a guard of blue-jackets to be permanently stationed on shore for my protection. Whereas, if the prince would accord me an interview, it would probably not last an hour, and we should relieve them of our presence the same evening. The messenger hurried off on hearing the disagreeable alternative I had proposed, and in less than an hour I saw that it had produced its effect; for a *norimon*, or native palanquin, appeared on the strand, being hurried along on the shoulders of its bearers, and containing a two-sworded official of a very different rank from the humble functionary with whom I had hitherto been in communication. He was accompanied by a man of a lower grade, and for a minute or two we vied with each other in the lowness of our bows and the *empressement* of our salutations. Then, with many apologies and compliments, I was informed that the Daimio was too ill to receive me; and in order to convince me that this was no sham illness contrived for the occasion, many details were entered into which were quite unnecessary, for they in no degree removed my suspicions. The most interesting items of information which I afterwards obtained in regard to this august personage were, that he possessed great influence at Yedo where his son was retained as a hostage for his good behaviour; that he was of gigantic stature—report said seven feet high; that he was afflicted with a cutaneous disease; and that he had one wife, twelve concubines, and forty-three children. As I found that he resolutely declined to receive me, I finally consented to an interview with his first Minister instead; but inasmuch as our appearance in the harbour had, according to my informant, already produced great consternation in the town, and as the peace of mind of the inhabitants would be still further disturbed by the presence of a foreigner in their streets—an event hitherto unknown—and as the building in which I was to be received lay at the other extremity of the town, I was requested to agree to the hour for the meeting being fixed for midnight. I was perfectly well aware that this was only an excuse for preventing me from seeing the town or its inhabitants; but I was too well satisfied at having succeeded so far to raise any objection — and after a further interchange of polite ceremony, I returned to the ship, having spent nearly four hours in the summer-house.

The view in Fatchio Bay as the sun set was enchanting; the heavy vegetation coming in places to the water's edge, in others clambering over rocks that rose precipitously from the sea; the prettily situated little town nestling among its gardens along the shore; the wooded slopes cut up into cultivated valleys and rising to a peak nearly two thousand feet above the sea, into which a little river emptied itself,—all formed a prospect that confirmed the good taste of the Russians in selecting the island for annexation.

In my interview with the official, although pressed to state the reasons of my visit, I had absolutely declined to do so to any one except the Prince himself or the Minister he might depute to receive me; so that doubtless the curiosity of the authorities was raised to the highest pitch, and the mysterious nature of my proceedings was calculated not a little to excite their suspicions; but this I considered a lesser evil than prematurely to reveal the object of my mission. About eleven o'clock the glimmer of Japanese lanterns at the summer-house told me that my escort had arrived to conduct me to the place of meeting, and that the natives intended to keep faith with me, in regard to which I had been in considerable doubt. I therefore put off for the shore, accompanied by the captain of the Ringdove and another boat containing a guard of a dozen blue-jackets, as it was not considered wise to make a midnight promenade through an unknown town totally unattended; moreover, I considered it advisable to invest the whole proceeding with as much importance as possible.

There were, as far as I remember, about twenty *samurai*, or retainers of the prince, with two or three *norimons* in waiting, and they looked rather timidly and suspiciously at the blue-jackets as they jumped on shore and formed in line; and indeed the leading official, who was the same with whom I already had an interview, informed me that their presence was quite unnecessary. But on this point I differed with him; and refusing to ensconce myself in a *norimon*, from which I should have failed to see even the little that was visible in the dark, I started off on foot, between two files of sailors, on my novel expedition.

It is difficult to judge distance at night except by time; but as we walked for more than half an hour, the distance traversed must have been at least three miles. More than half of this was through the straggling town, along narrow streets absolutely deserted. Every house had been closed by order, no living soul was to be seen, not even a light glimmered through the shutters. It was a brilliantly clear starlight night, so that I could see enough to observe that the place differed in no respect from an ordinary Japanese third-class town; so we tramped silently along, the stillness only occasionally disturbed by the barking of a dog, until we emerged into what seemed a straggling suburb, when we turned suddenly into a gateway, went along a short avenue, and entered a building the external characteristics of which I have forgotten, if, indeed, it was light enough to see them; and so along a passage, the walls of which were formed of paper screens, to an apartment in which stood a group of two-sworded officials. One of these, who proved to be the first Minister himself, now advanced to receive me. He was an agreeable, intelligent-looking man of about five-and-forty, very dignified and self-possessed in manner, and altogether a good specimen of his race. After introducing me to his colleagues, of whom there were four, if I remember rightly, forming, I imagine, a sort of privy council to the prince. I was conducted into another long narrow room, the walls of which were also of paper, and which had evidently been arranged with the idea of meeting the requirements of foreign taste. Down the centre of this room was a long low table, about two feet broad and twenty feet long, covered with red cloth, and on both sides were high benches, almost as high as the table, also covered with red cloth. It was lighted by four monster candles, each on its own huge candlestick, like those in a Roman Catholic cathedral. The first Minister invited me to sit at the head of this table, which I declined to do unless he sat by my side. This point of etiquette decided, the other functionaries, the captain and one or two officers of the Ringdove, seated themselves, and tea was brought in. In the centre of the table was the usual smoking arrangement, looking not unlike an inkstand, with a receptacle for the tobacco on one side, a fire-ball on the other, a pot to receive the ashes of the pipes in the middle, and the pipes themselves, with their diminutive bowls, lying like pens in the tray. As it only takes two whiffs to smoke a pipe, one smokes at least twenty in the course of a moderate visit. If my hosts were anxious to know the nature of my business, they manifested no impatience. We drank several small cups of tea, smoked several pipes, and made a great many inane and complimentary remarks, before I felt that I could approach the subject at issue, which I did at last with the incidental observation that I believed we were not the first strangers who had come to Tsusima, but that they had already had a visit from the Russians. To my surprise the Minister opened his eyes with well-feigned astonishment, and made the interpreter repeat the remark, as though he must have misunderstood it.

"No," he said, when it was repeated; "no Russians have ever been here."

I was fairly nonplussed.

"Will you explain to him," I said to the interpreter, "that I have had positive information that the Russians are now in Tsusima, and I have come here to see if it is true?"

"It is not true," he said; "they are not here, and have never been here."

This was the promising way in which our interview began. It lasted for more than two hours. At the expiration of that time, I had, as the result of a laborious confidence-inspiring process, into the details of which it is not necessary to enter, extracted from this same discreet and reticent functionary the fact that the Russians had been established in the island for six months; that they had built houses for themselves; that they had had a fight with the inhabitants, in the course of which one of the latter had been killed; and that the prince and all his Court were living in a chronic state of panic and despair. My informant further admitted that they had been desired by the Russians to keep their presence in the island a secret, under penalty of the gravest consequences; and that the reason he had denied that they were here was from the dread of punishment. Nothing could exceed the delight and gratitude manifested by all present at the prospect of being relieved of the presence of these unwelcome visitors; but they were still too timid to compromise themselves by giving us a guide to lead us to where they were. All they would say was, that if we went round to the other side of the island we should find a large harbour, and if we looked for them there we should find them. At that time this island had not been surveyed, and so our expedition partook largely of the character of one of exploration. The dawn was almost breaking when our nocturnal interview came to an end; but the streets were still silent, and the houses still hermetically sealed, as we passed between them once more on our way back to the ship.

Steaming out of Fatchio harbour, we coasted round the southern end of the island and along its western shore. As we did so, the highlands of the Corea were distinctly visible, and one could not but be struck with the commanding position which this island occupies strategically, situated as it is in the centre of the straits which separate the Corea from Japan, and which afford access into the Yellow Sea. We had coasted along half the length of the island, which is about forty miles long, when we observed a large opening, as though it were divided in the middle by straits, and into this we steamed. To our amazement we found ourselves in a perfect labyrinth of lanes of water. In every direction, to the right and left and in front of us, there spread an intricate network of deep narrow channels, divided by rocky promontories clothed with heavy timber. Large forest-trees sprang from the water's edge, twining their huge roots among the rocks, and drooping their foliage into the water. It was so deep even close to the shore that it was difficult to find anchorage; and our excitement was so great, in our desire to explore this strange and unknown water retreat, that we were off in boats before the anchor was down. We found, as we paddled along these singular channels, that we were in a harbour in which whole fleets might be concealed from observation—hidden away, so to speak, among the trees. Here and there the inlets expanded, so as to form capacious harbours, again narrowing, often to a breadth of scarce a hundred yards. There was no sign of human habitation anywhere; the only evidence of man were two Buddhist or Sintoo shrines, perched upon pinnacles of rock under the shade of huge wide-spreading trees, and approached by rock-cut steps. For hours we pulled about in this magnificent haven, never tired of wondering at its capacity, its safety from storms, its freedom from dangers to navigation, the extraordinary beauty of the scenery by which it was surrounded, the richness of the vegetation, and the absolute calm and stillness which seemed to brood over the whole landscape.

But all this time we saw nothing of the Russians. We passed from one deep creek into another, over the glassy surface of the water, only to exchange their unbroken solitudes, and to find some new and unexpected channel winding off in some fresh direction. At last, in one of these, our attention was suddenly attracted by some tapering spars that seemed to shoot out of the branches of a tree; and rounding a corner, we came upon the Russian frigate, moored literally, stem and stern, to the branches of a pair of forest giants, and, with a plank-way to the shore.

If we were startled to come upon her thus unexpectedly, our surprise can have been nothing to that of those on board at seeing an English man-of-war's boat pull into the sort of pirate's cove in which they had stowed themselves away. Indeed, the Russian captain afterwards told me that he had been so long in solitude that he could scarcely believe his eyes when we burst thus suddenly upon them, like visitants from some other world. However, he was too much of a gentleman to betray anything but pleasure and apparent gratification at receiving me, when I stepped upon his deck and introduced myself. He at once invited me most hospitably to his cabin; and while he entertained me with refreshments, we spent a few minutes in some very amusing diplomatic fencing. He was here, he said, for hydrographical purposes, and had made a survey of the island, in obedience to instructions. Looking out of the cabin window, from which was visible a frame-house with a barn-yard, in which was a cow and some poultry, I asked him if he combined agriculture with hydrography, as the one pursuit implied a more protracted visit to the island than the other. He admitted that he had been here for more than six months; that his survey was finished, but that he had received instructions to remain till further orders; and that, to pass away the time, and make himself comfortable, he was doing a little farming. I then went on shore to see his establishment. He had got a hospital for the sick, from which a Russian flag was flying, a dairy and poultry-yard, a Russian steam-bath, and a little cottage, in which to vary his residence from shipboard. There was a vegetable garden, and all the signs of a very comfortable little naval settlement, at least so far as it was possible for the crew of one frigate to make one. I gently hinted at the existence of treaties, and so forth; but he said that he was a sailor and not a diplomatist, and knew nothing about them. All he knew were his orders. He denied that he had had any dispute of importance with the natives, with whom, he declared, he was on very good terms—though, as their nearest village was at some distance, he saw very little of them.

The captain of the Possadnik turned out such a charming companion, and seemed so delighted to have his monotony varied even by an inquisitive *diplomat*, that I was quite sorry when the lateness of the hour warned me that I must return to my own ship, in which, as I explained to him, I should be absent for a day, so that it would be useless for him to attempt to return my visit at once, which, however, I promised to repeat. That night we steamed out to the offing, where the admiral was cruising in his flag-ship, and the next morning I went on board and reported my discovery. Soon after the admiral transferred himself to the Ringdove, and we steamed back to Tsusima harbour, finally bringing her to Russian Cove, as we named the Possadnik's settlement.

The Russian captain now came and called and dined with us, and we discussed the situation in the most amicable manner; the result at which we arrived being, that the admiral should himself go to Olga Bay on the coast of Manchouria, at which port the Russian admiral then was and present the diplomatic view of the situation to that functionary; obtaining from him the necessary orders for the evacuation of the island by the Possadnik and her crew. The captain of that ship assured the admiral that he would receive these orders with delight, as he was heartily sick of his exile.

Meantime our surveying parties had not been idle. It was found that the harbour or sound in-which we were, nearly divided the island into two; a narrow strip of land, not half a mile wide, alone connecting the northern with the southern half, each section being about twenty miles long and from ten to fifteen broad. I had no means of ascertaining the amount of the population; but as the island is very fertile, and is well peopled in parts, it probably contains from thirty to forty thousand inhabitants. From the wooded heights of Tsusima Sound, the Corea, distant about forty miles, is very plainly visible, and, in former days, the inhabitants of Tsusima kept up more intercourse with that country than did any other part of Japan, and the Prince maintained a garrison of three hundred men at its nearest port. He enjoyed a monopoly of trade, which consisted chiefly of tiger-skins, rice, hides, silver, and gold. The climate in summer was perfect, and even in winter it is extremely mild. The larger vegetation consists chiefly of evergreen oak, sycamores, maples, cypresses, and pines of different varieties. One of our officers, who had been to Manchouria, said that the conifers were of the type common in that country; while among the *feræ naturæ* the wild cats and deer differ from those of Japan. At high water the sea covers the -isthmus which connects the two islands, and stakes are put across it to prevent the passage of boats at low tide. The highest mountain on the island attains to the height of about 2500 feet.

P

Here, as the Russian paper observes, there is no fear of frost closing the harbour, which would form one of the finest naval stations in the world; while the agricultural and other resources of the island itself would make it a most valuable acquisition to any Power which might be lucky enough to obtain possession of it. Fortunately the Japanese are fully alive to its importance; and under existing treaties it could only be obtained possession of by an act of war, as the Japanese Government would certainly refuse to part with it for any pecuniary consideration, and the Powers which have treaties with Japan are pledged to ensure its integrity as against each other. From the cool way in which the Russian paper mentions the possible annexation of the island, no objections on this score seem to have occurred to it. "It would seem, therefore," it says, "unavoidable to preserve Vladivostock as the base of all serious operations; but to occupy and fortify Tsusima as a marine station well armed and provisioned." By being thoroughly forewarned of this intention, the Powers interested may possibly make it "avoidable"; and it would certainly be a gross breach of faith on their part towards Japan to allow the harbour to be occupied by force. The extreme importance of it to Russia as a winter naval station is indicated by the remarks of the Russian paper; while there is no Power more interested than England in preventing Russia from having a port in the Eastern seas open in winter. Our undefended colonies, our enormous commercial interests, would render resistance to such an act a necessary measure of self-preservation in the case of any European Power; but it is doubly so with Russia, of whose aggressive tendencies, unhindered by scruple of any sort, we have recently had such ample testimony. Every nation is entitled to consider an aggressive act of another nation, even though it is not immediately directed against its own territory, a justification for precautionary measures on the part of the Power threatened. It was for this reason that the late Sir Harry Parkes so persistently urged upon our Government the expediency of occupying Port Hamilton; and it is to be hoped, if it is now decided to evacuate that island in favour of China, it will be done under conditions which will not strategically weaken our position in these seas. That the annexation of Tsusima is as much part of the programme of the Russian Government, as the annexations of Khiva, Merv, and Batoum have formerly been, there is not the smallest doubt. Their first attempt to effect a quiet and unobtrusive occupation was, fortunately, frustrated in the manner above described. Admiral Hope at once steamed off to Olga Bay, and the result of his communication with the Russian admiral was an order for the immediate evacuation of Tsusima by the Possadnik.

These are the circumstances under which, in the words of the 'Vladivostok,' "the Russian flag was hoisted but subsequently withdrawn" from the island of Tsusima, and I trust that the hint will not be thrown away in view of future contingencies.

CHAPTER XII.

POLITICS AND ADVENTURE IN ALBANIA AND ITALY IN 1862.

THE circumstances under which I returned to England from Japan and Tsusima in the autumn of 1861, and the impaired state of my health, resulting from the wounds I had received during the attack on the Legation, induced Lord Russell, then Minister for Foreign Affairs, not to insist upon my immediate return to the East.

I was spending a few days at Vienna in the early part of the following year, when the Prince of Wales arrived on his way to the Holy Land, and kindly honoured me with an invitation to accompany him to Corfu, which was at the time the objective point of my journey. I accordingly proceeded with the party to Trieste, where we embarked on board the yacht which was in waiting there for his Royal Highness, and after visiting Venice, proceeded to Pola, Ragusa, Cattaro, Durazzo, where we had a wild-boar hunt, in which his Royal Highness was successful, and so on to Corfu, from which place I took steamer to Antivari—then a Turkish town—in the immediate neighbourhood of the since historic Dulcigno: the district which I was now visiting, has since been ceded to Montenegro. From here I rode to Scutari, the capital of Albania, and stayed with my old friend Captain Ricketts, at that time our consul there. I had formed the design of visiting the Miridits, a Roman Catholic tribe of Albanian mountaineers, who had excited my interest, both from a political and ethnographical point of view; but I found their chief, Bib Dodo Pasha, at Scutari, and his absence from his mountain home, where I should have been his guest, deprived the trip of advantages I should otherwise have enjoyed. Moreover I obtained from him much of the information of which I was in search. He has since died and been succeeded by his son, Prenk Dodo Pasha, who, if I mistake not, is detained at Constantinople as a hostage for the good behaviour of his tribe. The question of the future of Montenegro, Albania, and Epirus, with their divergent races, religions, and aspirations, in which I was then interested, is too large and complicated to enter upon here. It is destined before long to force itself for a final solution upon the attention of Europe, and it suffices here to say that if that solution is to be satisfactory, those engaged in bringing it about must acquire a more accurate knowledge of the local conditions, and the rival forces at work, than was possessed at the period of my visit. I was very much struck with the popular ignorance which prevailed in this country in regard to the revolt in Bosnia and Herzegovina, which finally led to the Russo-Turkish war. At the outbreak of that movement, the press, so far as I remember without an exception, assumed that it was a revolt of Christians against Turks, and I found the same impression existed even among members of the Cabinet,—the fact being that it was an agrarian rising of Slav Christian peasants against Slav Moslem landlords, very much analogous in many aspects to our own landlord and tenant question in Ireland. With this difference, however, that the British Government is able to put in force coercive measures if required, and is far more responsible for the maintenance of law and order in Ireland, than the Porte was in the case of the rebellious populations of these outlying Slav provinces. I was a guest for a day or two in Herzegovina at the country-house of one of these Slav landlords. He was a rigorous Moslem, but he could not speak a word of Turkish, and he was as hostile to the Turkish Government as his own peasantry were to him. It was a kind of triangular duel, in fact, which, since the transfer of the provinces to Austria, the Government of that country has had to solve. The more stringent measures they found it necessary to adopt, have had the effect of driving out the Moslem proprietary class, many of whom have taken refuge in the Turkish dominions; and curiously enough, two years ago, I found myself once more the guest of a Herzegovine Slav Moslem, who, with a number of his compatriots, had established himself on the ruins of Cæsarea in the Holy Land. Had they been among Russians, they could have made themselves understood in their native tongue. Surrounded by Arabs, they were strangers in a strange country—their only common tie being that of religion.

At the time of my visit to Scutari, fighting was in progress on the Montenegrin frontier between the Turks and the Montenegrins. I made a trip to the Turkish outpost, then on the island of Lessandria at the northern end of the Lake of Scutari, which has since been ceded to Montenegro. The steamer in which I took passage was conveying troops to this point, and the exciting incident consisted in our having to run the gantlet of a narrow strait, on the rocky sides of which Montenegrin sharpshooters concealed themselves, freely playing with their rifles on the decks of passing steamers. However, except for the captain and the man at the wheel, there was not much danger, as everybody either went below, or hid behind the bulwarks, during the few moments it took us to rush by at full speed.

From Scutari I took a boat and sailed down the Bojanos river back to the Bay of Antivari, thence returned to Corfu, spending some days there with Sir Henry Storks, then Lord High Commissioner. Thence I crossed over to Ancona.

The cordial sympathy which the British public had manifested for the people of Italy in their struggle for unity and independence had rendered England very popular at this time, and the name of Palmerston was a talisman in Europe. I had one or two curious evidences of the extremes of dislike and of affection in which this venerable statesman was held. At Trieste I met an Austrian officer who charged him with having imported guns under his own name into Italy during the Lombardy campaign. On my scouting this notion as absurd, my informant said that he had a gun in his possession which had been taken from the Garibaldians, and which would prove the truth of his assertion. This puzzled me so much that I requested to be allowed to see it, and accompanied him to his house to see a gun upon which "Palmer & Son" was engraved upon the barrel as its makers.

I was anxious to drive from Ancona through the Abruzzi to Naples, with a view of judging for myself of Italian rule in the provinces which Victor Emmanuel had so recently acquired from the King of Naples. The difficulty about the journey was the extreme insecurity of the roads. Upon my mentioning this to the general commanding the troops at Ancona, he most kindly offered to see that an escort was furnished to me through the only district which he said was in the least dangerous. I travelled by post, taking the coast road as far as Pescara, and then turning off to Chieti, a most picturesque town situated on a high hill-top, where I stayed two days, enjoying the hospitality of the officer in command of the troops, to whom I carried a letter of introduction from Ancona, and who was to provide the escort. As I was anxious to travel rapidly and to follow my own devices, I took four horses, and had no travelling companion but my servant B——, whom I have already mentioned in my account of the attack on the Legation in Japan. As he was as intelligent as he was faithful, I often on these occasions took him inside with me; and it was thus that one fine afternoon we approached the town of Salmona, our escort jingling merrily behind, and the four horses clattering over the smooth hard road in most exhilarating style. As we neared the town I perceived that some grand *fête* was in progress. Flags were flying from the windows, which were crowded with spectators, while the streets were lined with soldiers, and the distant strains of a military band were audible.

"We are in luck," I said to B——; "there is evidently some festival in progress."

As we drove along the street people cheered, and the

women waved handkerchiefs; but I was unable to perceive any object calculated to excite their enthusiasm. When we reached a square about the centre of the town the band struck up "God save the Queen," the troops presented arms, the carriage was suddenly stopped, and half-a-dozen gentlemen in full evening costume, with white ties and white kid gloves, approached hat in hand, with profound salutations. Their leader, who I afterwards discovered was the principal civil functionary, with many polite speeches requested me to descend from the carriage, and partake of a banquet which had been provided for me. It now appeared that all these military demonstrations were in my honour, and it became evident to me that I was mistaken for somebody else—an explanation which, in declining the proffered honour, I ventured to suggest to the mayor. He received it with a polite smile.

"We are well aware," he said, "that you desire to travel *incognito*, but we have been unable to regard this wish. We could not allow Lord Palmerston's nephew to pass through our town without making some demonstration of respect, in token of the great gratitude we feel for your illustrious relative."

"But," I persisted, "I have not the honour of being related in the most distant way to the great statesman."

"No doubt; we quite understand that under the circumstances it would not be possible for you to admit the relationship. I will not therefore again allude to it, but simply request you to honour the repast we have prepared for you with your presence, and receive an address, which will accompany one which we will beg you to transmit to Lord Palmerston."

During the time this colloquy was taking place, the mayor was standing bareheaded in the square, where a great crowd was collected, and I was sitting bareheaded in the carriage, feeling it incumbent upon me, when an unusually loud *viva* was shouted, to acknowledge it with a polite bow. The situation was too ridiculous to be prolonged; there was no alternative but to accept the inevitable. I promoted B—— on the spot to the rank of "il Signor Segretario," in which capacity he was taken charge of by a group of polite men in swallow-tailed coats, to his intense amazement, for I had no time to explain the situation to him, and we passed through a lane of spectators to a public building, in a long hall of which a table was spread for about fifty guests. It was quite a sumptuous repast, with champagne and all the delicacies of the season. There was a gallery in which were ensconced the beauty and fashion of the place at one end, and the band came in and played at the other. The mayor seated me by his side at the top of the table, while the Signor Segretario, still in a state of profound bewilderment as to what was happening to him, sat at the other. When the feasting was over the speeches began, and I was obliged, in my quality of Lord Palmerston's nephew, to reply, in execrable Italian, to the compliments which were lavished upon the policy of England in general, and of that statesmen in particular, and to receive two addresses, one to his lordship and the other to myself, with a promise that I would forward the former to its destination, which I did at the earliest opportunity, with a full account of the circumstances under which I had received it, to Lord Palmerston's great amusement.

Snugly ensconced in the bay, beneath what is known as the spur of Italy, on the shores of the Adriatic, lies the little seaport town of Manfredonia. It is a queer little out-of-the-way place, removed from the line of all travel, and very primitive in its manners and customs—at least it was then. I do not know how far railways and the general march of events may have affected it since. Notwithstanding its insignificance, we had nevertheless a British vice-consul there, to attend to the wants of the stray colliers or English merchant-ships that rarely visit the port. These vice-consuls in the smaller ports of the Mediterranean, are usually natives of the place, and at that time their remuneration consisted chiefly of fees, and other little perquisites, not always strictly legitimate, which they derived from their office. It so happened that I had an affair of some importance to transact with the vice-consul of Manfredonia, and I rode over one day from Foggia, where I had been spending a week, to see him. The whole of the Neapolitan States were infested at this time with bands of banditti, calling themselves Royalist troops, and, under cover of a political character which they did not possess, committing the most wholesale depredations. It was not considered, under these circumstances, a very safe proceeding to make the journey without an escort; but I achieved it without mishap, and putting up at a small *locanda*—the only one of which the town could boast—went in search of the vice-consul. A daub on a shield, bearing a faint resemblance to the lion and the unicorn, indicated his residence, and on knocking at the door it was opened by a dishevelled little girl.

"Is the English consul at home?" I inquired.

"Si, signor;" and she tripped before me up-stairs, and opening a door, ushered me into a room in which was a very pretty woman in bed. I started back at the intrusion of which I had been guilty.

"I told you I wanted to see the consul," I said sharply to the little girl.

"Entrate, entrate, signor!" exclaimed a mellifluous voice from the bedclothes. "The girl made a mistake. The consul is out, and will not be back to-day; but I am his wife, and he has left his seal with me. If you are the captain of a ship, and wish anything done, I can do it for you. See!" and she stretched out her hand, and lifted a seal from a little table by the bedside.

"I am sorry, signora," I said; "but I am not the captain of a ship, and my business is of a nature which can only be transacted by the vice-consul himself. When do you expect him back?"

"He may be a week, he may be more; it is impossible to say. I am sure, signor, I could transact your business if you would only confide it to me."

"I am equally sure, signora, that you could not;" and I explained to her its nature. "From which you will see that it is imperative that I should see your husband. Perhaps you can telegraph for him."

"Impossible, signor!" and with that she burst into a violent fit of weeping. "It is no use disguising the truth from you any longer. My husband deserted me more than a year ago, and I have no idea where he is."

"And have you been transacting the business of the consulate ever since?" I asked.

"Si, signor. There is very little to transact; but it is

almost all I have to live upon. Have mercy upon me, and do not let it be known to the English Government. It was I who used to do the consular business even when my husband was here. He was idle and worthless, and used to do many dishonest things, which I never do."

"I have no doubt," I replied, "that you are a far more capable and estimable person than your husband—indeed his present conduct proves his worthlessness; but unfortunately there is still a prejudice in the world in favour of official business being conducted by men. It is one which we shall no doubt get over in time: until then, I think it is the duty of any Englishman who finds that the British vice-consul has deserted his post and left his wife in charge, to let his Government know it, however capable, honest, and, allow me to add"—and I made a polite bow—"beautiful that wife may be."

I threw in the last words to gild the pill, but I evidently did not succeed, for I left her weeping bitterly; and I am afraid she did not remain long after this British vice-consul at Manfredonia.

I had scarcely taken ten steps from the door of the vice-consulate, and was still in a somewhat softened and reflective mood, when I was accosted by another little girl, who thrust a folded but crumpled piece of paper into my hand, on which was the superscription, "to English gentleman." Its contents were as follows:—

"Miss Thimbleby requests the pleasure of English gentleman's company to tea to-night at nine o'clock. Old English style."

"Follow me;" I said to the little girl, "and I will give you the answer." "Who in the world can Miss Thimbleby be?" I ruminated. "What a name for an old maid in a novel! It is morally impossible with such a name that she can be a young one." At any rate, it was evident that the invitation was one which should be promptly accepted. So I replied,—" The English gentleman has much pleasure in accepting Miss Thimbleby's kind invitation to tea to-night. Old English style."

I gave the girl the note and accompanied her with it to Miss Thimbleby's house, in order that I might know my way there later, and also because I thought it might give me some clue to the character of its occupant. It was a tumble-down old *palazzo*, with many evidences of departed grandeur, having probably two or three centuries ago been the town mansion of some large landed proprietor in the neighbourhood. Altogether its aspect rather gave me a pleasant idea of Miss Thimbleby, as being in all probability an antiquated respectable old person herself, in keeping with her abode. I refrained from making any inquiries about her at the hotel, as it was more agreeable to keep the edge of my curiosity whetted by conjecture, than satisfied by information; and at the appointed hour I repaired to tea in "old English style." On entering the house I found myself at the bottom of a very wide handsomely carved oak stair-case, at the top of which I could discern, by the dim lamp which lighted it, the figure of a little old woman like a witch, bobbing and curtseying all the time I was making the ascent. She shook hands with me with the affectionate cordiality of an old acquaintance, trembling either with excitement or with old age—for she was very, very old, well on in the nineties, she afterwards told me, but I forget her exact age. She had forgotten much of her English, having been in the country ever since the year 1804, when she had accompanied her brother, who was appointed English consul at Manfredonia in that year, to Italy. And here she had lived ever since. Her brother and his wife had died long ago, but she was in the receipt of a small pension from the English Government, which sufficed for her subsistence, and she was taken care of by sundry nephews and nieces, and by the connections of her sister-in-law, who had been a native of the place. Her brother had been connected with the Duke of York's expedition in some capacity, and her sister was the celebrated Mrs Jordan, the mistress of King William IV. Manfredonia was an odd place to come to, to gather the moss of British history, but I really felt as if I had made a discovery, when I learnt from this most venerable and highly respectable old lady that Mrs Jordan the actress's maiden name was Thimbleby. She showed me a letter from the Duke of York to her brother, and a paper with Nelson's signature, and many ancient curiosities which she had hoarded up. Tea in "old English style" seemed to consist of our partaking of that beverage tête-à-tête—for except the little servant-girl, I did not see a soul in the deserted old palace. In fact, the surroundings were so much in keeping with this strange old lady and her reminiscences, that I had a general impression of becoming fossilised. She insisted on talking English, profusely interlarded with Italian, and was extremely garrulous, but her sense of time had become so confused that she seemed in doubt in what century we were living. Thus she asked me at what hotel I was staying. I mentioned the name of the only tolerably decent one in the place.

"Ah," she said, "that is where the English always go when they come to Manfredonia."

"Why," I replied with some surprise, "I did not know that English travellers often visited Manfredonia."

"Oh yes," she said, "there was an English family staying there in 1829."

The ignorance of the benighted inhabitants of these small Neapolitan towns was something incredible. I spent several days as the guest of the mayors of the towns of Ascoli and Candela, situated in the Capitanata, which at that time was a hotbed of brigandage, and where, in company with a regiment of Piedmontese cavalry with which I was campaigning, I was quartered, with some of the officers, upon the inhabitants. I found the notions of the principal functionaries crude in the extreme upon all matters affecting European politics. This arose from the fact that during the reign of the late King of Naples they were not allowed to take in any newspapers. The mayor of one of these towns was ignorant that England was an island, and I found it difficult to give him any idea of the British Constitution. Yet this was a man who kept his carriage-and-pair, in which his wife used to drive about in silks and satins. It is true that her costume in the morning was of the most scanty and primitive description. None of the ladies thought of really dressing for the day until after the mid-day siesta, when they all regularly turned into bed, as if for the night, for a couple of hours. This was rendered necessary by the shortness of their nights, for we generally supped heavily about eleven, went to bed about one in the morning, and got up a little after daylight.

I was interested in inspecting a prison full of captured banditti. Here I saw the beautiful wife of a notorious chief of one of the bands, who had been captured, dressed in man's clothes, and using her pistol with such effect that she severely wounded a soldier before she was taken prisoner. Her husband, who escaped at the time, was afterwards captured; but there were several chiefs of minor distinction,—picturesque, bronzed, hardened-looking ruffians. The one with the most villainous expression, however, was the priest of one of the bands, who, still dressed in his ragged clerical costume, assumed an air of sanctimonious resignation, and who, I was assured, had presided over the roasting alive of a man who had been robbed, and other atrocities,—going through the ceremony of shriving the victims before their execution, and granting absolution to the murderers, in consideration of which his share of the spoil was always considerable. Upon two occasions I was present at an exciting chase after bands of banditti, one of which numbered over two hundred strong. As the detachment I was with was much inferior in force, they seemed inclined to show fight. However, when we charged they thought better of it, and scattering in all directions, gave us a run across country which was as exciting as any fox-hunt, but which only resulted in the capture of half-a-dozen of their number.

It is to be regretted that, owing to the insecurity of the country, Calabria, with its enchanting scenery, is a sealed book to the tourist. The habit of brigandage is so strong in the people, that nearly five-and-twenty years of the more enlightened rule of the Italian Government has been unable to eradicate it. It is engrained in the habits of

Q

the peasantry, nearly every one of whom, in some parts of the province, goes out with a band by way of a holiday for some weeks in the year. It was not a country adapted for the operations of cavalry, so I could only get glimpses of the scenery as we followed the enemy occasionally to the foot of the hills—for when hard pressed they invariably took to the mountains; but I saw enough to make my mouth water, and create an intense desire to explore its romantic recesses. Traversing the plain of Cannæ, with its battle-field, I crossed the Rubicon, and so made my way to Bari, and from thence by a very pretty road to Tarento, and so along the coast to Cotrone, both highly picturesque places, and well worthy a visit. From thence I crossed over to Sicily, and posted from Catania through the centre of the island, by way of Caltanizetta to Palermo, arriving there without mishap from brigands, apparently to the surprise of the inhabitants, who had not supposed that the journey was one which it was possible to make in safety. From Palermo I returned to Naples.

CHAPTER XIII.

CRACOW DURING THE POLISH INSURRECTION OF 1863.

ON my return from Italy, it became necessary for me to decide whether I should return to my post in Japan as *chargé d'affaires* or resign the diplomatic service. It was with great regret that I found myself compelled by family considerations to adopt the latter alternative, and abandon a career which had at that time peculiar attractions for me, and in which, considering my age, I had made rapid progress.

In January 1863 the Polish insurrection broke out, and as I had by this time acquired a habit of fishing in troubled waters, I determined to go and see it.

The proximity of the camp of Langiewicz to the Galician frontier induced me to hurry through Vienna in the hope of reaching Cracow in time to see the largest insurgent army which had as yet taken the field. That city had for some time past been the centre from which military operations were more especially directed, just as Warsaw had been, since the commencement of the movement, the seat of political and administrative action. It was, consequently, a point of attraction for unquiet spirits from all parts of Europe. Polish refugees, military and political adventurers, enthusiastic sympathisers, or reckless *condottieri*, were constantly passing along the line from Vienna to Cracow; and although my fellow-passengers were not numerous, I regarded them with a feeling of curiosity and interest which railway passengers in these prosaic days seldom think of according to each other. As, after a long cold night journey, the train moved slowly into the Cracow station, the groups collected on the platform seemed to share these sentiments with reference to myself as well as to my fellow-travellers. They peered curiously into every carriage, and had plenty of time to form their conjectures, as no one was allowed to leave the train until his passport had been examined; but it is only the innocent and unoffending traveller with a genuine passport who ever has it out of order,—a false passport is always a faultless document, and can be made to do duty in a variety of ways not necessary here to particularise. Far be it from me to insinuate that any of my respectable companions were thus provided, or betrayed to the inquiring gaze of a good many officials the slightest consciousness of having their heads in the lion's mouth. It is only when you show signs of alarm that the animal is likely to close his jaws; but there is a certain air of innocent effrontery, which may be acquired by a little practice, which disarms suspicion. I thought the people who came to see the train arrive seemed rather disappointed when we all passed safely through the ordeal, and drove contentedly away in the vain hope of finding a lodging. The hotels of Cracow are not of any remarkable excellence, even when they are half full; but when they are crowded to overflowing they are insupportable. Such was the condition in which I found them; and I was only rescued at last from a damp cellar, which I considered myself fortunate in obtaining, through the hospitality of my friend the late Count Adam Potocki.

The first news I heard was not encouraging to the sightseer. The army of Langiewicz had been destroyed the day before, and the Dictator himself had fallen into the hands of the Austrians. I thought, as I walked along the streets, that I saw the painful news written in the face of every soul I met. The sombre aspect of the population, clad in the deepest mourning, the haggard, careworn countenances of the men, the despondent look of the women, with eyes too often swollen from weeping, could not fail to produce a profound impression upon the most careless observer. At the first moment the shock was terrible. What will the Powers think? was the first question put to the foreigner, for every one felt that the disaster was in no way serious to the national cause, except in so far as it affected public opinion abroad; but inasmuch as foreign intervention was looked upon as essential to the ultimate success of the insurrection, men's eyes were ever more turned upon the state of feeling without, than upon the incidents which marked the struggle within, and they feared, with reason, that the impression might gain ground which it would be difficult afterwards to destroy—that the capture of Langiewicz would be a deathblow to the movement. Such, indeed, was the tone of the public press abroad when the catastrophe became known. In order that we may understand why the downfall of the Dictator was utterly without significance at home, it will be necessary to trace shortly the history of the movement, and the circumstances from which it principally derived its force.

I made a careful study of this at the time, which I recorded in the pages of 'Blackwood's Magazine.' Suffice it here to say, that for some years previously, the leading members of the Polish aristocracy had been earnestly engaged in considering how they might best advance the cause of the national independence without exciting the suspicions of the Russian Government, and for this purpose they had devised a species of moral crusade, the leader of which was Count Andrew Zamoyski, and the engine used, the celebrated Agricultural Society. The ostensible scope of this organisation was to develop the national resources of the country; but the questions which came under consideration naturally involved the discussion of social and administrative problems, the solution of which directly affected the civil action of the Government of St Petersburg. With branch societies in every province, its power and influence soon became widely felt, and the moderate party, as they called themselves, formed the most sanguine anticipations of the effect which a pressure thus legally exercised might have upon the Central Government.

Their hopes were dashed to the ground by the appearance of a new and important element, which threatened seriously to disturb the political and social aspect of affairs. Thirty years had now elapsed since the last Polish revolution, and the interval had worked a great change upon the face of Europe. To the superficial observer that change is purely mechanical; to those who connect cause with effect it is a great moral revolution. As the art of printing changed the current of men's ideas, and gave a stimulus to thought which produced the greatest theological convulsion of the age; so railways and telegraphs are working out the political problems of the day, and will mark an epoch in the moral history of mankind. It is impossible to estimate the influence which facility of transport must exercise upon those who, all their lives buried in the recesses of a remote province in some half-civilised country, are thus enabled in a few days to come into contact with the most advanced phase of existing civilisation. It is difficult to conceive the effect of the instantaneous interchange of enlightened and barbarous ideas, and to follow the varied channels which are thus opened to the spread of civilisation, forcing itself, like a rising flood, slowly but surely along wires and rails. As men's minds are differently constituted, it is a necessary incident to the progress of thought that it should often receive an undue impulse in an opposite sense from that in which it has been cribbed, cabined, and confined, and, passing the bounds of moderation, find an exaggerated expression in ill-regulated and enthusiastic natures. It is also natural that designing men should take advantage of this tendency to convert it to their own purposes, and that they should endeavour, by dint of method and organisation, to consolidate it into a power available for carrying out either their own selfish ends, or giving effect to their political theories. Hence there had been called into existence in almost every country in Europe a large class of society, whose representative men composed what was called "the party of action," and who had gradually acquired such power and influence upon the Continent, that the most successful monarch of the time perceived from the outset of his career the necessity of conciliating them by a certain qualified profession of their political opinions, and by a very large connivance in their secret schemes. The party of action of twenty years ago have since been superseded by a far more advanced body of theorists, they can scarcely be called politicians, recruited from a much lower *couche sociale;* but in those days they belonged mainly to the middle class, or, as in Poland, where the middle class properly so called does not exist, to that grade of society which corresponds to it in other countries—those persons, in fact, whether untitled nobility or not, who have no large vested interests in the country, but who are possessed of intelligence and education.

The growth of the urban population, and the diffusion of knowledge, with the increased facilities of its transmission by railway and telegraph, had widely extended this class in Poland of late years; and the party of action saw that a new field was open to its enterprise, and commenced some time before its political cultivation. They had considerably improved their organisation since their first effort in 1848 to carry out their European policy, and have since then incessantly and indefatigably laboured to prepare the nations for a more successful and unanimous attempt. It would be difficult for one not initiated to say in what countries their committees did not exist, or into what circles their agents had not penetrated. They were the *bêtes noirs* of the upper classes abroad, just as Jesuitism is the bugbear of Protestantism in England, and with far greater reason. As may readily be imagined, the more ardent spirits in Warsaw were speedily initiated into the mysteries of the sect. Committees were formed, a propaganda was set on foot, and the mine prepared here on the same scientific principles as had been followed in the case of Turkey, Hungary, and Italy. In February 1861 the first decided demonstration was made by this party in Warsaw. Then it was that the aristocracy, or party of order, as represented by the Agricultural Society, became really conscious of the existence of a powerful and dangerous rival, and a struggle took place for the pre-eminence. The disturbances which ensued led to the dissolution of the Agricultural Society; but the members, unwilling to abandon the policy they had marked out for themselves, formed a secret committee out of their number, with the object of counteracting the efforts which the opposition party might make to precipitate the revolutionary crisis. They believed that patience was all that was needed to ensure the ultimate independence of Poland, and trusted to the progress of civilisation, and to gradual measures of reform which they hoped by legitimate pressure to extort from the Russian Government, so to elevate the masses that the nation might be enabled to triumph at last by a moral victory. The younger and more ardent spirits who rallied round the other party, were not prepared to take this philosophic view of the situation: some of them even formed a third committee, and adopted Mieroslawski as their leader. The party of action, unable to control the forces they had set in motion, saw the necessity of preparing for the great struggle which was inevitable, and the summer of 1863 was the time fixed for the outbreak. The danger which threatened the Russian power in Poland was imminent. To avert it the Government resorted to the expedient of the Conscription Act, which contained lists of the suspected and dangerous youth of the country, who were thus to be drafted off to the army serving in the eastern provinces of Russia. By enforcing this measure in the depth of winter it was hoped that any outbreak would be rendered impossible; but Providence had willed it otherwise, and Poland escaped that year almost without a winter at all. The connection which subsisted between most of the *employés* and the committee rendered the secrecy which the Government intended to maintain with reference to the names of the conscripts impossible. Thus forewarned, those youths who found themselves doomed, determined rather to risk the chances of existence in the woods, than incur a certain exile in the deserts of Orenburg. In opposition to the earnest recommendations of their own committee, and without any kind of preparation for campaigning, a thousand young men suddenly betook themselves in January to the forests and morasses with which the country abounds; and, arming themselves as best they could, precipitated a struggle which, commenced at such a season of the year and under such auspices, seemed even to the party of action almost hopeless. But the mildness of the season favoured them: some unexpected successes kindled hope when it had ceased to exist. The committee of the party of action determined to make the best of it, and strained every nerve to procure arms and ammunition, and to increase the number of the bands. Soon one or two leaders became known to fame by the successes they achieved, and of these Langiewicz was the most prominent. Meantime the party of order stood aloof, awaiting the triumph to their policy which they considered certain to result from the failure of the premature outbreak. So far from these expectations being realised, the movement acquired greater proportions from day to day, until it became evident that the patriotic sentiment of the nation at large was roused, and that it would not do for the most powerful and influential class-to remain longer passive spectators. Negotiations took place between the committees, which resulted in the nomination of Langiewicz as Dictator, a good deal to the surprise of that leader, and under circumstances which have never been fully cleared up, and which seem to have partaken more of accident than design. The effect in Europe was in many respects favourable to the movement. It invested it with a character of permanence and stability abroad which riveted European interest far more decidedly than when it was under the direction of an unknown committee at Warsaw. At home, it enlisted in the cause the moderate party, who had resisted the direction of the opposition committee, and who accepted as a compromise the Dictatorship of a single individual. On the other hand, the measure was not without its dangers. By concentrating public attention too closely upon the fortunes of one individual, the success of the movement was apt to be too much identified with his fate, and any serious disaster to him or his army might compromise the success of the cause. For Poland, a still greater inconvenience attended the step. The very fact that the nomination of Langiewicz had satisfied the moderate party, and enlisted their sympathies in behalf of the movement, operated against him in the minds of those who had been the most violent opponents of that party, and who distrusted any leader who possessed their confidence, more especially when he was invested not merely with the military direction of the insurrection, but was possessed of civil powers as well. At the head of this faction, Mieroslawski, who already had many adherents in the country, hastened to place himself. It is unnecessary here to allude to the past history of this man, or to the disasters by which all his enterprises had been invariably characterised. He had only once taken part in active operations during the struggle, and his countrymen accused him of having exhibited cowardice upon that occasion, and thus lost the fortunes of the day; at all events, he left the band of which for a few days he had been the leader, and repaired to Cracow, in the neighbourhood of which city his rival Langiewicz was endeavouring to organise an army. In spite of the efforts of the Austrian police authorities, he managed to conceal himself successfully there, and to carry out those intrigues in the camp of the Dictator which at last conduced largely to his downfall. The prominence which had been given to Langiewicz, while it rallied to his standard volunteers from all parts of the country, was by no means an assistance to his military operations. His nomination was, in fact, premature, and his position an impossible one, even for a man of genius. For one of ordinary capacity, a fiasco was inevitable; it only needed a traitor in the camp to hasten the catastrophe. The first elements of authority were wanting. He possessed neither an army to carry out his military designs, nor an administrative machinery to give effect to his political views. Hunted from one wood to another, deprived of all regular means of communication, how was he to assume the functions of the Warsaw committee, and control or direct the movement throughout the whole country? In the absence of any regular base of operations, without artillery, commissariat, means of transport, or any of the appliances of a regular army, how was he to undertake a campaign against Russian troops? During the few days of breathing time allowed him by the Russians, after a most trying campaign, or rather series of forced marches, the youths of Galicia flocked by hundreds to his standard. Without even a nucleus of trained soldiers upon which to form them, without arms to put into the hands of these undisciplined men, without time to instruct them in the use of the few they had, Langiewicz found himself compelled once more to take the field at the head of a mob of about 3000 persons, most of whom had never seen a shot fired in anger, while some harboured designs fatal to his authority. The Russian tactics meantime seem to have been to allow a sufficient crowd to collect, and then to concentrate upon it an overwhelming force. On the 17th of March Langiewicz found himself surrounded by the Russians, and, after a short conflict, succeeded in keeping the enemy at bay, and passing the night on the field of battle. On the following day he was again compelled to accept battle, and again his army made up by heroic valour for their want of organisation. They had now been two days without food, their ammunition was expended, and the enemy, though beaten back with loss, was still receiving reinforcements, and closing round them. The moment was opportune for those who wished to work upon the feelings of men wearied and disheartened by hardship. The murmurs which had been heard in the camp swelled ominously. The Dictator found his authority questioned by his own men, while he had no means of closing their mouths with food, or of supplying them with ammunition to repulse another attack of the enemy. The position was one which would have demoralised a greater spirit than that which the partisan leader possessed. He determined to leave the orders which he considered best calculated to ensure the safety of the army, and to start himself in the middle of the night for another part of the country, with the view of appearing as Dictator in a new sphere of action. The following was the proclamation which he left to be issued after his departure:—

"BRAVE AND FAITHFUL COMPANIONS,—My office as Dictator requires my attention to various civil and military matters, and to the strengthening of our numerous bands fighting the Muscovite in other portions of the country, all of which require a better organisation.

"This necessity forces me to leave your ranks for a short time—those ranks in which I have been since the first night of the insurrection. I had hoped not to have been forced to leave you without sharing in a first victory: for this reason I sought a battle near Miechow; I stopped at Chrobierz, and fought the bloody encounter of Grochowiska.

"I do not take leave of you. The objects of my journey requiring secrecy, I cannot tell you whither I am directing my course. I take with me several officers to supply other detachments with commanders. Thirty lancers will accompany me as an escort, and will afterwards return to camp. I have divided my corps in two parts with distinct commanders, and I have given instructions to these.

"We have all sworn to fight. I shall keep my promise, companions, and expect obedience on your part, and a faithful service to the cause of our country.

"We will continue to fight Russia in the name of the Almighty until we obtain the liberty and independence of our country.   (Signed)   M. LANGIEWICZ."

The intrigues which existed in the camp rendered it impossible for Langiewicz to stay and see these orders carried out. He took most of his own staff with him across the Galician frontier, hoping to pass unobserved into the Palatinate of Lublin, and avoid the Russian troops by taking a short cut through the Austrian province. When day broke upon the hungry harassed men he had left behind, their indignation at finding themselves deserted by their leader knew no bounds. Only one detachment, commanded by Czachowski, which had left the day before, succeeded in getting through the Russian army and reaching the mountains of St Croix. A general panic seized those who woke on the morning of the 20th, which resulted in a scramble for Galicia. The plans for a division of the army were disregarded; the leaders who remained found themselves without authority; the *coup* was so unexpected; the desertion, to the great mass of persons who did not understand the intrigues which had forced it upon Langiewicz, seemed so base, that the whole army was demoralised, and retreated precipitately towards Cracow.

Many of them escaped capture by the Austrian patrols on the frontier, and reached that town wearied and disheartened, to spread the sad details among the anxious and gloomy population; but by far the greater number were brought in as prisoners by the Austrians, and lodged in the riding-school, and other public buildings in the town. On the day of my arrival Langiewicz was brought in a prisoner, and placed in the castle; but all access to him was forbidden, so I contented myself with going to the riding-school to see the *débris* of his late army. A company of Austrian soldiers grouped round the entrance kept off the crowd which had collected under the trees opposite the building, and which was composed of a large proportion of women. All were anxious, under various pretexts, to obtain admittance, but only a certain number were let in at a time, and these ostensibly only upon the ground of relations or friends being among the prisoners; but really no indisposition on the part of the Austrians was shown to relaxing as much as possible the strictness of their guard. The soldiers and the people seemed to understand each other perfectly, and a little patience and civility was all that was needed to gain admittance. The interior of the building presented a curious sight: about 150 ragged, half-starved, footsore young men were here collected together—some lying asleep on the straw, with which the floor was abundantly littered—others gazing listlessly at the motley groups which filled the body of the large room, or patching their torn garments or their blistered feet. Moving restlessly about were women in black, with anxious sympathising countenances, and with crinolines and shawls distended by articles of wearing apparel or creature comforts, which they had surreptitiously brought in for the famished and ragged insurgents. Here you saw an elderly female with her petticoats over her head, and two or three sturdy youths extracting articles from her under garments; there a gentleman was putting a half-clad figure into his own paletot, and watching the opportunity when they might slip out arm-in-arm past the good-natured sentries. Here was a knot of hungry men emptying a hamper and eagerly discussing its contents; in one corner, with very little ceremony, two lads were changing their trousers, and trying on boots. No sooner was a prisoner sufficiently transmogrified to pass for a respectable member of society, than he gave his arm to a lady and walked out under her escort with an assumed air of dignity and nonchalance, flattering himself, perhaps, that the Austrian guard did not know that he was escaping. The fact was that the Austrians had more upon their shoulders than they could comfortably manage. In one way or other nearly 2000 men had fallen into, or rather passed through, their hands; for a prisoner must have wanted ingenuity indeed who remained a prisoner long. Still, so far as appearances went, Langiewicz's army, like himself, was in captivity. The fact that an Austrian soldier had been killed the same morning by the Russians, who had violated the frontier in pursuit of the insurgents, was a circumstance which did not tend to render the Austrian soldiers unnecessarily severe with the latter. Indeed, a very strong feeling of exasperation had sprung up between the Austrian and Russian troops; while, as most of the Austrian regiments employed in Galicia had been recruited in that province, there was every inclination to be as lenient as possible in their dealings with the insurgents. As all those of the more respectable classes who had been with Langiewicz, had succeeded in escaping from durance during the first twenty-four hours, the men I saw were of an inferior condition. I conversed with many who were either domestic servants or artisans, and was surprised to find into how low a grade in society the patriotic feeling had spread. Most of them were from the kingdom, as Russian Poland was always called, and as they had no friends in Cracow

R

some of them manifested no particular anxiety to escape, as without clothes or money their predicament would not be much improved. However, a subscription was speedily got up in the town, charitable ladies bought food and raiment, and ultimately the greater number were provided for somehow or other. One man I observed whose Tartar physiognomy plainly showed a different origin from that of his companions; he turned out to be a deserter from the Russian army, belonging to one of the eastern provinces of the empire. He was quite unable to make himself understood, but seemed perfectly contented with his lot. Soon the presence of so many refugee insurgents became apparent in the streets of Cracow. It was not difficult to tell those who had been in the wars—a very few weeks of hardship and exposure leave their traces on the face; and even though nothing in the dress indicated the recent occupation of the wearer, it was not easily to be concealed; but many were either without means of disguising themselves, or did not care to take the trouble to do so. The day of mystery had gone by; the whole town was in a ferment; committees were sitting; insurgents expatiating on the past or future; gossips retailing news; women engaged in acts of benevolence and charity. Everybody was in black, every countenance was gloomy and anxious, and a feeling of despondent restlessness pervaded the community. There is a quaint old square in Cracow, with a cathedral on one side, some public buildings on the other, and a large covered market-place down the centre. Here peasant women crowd on market-days in picturesque dresses, and sell vegetables; at other times they leave it to excited groups of patriots. There was always a sort of movement going on here, and if you got tired of the solitude of your chamber, you could go out and find in a moment some melancholy friend with whom to discourse on passing events, or from whom the last piece of exciting intelligence might be gleaned; but the question, as I have already said, which chiefly agitated the public mind at this moment, was the effect likely to be produced abroad by the events which were now transpiring.

I have endeavoured, in as condensed a form as possible, to give the history of the movement up to this point, to convey some idea of the condition of feeling in Austrian and Russian Poland, as influenced by the different systems adopted by the two Governments, and to narrate the circumstances which produced the actual situation of affairs as they existed on my arrival at Cracow. It will easily be perceived now, why on calm consideration the cause itself did not seem in the eyes of those who were most interested in the movement, and most capable of judging, to have suffered by the capture of the Dictator. In the first place, the fusion of parties, so essential to its ultimate success, was in a great measure achieved by the nomination of Langiewicz. During his brief reign the aristocracy had more or less become compromised in the insurrection, and could not, even if they had desired, now abandon it. In the second, with the fall of Langiewicz, his dangerous rival, Mieroslawski, disappeared, at all events for the present, from the scene. The party whose bond of union was antagonism to the Dictator, ceased to exist when he resigned his functions in that capacity, betrayed by Mieroslawski. Discredited by his previous achievements, the latter was now execrated as the prime cause of the late disaster, and not even the most advanced members of the party of action would venture to acknowledge him as a colleague. A general sentiment of cohesion was produced by the very exigencies of the situation. The crisis was too grave to indulge in petty animosities, or allow petty ambition to triumph. For the moment there was a universal rush to the rescue, an earnest desire to see where the mistake had been, how it was to be remedied, and to think what it was best to do next; but, as usual when there is no leader of decided eminence, there were a great many different opinions upon the subject. Before people had had time to reflect, there was an impulse to appoint another Dictator; and in spite of the failure of the last, there were those who thought themselves capable of filling the office. Persons like myself, who were necessarily not thoroughly informed as to the nature of the various projects discussed by the committees which sat at Cracow, could only follow vaguely the course of events, or obtain a confused notion of the difficulties which at such a crisis must always to a greater or less extent impede the current of affairs. It was impossible for the two great political sections which had hitherto always found themselves in antagonism, to forget completely their old prejudices; and though they were animated by the best intentions, and were most anxious to conceal from strangers any want of harmony in their councils, it would be contrary to human nature to suppose that they both took the same view as to the most expedient measures to be adopted. It is useless now to recur to the points of difference which arose, as they were all settled more or less satisfactorily at last, and both sides were driven by the nature of the emergency into making concessions for the common cause. The truce was precipitated in an unexpected way by the appearance of the following proclamation issued by the Warsaw Central Committee, resuming the functions which they had abdicated on the nomination of Langiewicz :—

"WARSAW, 27th *March*.
"PROCLAMATION.

"The Central Committee, as National Government, informs the nation that, in consequence of the arrest of the Dictator, Langiewicz, by the Austrian Government, the supreme national authority has been resumed by them. With a view to guarantee the country from the confusion that might arise from attempts to seize the supreme power by any single individual, the assumption of dictatorial authority, or of any other form of government, whether at home or abroad, is declared treasonable."

There were doubtless those at Cracow who were disconcerted at the suddenness of the measure, which was in fact the act of a single individual, since killed in a duel, but which produced a good effect in one respect, that it recalled to the minds of the Cracow people the existence of a very influential body at Warsaw; for it was not unnatural that, Cracow being for the time the centre of the movement, the persons interested in it there should have assumed to themselves the initiative. Anything, however, was better than chaos; and for the first three or four days after the resignation of Langiewicz, there was a period when everybody wanted to do what was best, but no one knew how to do it, and there was no one to tell them. Now, at least, there was a *point d'appui*. No doubt there were prejudices to be got over on the part of those who had all along objected to the direction of affairs being undertaken by any secret society; on the other hand, their alternative had been tried and had failed. The only thing remaining was a compromise between the two rival committees, and discussions to bring this about occupied the leaders of the parties during that moment of lull which succeeded the downfall of Langiewicz. The pressure of public opinion without, no less than the magnitude of the crisis within, tended to facilitate this fusion. Both parties felt that the eyes of Europe were upon them; that nothing would be more fatal to the good opinion they desired to obtain than the idea of any split in the camp. The aristocracy were extremely anxious to dissipate any impression which might exist abroad that the movement was revolutionary in the democratic sense of the term. They were fairly committed to it, and could best prove its true character by going thoroughly along with it, and using their influence as best they might with those they had formerly opposed. Their antagonists were too glad to obtain such valuable co-operation to make any unnecessary difficulties. They too decided on substituting for political theories, practical execution; and both sides at once recognised the strength which such a union would give them, and the beneficial effect it would produce upon foreign cabinets. Henceforward there was to be no party of action, no moderate party; each and all were to combine to make Poland independent of Russia, and to allow no sectional jealousy to interfere with the one great national aim.

There was one other respect in which the experience gained during the Dictatorship was most useful. The inexpediency of massing together large bodies of undisciplined men had been made apparent by the disaster which befell Langiewicz's army. Hitherto the Poles had regarded with feelings akin to discontent the scattered bands which might harass the enemy, but could not signalise the insurrection by any grand military operation. Unused to guerilla tactics, and imbued with the traditions and associations of regular warfare, their ambition was to form an army which might meet the Russians in the field, and settle, by a few decisive actions, the fate of their country. Any such hope was now clearly delusive: circumstances rendered the formation of an army impossible, and victory must be considered to consist, not in meeting and defeating the enemy, but in coexisting with him, and keeping the country in a state of chronic disorganisation. Cracow was the natural and most available centre for concerting the measures necessary to this system of partisan warfare, and it was therefore my first point of observation. After I had learnt all that was to be discovered here, I determined to push on to Warsaw.

CHAPTER XIV.

EXPERIENCES DURING THE POLISH INSURRECTION:
WARSAW.

If it was impossible, without visiting Poland, to obtain an accurate idea of the true character of the insurrection, and of the nature of the obstacles with which it had to contend, it was still more difficult for me to convey in any satisfactory form the result of my observations. As an essential condition to the ultimate success of the movement was secrecy, a stranger must enjoy peculiar advantages to acquire information of any real value, and could only expect to be let in behind the scenes upon the assumption, not merely that he was thoroughly trustworthy, but that his sympathies were entirely with the insurgents. He was thus naturally expected to tell only what might advance the cause, and to colour, with a pardonable enthusiasm, his narration of the events which have come under his notice. Under no circumstances was he regarded as an impartial observer, whose only object was the discovery of truth: if he was not a frantic and unreasoning partisan either of one side or the other, he could be nothing else than a political spy. In that case, it was probable that both parties would tell him just so much as they thought proper, and might possibly also take great pains to mislead him where it might seem to serve their ends. Neither Russians nor Poles would ever believe that an Englishman should have no other object in visiting them, than that of relieving the monotony of the London season by a little mild excitement likely to be afforded by the investigation of the country in a state of revolution, or that he should be animated by the still more natural and worthy motive of improving his mind, and forming his own opinions upon the political events of the day. That he should travel on beaten paths for the mere purpose of sight-seeing, is in their eyes a silly English eccentricity, to which they have got accustomed; but that he should take an abstract interest in the moral, political, social, or religious condition of foreign nations, is to them incomprehensible. That one should not be contented with learning geography at school, but choose as a pursuit the observation of men, and the study of the working and effects of their institutions in different countries, is in their eyes simply ludicrous; and yet it is only the exploratory tendency cropping out in another form. Instead of plunging into the centre of Africa to discover the source of the Nile, like Speke and Grant, why not dive into the sources of revolutions? Why confine exploration to physical geography, when there are so many moral and political geographical problems yet unsolved? When does human nature lie more open to philosophical examination than when convulsed by mixed and violent passions? When is the value of political institutions better tested than during a revolution? When is the national character more easily read? What is more exciting than the acquisition of knowledge when everybody conspires to retain it from you? What more interesting than those speculations upon the future, to which the most critical moments in a nation's history give rise? There was a fermentation in political opinion upon the Continent in 1863 which promised to be a fruitful source of revolution, but each movement would owe its origin to different causes; it would be marked by its own special conditions; and just in proportion as his former experience has enabled the observer to arrive at just and accurate conclusions, would he find an interest in bringing his knowledge to bear on each successive occasion, and thus be better able to examine, with the calm and impartial scrutiny of a surgeon, the seat of the disease, watch its progress, and predict its result.

The happy privilege which Englishmen possess of being able to travel without restraint, and to express their opinions openly and without reserve, is calculated to puzzle and mislead foreigners who have lived in the retirement of oppressed nationalities. The impossibility of being frank and open among themselves, renders them suspicious of those who come without *arrière pensée* to visit them, and have no reason to disguise their feelings on political subjects.

Thus, I was not surprised to find in the 'Czas,' a Polish newspaper published at Cracow, the following paragraph, sent to it from Warsaw, on the occasion of my visit to that city, by its special correspondent, who evidently could not conceive it possible that I should go there at such a time for my own amusement, and, when there, that I should say what I thought:—

"WARSAW, 25th *April*.

"I have some further news to announce to you respecting ——, the Englishman who, ostensibly in the character of an ordinary tourist and observer, but really, I believe, with an object well known to Palmerston, has arrived here to have a nearer view of us. In general, he expressed himself with great hostility towards France; he thinks we ought to turn out the Russians by every possible means—even the least proper; at the same time he tried very hard to frighten us by detailing the sad consequences of an eventual French intervention, pointing out with much indignation the traditional policy of the Napoleonic race, whose members, while constantly making use of us, always ended by leaving us to our own efforts. He expressed much love for us in the name of the three United Kingdoms of Great Britain: it was, however, not difficult to perceive beneath this fine appearance of sympathy a much deeper object."

In other words, I only expressed the sentiments of nine Englishmen out of ten, when I told those Poles with whom I conversed that they possessed the sympathies of the English generally, and that they would retain those sympathies more surely by trusting to their own efforts alone to expel the Russians from Poland, than by looking to the French Emperor for assistance, while, like the Italians, they might feel the weight of their obligations to France little less oppressive than the tyranny from which they escaped, if they owed anything to her. It was indeed rather trying to the temper of a Briton to be informed at every turn that England was the only obstacle in the way of the reconstitution of Poland, and that our selfish policy prevented a magnanimous and disinterested Power from liberating the Poles, and advancing the cause of progress and humanity in Europe. The familiarity of the Poles with the French language, and the traditional and historical associations connected with France, drew their sympathies strongly towards that country. Deriving all their ideas of European policy through French newspapers, they were in general ignorant of any other views than those which were put forward in them, and united a profound respect for the French Emperor with an intense admiration for the people he governed. It is difficult to say whether my supposed capacity of political intriguer facilitated or impeded my very harmless investigations: on the one hand, I found no difficulty whatever in hearing a vast number of political opinions, but there was no great variety in them, and an utter absence of facts. I was perpetually grasping at shadows; the realities were there, but they were difficult to lay hold of. There was a great deal going on while I was at Cracow; bands were forming, people were plotting, and important measures being adopted, and yet a stranger, while overwhelmed with kindness and hospitality, was groping in the dark. Perhaps this was only natural, and the prudence and reticence which characterised the leaders of the movement had been taught by bitter experience; but it stimulated one's faculties all the more, and I regret that the most interesting items of information which I ultimately obtained I am not, even at this distance of time, at liberty to disclose. The delicacy of the situation arose out of the relations in which the Galician Poles, who were co-operating in every possible way with those in Russia, stood with reference to Austria. It was of the utmost importance that the measures undertaken in Cracow should be of such a nature that the jealousy or suspicion of the Austrian Government should not be aroused — that nothing, in fact, should be done which should induce the Austrian Government to interpose greater difficulties to the formation of bands and the transmission of arms than those which already existed. Cracow was essential as a base of operations; the policy of Prussia had increased the value of Galicia in this respect; and the most serious blow which the movement could receive, it was in the power of Austria to inflict. Every day almost indicated some change in the policy of this latter Power. At one moment the restrictions were relaxed, and there seemed a tendency to give the greatest latitude to the stipulations which exist between Russia and Austria, in favour of the movement; at another the reins were unexpectedly tightened, and people who had been encouraged into imprudence found themselves sufferers for their temerity. It did not do to trust to appearances. Sometimes they seemed to doze at Vienna, but it was only to wake up suddenly with a start. No doubt this sort of spasmodic action on the part of the Austrian Government was in a great measure forced upon it by the representations of M. de Balabine. The Russian Minister at Vienna was better served by his agents at Cracow than Count Rechberg, probably because he paid them better. Indeed, the Austrian police in Galicia had a profitable time of it, as in addition to their regular pay they were largely subsidised in secret by the Russian Government. Cracow swarmed with spies in Russian pay, and thus the Government at St Petersburg was kept far more accurately informed of the proceedings of the insurgents who were in Galicia than of those who were in Russian Poland, inasmuch as it was always easy to find Germans who would serve as spies—not so easy to find Poles. It was necessary, then, to make arrangements for the collecting and arming of bands with all possible secrecy, and every description of device was resorted to in order to elude the vigilance of the Austrian Government and the observation of the Russian spies. In order to appreciate the difficulties incidental to the equipment and despatch of a band under these conditions, we must consider in detail the *modus operandi*. First of all, inasmuch as the Russians lined the Galician frontier in considerable force at the time of my visit to Cracow, it was necessary for any band which crossed into the kingdom to be sufficiently numerous to be able to repel the troops they might encounter on the other side. Of course, just in proportion to the size of the band did the difficulties increase. It was impossible to form them in Cracow. All that the leader could know through the recognised channel was, that a certain number of men had enrolled themselves as his followers. Most of them, perhaps, he had never seen. Some had obtained arms from their own sources, others were directed to the quarter from whence they could be in secret supplied. In the middle of the night groups of young men might occasionally be seen stealing out of Cracow in different directions, and making their way to the frontier. As the country is undulating and well wooded, the impossibility of the Austrian patrols guarding its whole extent on a dark night is manifest: besides, there can be no doubt that the patrols would often look the other way when they suspected that insurgents were crossing in the vicinity. At daybreak the band would have arrived at the rendezvous—perhaps a wood a mile or two inside the frontier. Here they would be joined by, the leader, who would look over the men and material he found at his disposition, and examine their nondescript arms. Two or three waggons loaded with ammunition, which had been dragged along by-lanes and passed the frontier in safety, would now be unloaded, and their contents distributed. Sometimes all their munitions of war would be intercepted, and the band, after having crossed, would be obliged to return, and await a more auspicious occasion; but supposing the spot to be happily chosen, and everything to have gone smoothly thus far, the next object was to lie *perdu* as long as possible, and hidden from Russian observation. A day or two thus gained was of infinite value. A messenger would go back to Cracow, to report proceedings. More men, arms, and ammunition would cross over next night, while the day would be occupied by the leader in the endeavour to impart some kind of discipline to the men, and in instructing them in the use of their weapons. With a new raw band the leader was unwise if he removed from his base of operations, which was Cracow, a day sooner than he was obliged. But he could not hope for a respite of more than three or four days; he then found himself called upon to exercise all his ingenuity to avoid meeting the enemy, which is beginning to close round him; for the peasants, not well disposed in these parts, are not long in conveying the news. However, he has supplied himself with a few carts and horses, though, as his men have no clothes except those they have on, and carry a great proportion of their ammunition, his necessity for land-transport is not very great. If he could manage to get away into the mountains of St Croix, or to bury himself in some of the woods and morasses with which the interior of the country abounds, he was comparatively safe: if his band was not too large, he found no very great difficulty in procuring supplies; and if he was a prudent leader, his whole object was to keep out of the way of Russians for weeks to come. As it was of the utmost importance that he and his men should get to know and have confidence in each other, and acquire some slight knowledge of the kind of work before them, at first he confined himself to operations on a very small scale, and contented himself rather with a trifling success, than with risking the *morale* of the band by attempting too ambitious an enterprise. Such had been the experience of Jezioranski, Lelewel, and other leaders. But the majority of the bands which left Cracow were not so fortunate. Either they were unable to convey their ammunition across the frontier, or they were attacked so immediately after crossing that they were not in a position to defend themselves, and although behaving with great courage, were obliged to fall back before disciplined troops. Sometimes on these occasions they succeeded in burying their arms, more often they fell into the hands of the Austrians, who made prisoners of them as they retreated in confusion upon the frontier. Such was the fate of a portion of Gregovicz's band, which was attacked so close to Cracow that the firing could be heard in the town. Unfortunately, as I left the same day, I was unable to go to the frontier to witness the skirmish, which, however, though it resulted in the dispersion of the band, was more serious in its results of killed and wounded to the Russians than to the Poles. A large city naturally possesses greater facilities for the despatch of a band than the country villages; but, on the other hand, the Russian troops were generally collected in greater numbers on the frontier in the neighbourhood of Cracow than elsewhere. Bands were therefore often formed at other points, but here greater circumspection was required. The men were lodged in farm-houses, or even camped in woods, for a night or two on the Galician side.

In spite, however, of every precaution and of the most cunning devices, a great quantity of arms were constantly being seized *in transitu* by the Austrian Government; and it was calculated that it was necessary to add a sovereign to the price of every rifle or musket conveyed in safety across the frontier, after all other expenses were paid, in order to cover the loss sustained by those intercepted. It is almost impossible to estimate rightly, unless one has been upon the spot, the enormous disadvantages under which the insurgents laboured in being deprived of any safe base of operations. They were perpetually exchanging the frying-pan for the fire. The position of an Austrian Pole who took part in the movement was bad enough, but that of the Russian Pole was still worse. The Austrian who had been fighting with the insurgents, when desiring repose, could at least return to his home, and hope to remain there unmolested; but the Russian no sooner found himself a refugee in Cracow, than he had to scramble across the frontier into the kingdom for safety. I have conversed with some who belonged to

Langiewicz's army, and had succeeded in reaching Cracow; here they were lying hidden, afraid of being arrested and thrown into prison, for the Austrian Government drew a broad distinction between their own and Russian subjects. The latter they were bound by the convention to arrest, if not to give up. It is due to the Austrians to say that they did not interpret this obligation too strictly; but if a Russian Pole would persist in living in Cracow, he could not expect unlimited grace. The consequence was, that his only plan was to put his head back into the lion's jaws, and make the best of his way to the nearest insurgent band in the kingdom with the least possible delay. Unfortunately for the Poles, although they have shown the greatest aptitude as contrabandistas, they do not seem to possess an equal instinct for guerilla warfare. In this respect their habits are French: they like fighting in masses, they glory in the rules of regular warfare, and, with a strong military instinct and unlimited courage, insist upon undertaking operations upon a larger scale than the conditions under which they are fighting will admit of. It was rare to find a chief who could resist accessions to his band, which at the very moment possessed neither discipline, ammunition, nor food; rarer still to find a man who would not sacrifice half his band for the glory of taking a couple of cannon, which would be of no earthly use to him after he had got them. The disastrous attack of Miechow was perhaps one of the most painful illustrations of this blundering style of warfare. The insurgents could not be brought to understand that the great object of guerilla warfare is to be invisible—that victories are only one shade less disastrous than defeats, because you cannot afford the men they cost—that while discipline was necessary to keep a band in order, drill is absolute ruin to it, because the men will immediately fancy themselves soldiers — that excess of courage is a positive nuisance where you want to teach men the art of killing others without being killed themselves—that large bodies of human beings without guns are only food for the artillery of the enemy; whereas if the whole country is kept alive with scattered guerillas, their artillery arm is paralysed, for you give them nothing to fire at.

Thus there was an absence of ingenuity in their mode of conducting their operations. The essence of partisan warfare is *ruse*, but very little strategy was displayed; while it is due to the insurgents to say that their proceedings were always characterised by the utmost humanity. They almost invariably, after depriving their prisoners of arms, restored them to liberty; and some of the leaders even expressed horror at the idea, which very naturally occurred to me, that they should follow our example in the Crimea, and choose the Russian Easter, when the enemy would be engaged in celebrating that feast, to make a general attack upon him. I received abundant and convincing testimony that no such scruples of humanity animated the Russians, who committed atrocities which were not justified by the exigencies of the situation, and who could not complain if the Poles were driven to retaliative measures, as severe as those which we inflicted upon the rebels during the Indian Mutiny.

Again, the desire for military distinction is a principle so firmly rooted in the heart of every Pole that it sometimes interferes with his love of country. Not only does the leader despise the petty achievements to which a guerilla warfare should be confined, and from which he cannot acquire renown; not only does he love to augment his band even at the sacrifice of its efficiency, but he finds it difficult to hear of the success of rivals without a certain degree of jealousy: his ambition is to be the commander-in-chief of a Polish army; and although this struggle had been the means of calling forth in many instances a display of magnificent self-sacrifice, and neither life nor liberty were considered where the interests of the country were concerned, there could be no doubt that a danger existed of personal feelings being excited among the leaders, which prejudiced the success of the cause they all had at heart.

I crossed the Russian frontier at two points while at Cracow, but upon neither occasion did I see any troops. The nearest barrier was Michaelowice, and here there was a mile or so between the Austrian and Russian guardhouses. At the former was a patrol, and we were a good deal cross-examined before we were allowed to pass it, although promising to limit our explorations to a short drive. A number of peasants' carts laden with country produce was all we met, and my curiosity was considerably excited as we approached the Russian barrier, as it had been reported that the enemy was still there. However, beyond a dirty Jew leaning over the bar which crossed the road, and a few mangy curs, the place was deserted. Not a soul inhabited the handsome block of building, the official character of which was denoted by the Imperial eagle; the windows were many of them broken, and all was silent and forlorn. Taking courage from the desolate aspect of this post, we ventured on, and found ourselves in the kingdom. The coachman now began to think that we had gone far enough, but the temptation was too great to turn back at once, and we continued till we reached a hill from which we obtained a good view of the surrounding country. Not a Cossack was to be seen, scarcely a living creature; still the silence might be treacherous, so we turned back, to the immense relief of our coachman, whose speed was considerably accelerated until he found himself once more safe in Galicia. Practically, travelling in this part of the kingdom was impossible, except by railway, and then it was uncertain. Every peasant had a right to stop any one dressed respectably whom he might chance to meet, and bring him up to the nearest Russian post. One gentleman whom I saw, and who was harmlessly proceeding to his farm, was thus arrested, and he informed me that the Russian officer blamed his captors for having brought him in alive. They were informed that they would be considered to have rendered better service, if they would spare the Russians the responsibility and trouble of executing persons. As my informant could under no pretext be considered an insurgent, he was allowed to go; but so unsafe were the streets of the small town in which he lived during its occupation by Russian troops, that he was obliged to beg two Russian officers to accompany him across the road, as a protection from their own men. I. was prevented, from the utter disorganisation of the Russian army upon this frontier, from visiting Micchow, then the headquarters of General Szachowsky, as, although

I might have obtained a safe-conduct from this officer, it was not considered by the Russians themselves a sufficient protection. Even the wives of Russians employed in the kingdom were removed from places likely to be occupied by the Imperial troops. There is no doubt that this insubordination was due to an order issued by the Grand-Duke Constantine at the commencement of the outbreak, in which the men were enjoined not to place too much confidence in their officers. It seems that the Government had some reason to suspect the fidelity of the latter; certainly such an order was not likely to confirm it. The result was, that in several instances officers have been shot by men; and the account which Mr Bielski, in whose veracity I have every confidence, gave me of the attack upon his own country-house at Gibultow, vividly illustrated the utter demoralisation of the Russian army.

It would appear that the proximity of Langiewicz's camp induced four of the insurgents to pay him a visit, the more especially as his own son, who had joined the army of the Dictator, was of the number. Mr Bielski, who had a wife and daughter, was naturally alarmed at such dangerous visitors, and implored them not to prolong their stay, as it was known that the Russian army was in the neighbourhood: however, they lingered a little, and were just preparing to start, when a number of Cossacks and infantry were seen approaching from all sides. The first impulse of Mr Bielski's guests was to jump upon their horses and escape; this, however, they found impossible. A gentleman, unconnected with the insurgents, who was a visitor in the house, managed to jump into a bed and feign illness, the others endeavoured to hide themselves in a ravine. Of these Mr Bielski's son alone eluded the vigilance of the Russians, who, having secured his three companions as prisoners, now approached, in order to ransack the house. Meantime the ladies had taken refuge in the chapel, where they were praying, while Mr Bielski went out to try and parley with the officer. As, unfortunately, he had a boil on his face, and a handkerchief stained with blood round it, he was mistaken at first for a wounded insurgent, and the officer could with difficulty prevent the Cossacks from shooting him. Seeing that his life was in danger, he hastily retreated, and the house was entered by two officers and six men. Those outside clamoured furiously for the work of destruction to begin, shouting *Rubac!* (pillage), *Rezac!* (murder), *Palic!* (burn); and for more than an hour did the horrified inmates listen to these ominous cries, expecting every moment that the officers would cease to have any control over the men. Meantime the house was searched, the six Cossacks filling their pockets with everything that appeared of any value, and utterly disregarding the threats and injunctions of the officers. The gentleman in bed was turned out, and every room ransacked, the officers apologising for the painful task which was forced upon them, and the impossibility of executing it in any other way. Ultimately, but not until the officers had threatened to shoot the men, one of whom replied that his carbine also contained a ball, they were induced to leave the house. As they were leaving, Mr Bielski, who felt some gratitude to the officers for their endeavours to mitigate the ferocity of the men, offered one of them cigars. On their being declined, Mr Bielski said ironically, "Why do you refuse them? do you think they are poisoned?" On which the officer answered, "Had they been poisoned, I would gladly have smoked one, and thus relieved myself from any more of this hateful work."

A violent altercation next ensued between the officers and the men outside, who refused to take charge of the prisoners unless they were first allowed to plunder the house. When at last the latter were removed into the highroad, they found a certain Mr Finkenstein, who was a British subject, and a lady in a cart, surrounded by soldiers. What then transpired I had from the lips of one of the prisoners, who declared that he heard an officer give the order for their massacre. Mr Finkenstein, on the other hand, assured me that the officer, who was endeavouring to protect him, presented a revolver at the men who first attacked him: however that may be, the whole party were attacked—three of the Poles were killed on the spot. My informant, after receiving thirteen wounds, managed to shelter himself under Mr Finkenstein's waggon, out of which Mr F. was dragged and left for dead, with thirty-two wounds, the lady who was with him having been stabbed in three places.

Another history, the details of which were of the most harrowing description, was narrated to me by Mr Woyciachowski, whose son was murdered before his eyes, but that has already appeared in print. Indeed, there was no lack of evidence in Cracow confirmatory of the worst accounts we read at the time in the public prints of the barbarity of the Russian soldiery. The hotels were crowded with refugees, all of whom had some instances to relate; while the hospitals were filled to overflowing with young men, not merely wounded in the ordinary course of fighting, but often covered with wounds they received after having been captured and disabled. Unfortunately, the length of the interval which usually elapsed between the time when the wounds were inflicted, and when they could be attended to, caused them in a very undue proportion to terminate fatally. Not a day passed without my being attracted to the window by the mournful chant of a funeral procession, winding its solemn way to the cemetery outside the town, one portion of which was devoted to the interment of those killed for the national cause. Almost every evening I met in that gloomy society persons who had some new tale of distress to recount, or the loss of some near relative or friend to bewail. Still there was no symptom of flinching; those who were recovering from their wounds were only yearning to be back to the scene of action. The hardships they had undergone could not deter them from seeking to rejoin their comrades who were in the field; and the hotels swarmed with ardent young men either just returned from camp for a moment's respite, or just starting to take their share in the movement. It was difficult to be an indifferent spectator of so much misery and so much devotion.

The concentration of Russian troops in the neighbourhood of Cracow, and the obstacles in the way of despatching bands from that city, had induced the insurgents to commence operations upon other points of the frontier, so I went to Lemberg to see what was going on in the eastern part of Galicia. A ten hours' railway journey takes one to this outpost of Austrian civilisation. The contrast between the provincial capital and the old city of Cracow is sufficiently marked. Containing a population of nearly 90,000 inhabitants, Lemberg possesses none of the grand historic associations of Cracow, and can boast none of its picturesque effect. The houses are large white palatial structures, the shops gay and well furnished, the streets broad, and the city generally modern-looking and handsome. In Cracow the whole world seemed to live in the central square and the streets running into it. Everybody knew everybody, and everybody was in the movement: nothing else was thought of or talked of; youths in unmistakable insurgent costume were swarming everywhere, and the committees were in constant deliberation. In Lemberg the streets were busy with people going about their usual avocations. For all that a stranger could discover, there might have been no national movement in existence: except the predominant black, there was nothing to indicate Poland. It is true that its official character obliges a number of Germans to live at Lemberg, and that the large garrison may give a greater air of animation to the scene; but one felt, on walking about the streets, that one had got out of the movement. Nevertheless there was something going on, and arrangements were being made here as at Cracow to equip bands.

The weather was so bitterly cold during the period of my visit to Lemberg, that the camp of Lelewel, which I had intended visiting, and which was just upon the other side of the frontier, in the Palatinate of Lublin, was dissolved. It was almost impossible to keep the field with the driving snow and piercing wind, which seemed to penetrate one's whole system. It should be remarked, that the dispersion of a band by no means implied its extinction. When either an overwhelming force, inclement weather, or the absence of supplies or ammunition, rendered it impossible for a band to keep the field, they buried or concealed their arms; and, if in the neighbourhood of Galicia, crossed the frontier, and rested themselves for a while, or, if in the kingdom, scattered temporarily, but only to reunite at a given rendezvous on a more convenient occasion. Thus at Easter numbers of insurgents went home and spent the feast with their friends and relations; and just at the moment of my visit to Lemberg there was a lull in affairs in consequence. After staying a few days, I therefore decided upon going direct to Warsaw, and proceeded to arrange my luggage, in anticipation of the ordeal to which I understood travellers were subjected on entering Russian Poland. I was reluctantly compelled to refuse to be the bearer of sealed letters, as of course the only safe means of communication between Poles was by private *entremise;* and they were so skilled in concealing correspondence that the Russians seldom succeeded in intercepting the letters. I did not feel the same confidence in being able to elude the vigilance of the frontier officials, though, had I possessed my subsequent experience, I need not have been so prudent. The force of circumstances had obliged the Poles, when they wrote by post to each other, to convey their political intelligence in the shape of domestic details, so cunningly worded that they possessed no meaning to any one not initiated in the family affairs, and the ideas which they can be made to represent. The number of deaths, funerals, illnesses, and misfortunes, which occasionally overtook a family, would appal a stranger who read the letter, and did not know that these domestic afflictions were only fabricated to convey news of national disaster.

As the through trains from Cracow to Warsaw had ceased to run, I was obliged to pass the night at the miserable frontier station of Graniza, where a gaunt building, inhabited by a deaf old woman and a sulky barefooted maid, did duty for a hotel, and where my evening meal consisted of junks of ham and tea, and my bed of a very narrow stretcher, with thickly-populated dirty sheets. Only two other travellers were in the train, and they were both insurgents, on their way from a camp to spend Easter at home, as I afterwards discovered. None of us had any difficulty with our passports, and my luggage was subjected to a mere formal examination. My companions dispensed with any such encumbrance, and walked about the platform, on which a company of ill-favoured Russian soldiers were drawn up, with the utmost effrontery.

The fact that insurgents were reported to be hovering about the line, that they had already interrupted the communication upon several occasions, and that they had a disagreeable habit of firing upon the trains as they passed through the dense pine-woods, invested railway travelling in Poland with a novel sort of interest. Only three days had elapsed since the bridges destroyed by the insurgents had been repaired, and we did not know that we might not find some new interruption established.

At eight o'clock A.M. we collected on the platform. When I say "we," I mean one company of Russian soldiers who were in permanent occupation of the station —one company who mounted the open fourth-class carriages, and were to be considered as our protectors—an officer with a revolver, and three soldiers, who got upon the engine to see that the engineers and firemen did not play tricks — the two above-mentioned insurgents, who were not deterred by the presence of the Russian escort from going to Warsaw to see their friends, and who had only left their camp two days before—and a small group of Polish, railway officials, who, I presume, had no more idea than the Russians of the real character of their passengers, otherwise they would have insisted upon asking to see the tickets the insurgents had no money to purchase; for we will not do them the injustice of insinuating any complicity with their penniless compatriots; though the chief of a station on another line, I won't say where, did inform me that he could take ninety guards and *employés* off their duty at any moment, and make a band of insurgents of them, only he thought they were more useful passing insurgents up and down the line under the noses of the Russian troops.

With a puff and a shriek we dashed off with our light freight over the dreary flat country, across vast open plains thickly dotted with habitations and with peasants tilling the ground, through dark woods, across marshes, and over trestle-bridges, till we got to a station where another company of grim, dirty, Mongol-looking soldiers were waiting to receive us, and a few wild-looking Cossacks, with horses fastened to trees close by, were lounging about; while in the fields, a few hundred yards off, pickets were posted: for the insurgents like dashing suddenly upon isolated stations where a company of men may be surprised; then they have been known to jump into the train and make it take them up or down the line as their fancy may direct.

They have played all sorts of pranks on the railways; hence the strong guard, consisting of seldom less than a hundred men, by which each train is accompanied. The spruce officer, with spotless uniform and patent-leather boots, looks rather out of place in these wild regions, and in command of these wild, Tartar-looking men; and we cannot wonder that sometimes they will not obey his orders, and that lady-passengers do not much like trusting themselves along a line where there is more to be feared from the troops who protect, than from the insurgents who threaten it. The mayor of a small town sent the following rather characteristic account of events which transpired in his arrondissement: "At twelve o'clock on such a day," he reported, "'the destroyers of order' (insurgents) arrived; they took so much flour, so much brandy, so many pigs, &c., for all of which they paid, and they then retired: and at four o'clock in the afternoon of the same day, 'the preservers of order' (Russians) arrived; they took so much flour, so much brandy, so many pigs, &c., for which they did not pay; they then burned the town to the ground and retired."

At every station there is the same smart officer and the same company of soldiers; two or three times between the frontier and Warsaw the escort is changed, and as we proceed more passengers get in. Every soul, man or woman, is in the movement, and talks about it freely; they hand photographs of celebrated insurgents about, and upon one occasion the man whose likeness was being discussed was sitting placidly opposite, and did not attempt to conceal from his neighbours that he was the very individual whose figure, bristling with revolvers, we were inspecting. There can be no greater proof of the unanimity of the popular sentiment than the mutual confidence which all classes display in each other, and the freedom with which the most compromising topics are discussed. When surrounded by Russian soldiers, insurgents who were lounging about the platforms were openly pointed out and introduced to me. I felt the only coward of the party, and could scarcely believe that all the rest of the people who were in the secret were to be trusted. Upon one occasion, I saw the insurgent whom we had recognised by his photograph, in the most amicable and confidential conversation with the Russian officer commanding the company, and was laughed at for excessive caution when I expressed my surprise at his imprudence. I afterwards learned that no fewer than 3000 insurgents on leave from their bands had arrived by the three different railways which centre at Warsaw, to spend Easter in that city, and that so inefficient were the police, or rather so much implicated themselves in the movement, that the Government could not lay hands on any of them. One young man, who had been wounded in an encounter with Russians, was actually lying ill of his wound in Warsaw, and being attended for it under the nose of the Russian authority. How, upon our arrival at Warsaw, all those who had come with us managed to get passports which should satisfy the authorities, was a mystery; but my friend of the photograph, who had never from the beginning owned a ticket, was careering along triumphantly in a cab, before I had extricated myself from the police formalities.

Before the Government adopted the plan of sending escorts with the train, it was stopped one day by the insurgents, about fifty of whom availed themselves of it. As it approached the station, the engineer perceived that the authorities had got some suspicion of its contents, and that the platform was lined with troops. There was still time to allow the occupants to creep out of the doors on the opposite side, and hide themselves in the luggage-van. This operation was barely accomplished before the train slowly entered the station. No suspicious passengers were found in the carriages, and the officer was at a nonplus, when it occurred to him to search the luggage-van. No sooner did the engineer hear the order given than he quickly attached the van to the engine, and, detaching the rest of the train, steamed down to get water, taking the luggage-van with him as if by mistake. After watering the engine, he was obliged to come back to the station; and as they had been all the time in sight of the troops, no opportunity had been afforded to the insurgents to escape. Their situation was becoming critical as they re-entered the station; but, to the astonishment of every one, the guard again re-attached the empty train, and off it went at full speed. No sooner did the train arrive at a turn which hid it from the station, than the van was opened, the insurgents jumped out, and the train once more entered the station amid a general volley of abuse, the guard accusing the engineer of stupidity, the engineer laying the fault on the guard, and all, secretly amused, indulging, for the benefit of the Russians, in the loudest mutual recrimination.

Upon another occasion the line had been destroyed by the insurgents, and a party of engineers were sent down to repair it. In the day they worked at the demolished bridge, but in the night they proceeded to another bridge farther on, which they broke down, and next day pointed out to the Russians what they pretended had been a fresh work of the insurgents. These latter naturally aimed, in the first instance, at supplying themselves with funds; and two or three young men called upon an official one day to hand over the treasure-chest of a small town. As they were too few in number to resort to force and make a tumult, they were rather disconcerted at his refusal, and were going away without it, when he called them back and said, "I can't give you the box unless you present a pistol at my head." This was done at once, and the box handed over. The youths, being inexperienced, then asked him for the keys, which he also refused. Here was another puzzle; and the good-natured official was actually obliged to remark, "I shall certainly not give you the keys, nor can you get the money unless indeed you break open the lock." In this fashion did the Polish officials of the Russian Government serve their masters.

The air seemed heavy with suspicion when I at last got away from the station, with the sort of feeling of having escaped some danger, and of being still a very guilty personage. I imagined that everybody was narrowly examining me, and that all the waiters in the hotel were spies. And when I drove along the wide streets, crowded with foot-passengers in black, and met here and there a patrol of Russian infantry, or a few Cossacks with ragged ponies and long lances, there was something in the close proximity of these antagonistic forces which gave me the same sort of sensation I once experienced in America, when a gentleman informed me that the barrel upon which I was sitting smoking a cigar contained gunpowder.

The two first essentials to the traveller's comfort in Warsaw were, a lantern, and a permit to be out after ten o'clock at night. After seven the streets presented a most singular aspect; everybody was compelled to carry a lantern, and the town seemed inhabited by a population of lively glow-worms. After ten o'clock all this disappeared; here and there at long intervals a stray lantern might be seen, but the bearer of it carried in his pocket a permit to be in the streets at all. Very few Poles carried these, as it implied too great a familiarity with the Russian authorities, and loyal Poles prided themselves upon not having sufficient interest to obtain one.

With a pair of coloured trousers and a hat, however, one might do a good deal without a permit, as no native would be seen in either the one or the other. The wearer, therefore, must expect black looks from the townspeople; but, *en revanche*, he was not so likely to be molested by the police. Upon one or two occasions I was out late without a permit, but escaped observation by getting into the deep shadow when any one passed. I found several people doing the same thing: they were apt to bolt to some other corner on a new arrival, and it became quite an interesting amusement to dodge about, not unlike the game of "post," the usual forfeit being a night in prison. The police, however, were not stricter than was necessary to keep up appearances, as they were all in the movement: one of them informed a friend of mine that the muzzle of a rifle he was endeavouring to smuggle home beneath his greatcoat was visible above the collar, and he had better hide it before the patrol came, for the patrol were disagreeably personal in their investigations, particularly when they were not sufficiently educated to read the permits.

In spite of all their endeavours, the united exertions of the Grand-Duke Constantine, General Berg, and the Marquis Wielopolski were incapable of suppressing the Central Committee, or of preventing that occult body from governing not only Warsaw, but Poland, just as it pleased. It made use of the Government telegraph for the transmission of its information, of the Government post-office for the forwarding of its despatches, of the Government machinery for the promulgation of its orders, of the Government clerks for the obtaining of official information, of the Government police for carrying out its secret designs —in fact, of everybody in Poland, whether in Government employ or not, except the Russian army, the Marquis Wielopolski, and the peasants of some districts. The proclamations of the Central Committee were freely circulated, and passports issued by it, which facilitated the movements of the stranger anxious to visit their camps, but involved his speedy execution if they were discovered upon him by the Russian soldiery. I therefore declined burdening myself with so dangerous a document. At the period of my visit, among other proclamations issued by the Central Committee, was one warning the people against spurious documents emanating from the Russian Government, but which purported to be promulgated by the Central Committee, and to which a stamp in imitation of the one used by that body was appended. The idea of the authorities in resorting to this ruse was characteristic;

but the stamp was badly imitated, and though for the moment it created some little confusion, the public were soon on their guard against similar forgeries. Another notification announced the death of two persons who were executed as spies in the streets of Warsaw by order of the Central Committee; the warrant for their execution was found pinned upon their dead bodies. It is probable that the police on duty at the time looked the other way.

Perhaps the most remarkable feature of the whole of this movement was the continued existence of this Committee for more than a year, in spite of all the efforts of the Government to suppress it. The authority it wielded over the Poles was marvellous. Every order was executed as soon as it was given, and it possessed the confidence of the country so completely, that an order from it at any moment would have suspended operations. Many are the stories told of the mysterious working of this secret council. Some asserted that it consisted really of only one man, who was known only to two other men, who in their turn were known to four others, and so on, each set being bound not to reveal the particular link in the chain with which they had to deal, so that the first man would be unknown to the four. But these were the fables with which wonder-loving gossips delighted to amuse strangers. The fact is, that the members of the Central were very well known to a great number of persons, and that practically it was merely a sort of upper house to the more active and intelligent spirits of Warsaw, who discussed in private the measures to which the Central Committee gave effect. Latterly the aristocratic element predominated in its councils, and there was probably scarcely a single individual on the Committee at the close of the movement who was on it when it was commenced. This was not on account of any wide divergence of opinion, although there was an essential difference in the views of the two parties, so much as in the fact of every original member having been either executed, imprisoned, exiled, or obliged to join an insurgent band. The odd thing was, that there was no difficulty whatever in communicating with it. It lived nowhere, but was to be found everywhere. A band of insurgents having occasion to take some forage, &c., from a peasant, gave him an order for payment on the Central Committee. He being as ignorant of politics as most of his class, came into Warsaw and asked the first person he met which was the way to the Central Committee: people laughed and passed on; at last he went to the Russian police-office and inquired there, ingenuously remarking that he had a claim on it for some money. The police could give him no assistance; but requested him, should he ever find the Committee, to come back and tell them where it was. So he wandered disconsolately on till he came to a group of persons in one of the public squares, and asked one of them if he could direct him to the Central Committee. The gentleman he addressed took him at once up a by-street and inquired his reason for wishing to find it, on which the peasant pulled out his order for payment for forage received by insurgents. The gentleman immediately took the order, pulled out his purse, paid the money, and made the man put his mark in pencil to a formal Central Committee receipt which he had in his pocket. Half an hour later a body of police were crossing the square under the guidance of the ungrateful rustic, and minutely examining the by-streets; but the group of persons had vanished, and the gentleman who had represented the Central Committee upon the occasion was nowhere to be seen.

A glacis, about half a mile wide, separates the city of Warsaw from the citadel. It was filled to overflowing with political prisoners, and every morning crowds of women were to be seen clustered round the prison doors, who had brought comforts to their relatives and friends, with whom, by special favour, they were sometimes permitted to communicate. In the event of a popular movement in the city, the guns of the fort could lay it in ruins; but it would not offer any very formidable resistance to the siege operations of a regular army. A barrier round the town was guarded by Russian sentries, and they examined minutely the passes of persons who might wish to go into the country for a drive. This was, however, a luxury very rarely indulged in by the inhabitants, partly because a pass was not a very easy thing for a Pole to get, and partly because the country, even close up to the city, was by no means safe. The insurgents came to within two or three miles of it, and Cossacks, not very scrupulous in their treatment of harmless wayfarers, scoured the neighbourhood. The insurgents themselves, however, found very little difficulty in going in and out of the town as they pleased. The sentries were all to be bought, and in the night could easily be induced for a consideration to look the other way while their enemies were passing to or from their camps. Indeed, so ready were the Russian soldiers to provide themselves with the means of procuring brandy, that they willingly sold their ammunition to the insurgents, and were only prevented from selling their arms as well, by the impossibility of accounting for the absence of them to the military authorities.

General Berg was sent expressly from St Petersburg to assist in the military administration of Poland, and arrived in Warsaw about the same time as myself. He is reported to have said, after his first week's experience of the difficulties with which he had to contend, from the unanimity amongst all classes of Poles, whether employed by the Government or not, in favour of the movement, that there was only one other man in Warsaw upon whom he could depend besides himself, and that this was the Grand-Duke Constantine. The remark was aimed specially at the Marquis Wielopolski, the Civil Governor, between whom and General Berg an intense jealousy existed, notwithstanding the fact of both being included in an order from St Petersburg, which commanded the inhabitants of Warsaw to take off their hats whenever they met either the Grand-Duke, Berg, or Wielopolski. The poor "Marquis," as he was called, *par excellence*, because he was the only noble of that rank in Poland, enjoyed a most unenviable distinction amongst both the Russians and his own countrymen, the Poles. The former distrusted him because he was a Pole, and was engaged in the revolution of 1830-31; the latter called him a traitor, and the author of all the misery which had latterly fallen upon their unhappy country. It was sufficient for the "Marquis" to propose a measure to ensure the opposition of Berg; but as the latter had also an opponent to his policy in the Grand-Duke, Wielopolski had in the long-run been triumphant.

However much it was to be regretted that the most remarkable Pole which this century has produced, should have placed himself in a false position with reference to his country, we are bound to accord him a certain qualified admiration. There was something grand in his imperturbable stubbornness, in his egregious self-sufficiency, and in his indomitable courage. In his ponderous figure, massive brow and chin, and shrewd eyes, there was an individuality that imposed upon those who came under his influence. His appearance reminded me at the same time of Yeh and Cavour, and his character did not belie his looks. It contained about equal proportions of the Chinaman and the Italian; with the pride and obstinacy of the one he combined the *finesse* and intelligence of the other. Stolid and reflective, he elaborated a policy repugnant to his country, and trusted to the strength of his will and the inflexibility of his character to force it upon the nation; but he overestimated his power, the nation refused to bend, and Wielopolski, too proud to yield, became the servant of Russia. Phrenologically speaking, the inordinate development of the organ of self-esteem has neutralised all the grand qualities which might have made him the saviour and the blessing of his country. The scheme to which he sacrificed his own reputation and his country's wellbeing, was a vast conception, and seems to have been suggested by the Galician massacres in 1846. Then it was that he addressed to Prince Metternich a celebrated letter, which ended in an exordium to his countrymen:—" We must take a line. Instead of the irregular and haphazard course we have been hitherto pursuing, we must, by a bold stroke which may cause our hearts to bleed, substitute for it a line of conduct which is safe, and which is marked out for us by events." And then he proposed to Poland to abdicate its pretensions as a distinct nationality, and to put itself at the head of Sclavonia. His idea was, in other words, that the superior moral and intellectual resources of Poland should be directed to the annexation of Russia—that the Poles, identifying themselves with the aspirations and aims of the Sclavonic nationalities, should, as their most civilised representative, control the destinies of Eastern Europe. "The nobility of Poland," he writes, "will surely prefer to march with Russia at the head of a Sclavonic civilisation, young, vigorous, and with a great future before it, than to be dragged, jostled, despised, hated, and insulted at the tail of a decrepit, intriguing, and presuming civilisation." But the Poles, however much they might hate Germany, could not make common cause with Russia against it. They still clung to the traditions of their former independence, and preferred rather to fight single-handed against three enemies, than to identify themselves with one in the hope of crushing the other two. Wielopolski was too enamoured of himself and his plan to abandon it. If Poland declined to found Panslavonia, Wielopolski would found it by himself; and he went to St Petersburg to take the preliminary steps. The first was the subjugation of Poland by force, as argument had proved of no avail; and in order to carry this out thoroughly, he succeeded in getting named the governor of the country. Of course he found himself placed in a position of direct antagonism with the whole nation, and could only rely on Russian bayonets to give effect to his will.

This he never scrupled to do. He never hesitated to trample on anything, so that he could keep his own head erect. It became a struggle between the nation and the man. We cannot but wonder whether there was not a fiercer struggle going on within the man himself. Did he never feel, now that he had laid the country he so undoubtedly loved, prostrate and bleeding at his feet, one twinge of remorse? Did he never think of the day when he fought for the liberties he was now crushing, when he was the ambassador to England of the same people, engaged in the same struggle that they were now, and when he pleaded for them so eloquently? Did he never inwardly curse that pride of his nature which so blinded and hardened him that he thought he could change the aspirations of a nation, and did not shrink from massacring them when he failed? Unfortunately, Wielopolski had not been long in Warsaw before his *amour propre* became involved in another direction. He had assured the Emperor that he understood the Poles, and could govern the country; but every day was proving the contrary, and the imminence of an outbreak threatened altogether to destroy his credit and his prestige. Then it was that he proposed the Conscription Act in the dead of winter. No wonder his countrymen called him traitor. And they were right. A man who will not sacrifice his own pride to the good of his country is a traitor—not, perhaps, in the worst sense, but in one equally fatal to the cause he ought, if necessary, to die for. And Wielopolski would have died sooner than give in; so he clung to Warsaw, and drove about the streets surrounded by a Russian escort to protect him from the bullets of his countrymen.

Notwithstanding the rigorous measures adopted by the Russian Government, and the stringency of the rules to which everybody was obliged to conform in Warsaw, there was an entire freedom in the expression of opinion. It is only before a popular outbreak, when public feeling, seething and fermenting, has not yet found a vent, that people are afraid to speak. When the surface is still calm, any solitary individual venturing to express an opinion is at once seized, so that it is generally difficult beforehand to predict a revolution. There is always a moment of lull, and the police are doubly active, while the masses are nerving themselves silently for the final effort. No sooner is that made than the tongues of the most prudent are loosened. In proportion as the prisons are filled, and arrests increase, do men become reckless, until the Government gives up in despair the attempt to control the freedom of speech. When one common sentiment animates a whole population, and each individual is determined to express it, imprisonment becomes impossible. Thus it happened that treason and revolution, so far as Russia was concerned, were openly talked in Warsaw; spies were of but little avail, because they would have been obliged to report everybody in the town for the same offence. But the office of a spy was not coveted; even Jews were not to be bribed. The police of the Central Committee was so much more efficient than that of the Russian Government, that sooner or later the doom of a spy was certain. So far, then, as the liberty of discussing openly the situation was concerned, there was no difficulty. Every one was glad to give a stranger the benefit of his patriotic opinions. The Warsaw Society met at each other's houses;

triumphed over the news of victories gained by insurgents; mourned over defeats; anathematised Russia in general, and Berg and Wielopolski in particular; canvassed the probabilities of aid from without, and the expediency of the policy to be adopted by the Central Committee. It was strange to be in a room with thirty or forty persons, all of whom were uttering sentiments which would have infallibly consigned them to Siberia if they had been heard by a Russian; and yet so thoroughly confident of each other, that no man hesitated to say exactly what he thought; and interesting to observe the phases of character as indicated by the nature of the views expressed—some so sanguine of the power of the internal forces at work that they were comparatively indifferent to foreign intervention; others so earnestly anxious for an indication from any Western Power of a disposition to take up their cause; some gloomy and despondent of the whole affair; some alarmed at the strong infusion of the middle-class element, to which the movement owed so much of its force; all interested in hearing what impression a stranger had received, and in discovering what he considered to be their ultimate chances of success.

It was indeed difficult for a traveller to arrive, on such short notice, at any definite conclusion; but no one could be long in the country without perceiving that one ingredient most essential to a successful revolution was wanting. The leading spirit had not appeared—the movement had not yet found a living representative. For a moment, persons looking on from abroad expected to find in Langiewicz a second Garibaldi, but Poland did not produce either a Garibaldi or a Cavour. The Central Government at Warsaw proved itself a most admirably contrived machine for the management of internal affairs, but the wisdom of its measures was not in proportion to the adroitness which was exhibited in carrying out its organisation. To make it effective it should have been the tool of one man, and he a man of consummate genius. In supreme moments, if the ship is to weather the storm, it must be steered by one hand and one head; and it does not seem that there was any political leader of surpassing ability, who, by means of the Central Committee, governed the country. Hence the very composition of the National Government underwent change, and there was not that consistency and decision in its policy which would have given confidence had it been under the guidance of one man.

Hitherto my observations had been confined to the men of council. I now wished, before leaving the country, to see the men of action at work in the field.

CHAPTER XV.

A VISIT TO AN INSURGENT CAMP.

SCARCELY a week had elapsed after my arrival at Warsaw, before the opportunity which I had so long desired, and had vainly attempted to find in Galicia, presented itself of visiting a camp of insurgents. I therefore got my passport *viséd*, as though I were going to leave the country altogether, and went through the usual police formalities which were necessary for that purpose; then I took a ticket for Berlin, and bade adieu to Warsaw, without exciting any suspicion. After travelling a few hours, we arrived at a station, too small and lonely for the Russians to care to defend it with the usual company of soldiers. My companion was a Polish gentleman, who did not take so much trouble to disguise our destination as I could have wished; and there was probably scarcely a passenger that saw us alight who did not guess where we were going. A light open country cart, without springs, but plentifully provided with straw, and drawn by a pair of spirited young horses, jolted us first along a rough road, then through a small town inhabited entirely by Jews, where greasy-looking women inspected the heads of their progeny in the sun, and their fathers, in long coats, long beards, and long curled locks, smoked long pipes in all the luxury of *dolce far niente;* for this was their Sabbath. Then we dived into a pine-and-birch wood, dexterously threading our way between the trees—for there was no road—and so again out into the open, till we came to a most picturesque old chateau, with "bridge, and moat, and donjon keep;" but prudence prevents my describing it so accurately as I could wish, for fear of compromising my host. The camp we had expected to find in the neighbourhood had moved, so we determined to drive on and spend the night at a country-house about fifteen miles distant. My host could, indeed, not offer me very much hospitality, as he found that, during his absence in Warsaw, nearly all his servants had disappeared and joined the insurgents; his cook was at this moment exercising his culinary talents for the benefit of a band; his groom, mounted on one of his master's best horses, was perhaps chasing a Cossack, while the footman might be leading a body of scythemen on to glory. However, the coachman had remained, being an elderly individual, with a wife and family. It was twilight ere we were *en route*, this time in a civilised landau, which needed four strong well-bred horses to drag it along the deep sandy roads. We kept a bright look-out for Cossacks as the shades of evening closed in upon us; but latterly the insurgents had taken so much to night-work, that the Cossacks preferred staying at home to incurring the risk of meeting them, so that we felt pretty safe, and arrived, without any other incident than one or two false alarms, at our journey's end, just as the family were going to bed. Their astonishment at the arrival of an English traveller on so strange an errand soon gave place to the rites of hospitality, and before going to bed the programme for the following day was already arranged. My new host was a small country gentleman, too devoted to his farm and his country's cause to take refuge, like many of the larger landed proprietors, in Warsaw. His wife was a genuine specimen of a Polish woman, enthusiastically patriotic, high-couraged, self-sacrificing, and energetic in giving aid and encouragement to the insurgents. Though living in the midst of a perpetual scene of guerilla warfare, and liable at any moment to be subjected to outrages such as those which she believed had already been perpetrated on her countrywomen by the Russian soldiery, she showed no symptom of flinching or deserting her post. Already, upon several occasions, at all hours of the day and night, her house had been invaded by Cossacks, who only abstained from massacre and pillage because no evidence could be discovered of complicity with the insurgents. Fortunately the house lay a little distance off the highroad, and was therefore often passed unperceived by the Russian marauding parties: but the occupants could never feel themselves safe; and as every day brought tidings of unsuspecting families falling victims to the rapacity and lust of a disorganised soldiery, the chances of this unprotected little mansion escaping seemed diminished. It was, indeed, little better than a farmhouse, and consisted of only one storey; but it was surrounded by a well-stocked steading, and fields that bore evidence of a master's eye and careful cultivation. In one direction, a long unbroken line of dense pine forest shut out the horizon: in the other, sandy undulating downs stretched away indefinitely. The scenery would have been tame and uninteresting, were it not that its wild desolate character gave it a peculiar charm: this was heightened by the circumstances under which we saw it. A solitary horseman appearing upon the distant landscape caused as much sensation in the household as a suspicious-looking craft in the West Indian seas would to a Spanish galleon in the days of Kidd. There was a constant succession of emotions; and I thought my hostess must have been endowed, in the first instance, with strong nerves, to have been able to undergo the constant wear and tear to which she was daily subjected. An ardent devotion to the cause, and a plentiful indulgence in large, strong cigars, however, sustained her through the various exciting events by which her life was checkered. There can be little doubt that the constant proximity of danger at last renders one callous to it, and that by a providential arrangement the nervous system becomes so accustomed to tension where it is sufficiently protracted, that in the end it ceases to suffer from it. I sat up till a late hour listening to "the sensation anecdotes" which formed the staple of my host's conversation—stories of the robbery and pillage of neighbouring houses by Russians, of deeds of heroism performed by individual insurgents, of skirmishes which had already taken place, and of those which were daily anticipated—of friends who had been arrested, of others who had joined bands, of others who were killed or wounded, of the movements of the insurgents, of farms visited, of horses taken, of peasants hung, of arms concealed—of every variety of incident with which such exciting times must necessarily abound. It was long past midnight before I sought the detached building which contained my bedroom. As I crossed the lawn, the sound of a distant chorus fell faintly upon my ear. I stopped to listen. It was a bright calm moonlight night, and for a moment all was profoundly silent; then gradually the swelling strains of the magnificent Polish national anthem broke the stillness for a moment, and died away again in the extreme distance. We had to listen intently to catch the notes; but it was evident that many voices joined in that midnight chant; and as the sounds grew fainter, we found that they were not stationary. It was, in fact, a body of mounted insurgents on a midnight raid; and as at the moment the nearest Russian force was supposed to be at least four miles off, they were beguiling the way by almost the only song a Pole ever sung in those days—the prayer for the deliverance of his country. I thought, nevertheless, that the proceeding, though most romantic in its effect, was somewhat rash, and was confirmed in this impression by the next sound which broke the nocturnal silence, and which was nothing less than the sharp report of a rifle. To a person not accustomed to them, it must be admitted that these were somewhat disturbing influences under which to court repose; however, the day had been a long and an eventful one, so exhausted nature soon triumphed over every other sentiment, and I fell asleep while vainly endeavouring to keep awake and listen for the report of another shot.

Breakfast is almost as substantial a meal in Poland as it is in England, and the disturbed state of the country did not prevent my hosts from loading the table with most excellent fare. The master of the house was in a condition to do full justice to it, for he had already made a pilgrimage to the camp to prepare the way for my visit. It was indeed necessary that the band should have some information as to my object and intentions, for in spite of the severe measures adopted by the insurgents, there are spies in every form and under every guise, against whom they are constantly on their guard; and it was some time after my arrival before even my hostess could divest herself of some suspicion as to my real character. It chanced to be Sunday, and a number of peasants came on their way to church to pay their respects to their master. They were fine stalwart men, with long coats, big boots, round caps trimmed with fur, and honest cheery faces, not by any means devoid of intelligence. Their mode of salutation is to touch the ground at your feet with their caps. They looked with considerable interest at the English traveller who had come to this out-of-the-way spot to see what was going on. Nor did my host neglect to take advantage of the circumstance, and instance it as a proof of the sympathy which England felt for the cause of Polish independence. I asked the most intelligent-looking among them why he had not joined the insurgents? He answered, with a sly look at his master, "Because my master has not. When my master does, I will." From what I could gather, the peasants of this part of the country were not indisposed towards the insurrection; but they had been too long accustomed to regard the power of Russia with an awe amounting almost to superstition, to venture, at the outset of the movement, to set it at defiance. It was only natural that they should feel no very keen interest in the success of a cause which would produce no immediate material change in their condition. It is not until a man becomes more or less educated that he knows the difference between one form of government and another; but whether the seat of government be Petersburg or Warsaw, and whether the head of it be a Russian emperor or a Polish king, makes very little difference to the rustic, who would be at the tail of the same plough, driving along the same furrow, whoever was the supreme authority. The only questions which touch persons of this class are those connected with religion or with property. A peasant will be profoundly indifferent whether he is under a responsible or an irresponsible government; but when it comes to making the sign of the cross with three fingers or with two, he enters keenly into the question at once. Thus in Samogitia and other parts of Lithuania the peasants were the prime movers of the insurrection, because they were compelled to become members of the Russian Greek Church, and to abandon the United Greek persuasion, to which they originally belonged. As they were pagans only three hundred years ago, they were the more tenacious upon the point, and had taken advantage of the movement in Poland to rise all through the provinces. Russia had lately succeeded in exciting some of the Greek dissenting sects to attack the Roman Catholic proprietary, and had inaugurated a system of *jacquerie*, which had been productive of the most frightful results in Lithuania and the provinces. That this policy of annihilation emanated from the highest sources, is proved by the following paragraph contained in the instructions issued by the Czar to General Mouravieff:—" His Excellency should take every opportunity of acquainting the peasants with the paternal intentions of the Czar towards them, and of demonstrating that the landowners are their enemies and oppressors. If his Excellency considers it advisable, he can also furnish arms to those among the peasants who are attached to the Czar and to Russia." In other words, having demonstrated to the peasant who was his natural enemy and oppressor, he was provided by a considerate Government with the means of exterminating them from off the face of the earth, and encouraged to do so by the prospect of plunder which this process would ensure to him.

In the kingdom of Poland, where the tenure of land is not the same, and the peasants are already proprietors of the soil, the Government could not hold out the same temptation to them to murder their masters. In fact, the National Government had outbid the Czar in an attempt to secure the goodwill of the peasantry; for whereas the latter had been obliged to pay into the Imperial treasury a certain proportion of their profits, to be accumulated into a sum for the redemption of the land which formerly belonged to the nobles, and out of which they were to receive compensation, the National Government proclaimed that this obligation was no longer binding upon the peasant, who would thus become a landowner without ever having paid for his property. The struggle between the Poles and the Russian Government for the goodwill of the rural population began with the Agricultural Society, and there can be no doubt that the efforts of that body, and the subsequent policy pursued by the National Government, did much to conciliate this large and important section of the population.

For example, the hostility of the peasants to the national movement in the district I was now visiting had been loudly insisted upon, by the few persons I had met who were themselves indifferent to the cause of Polish independence; but we received practical evidence to the contrary when our arrangements for visiting the camp were completed. As some friends from a neighbouring country-house were expected to come and spend the day, we delayed in the hope of their joining, and finally started in four light open country carts, each drawn by four horses, for the recesses of the forest, which rose in a sombre mass upon the distant margin of the cultivated plain.

It was not to be supposed that we could thus ostentatiously depart without every servant in the house being aware of our destination; indeed there was a flutter and excitement in their movements which plainly showed the interest they felt in the expedition. The coachmen looked eager and self-satisfied, and there was quite a group collected to see us off. With the loud cracking of whips our primitive *cortège* dashed off along the sandy roads. There were no less than seven ladies of the party, looking brave and animated, for the expedition was a novelty even to them. Notwithstanding the constant proximity of insurgent camps for months past, upon no former occasion had any of them ever ventured to visit one. Now their eyes sparkled and their faces flushed, as they felt the risk they were incurring, and calculated the chances of a safe return. We passed through two populous villages, every man and woman in which knew where we were going, and ran to see us pass; and any of whom would have received a large reward had they carried the intelligence to a Russian force of six thousand men, quartered in a town not five miles distant. Had they done so, and had we encountered a party of Cossacks on our way back, the murder of every member of the party was a moral certainty.

Even the men did not feel quite comfortable at the possibility of such a contingency, and could only express their belief in the loyalty and affection of the peasants. When it is remembered that these latter were invested with the functions of police, and were actually liable to be severely punished for not informing against us, it cannot be said that the rural population, in a district where they had the reputation of being most hostile, were so very decidedly opposed to the movement.

At last we arrived at the outskirts of the wood, and came to a farmhouse, where the proprietor, a sort of gentleman-farmer, was waiting to be our guide. This man and his wife, a large fearless woman, were practically the commissariat department of the neighbouring camp. He made all the arrangements for the purchase and transmission of supplies; and while he had placed all his resources at the disposal of the insurgents, and nearly ruined himself for the cause, he was daily risking life and liberty by the active and energetic assistance he afforded in giving information, conveying intelligence, and making himself generally useful. In everything he was ably and courageously seconded by his wife, who would not hesitate to drive a cart of provisions into the wood by herself, and was unremitting in motherly care and kindness to the members of the band, many of whom were young enough to need it, and whom she regarded with as much affection as if they were her own family. It was only to be expected that they cordially reciprocated these sentiments.

Half a mile from this farm we plunged into the woods. The country here was thinly populated; the last village we passed was four or five miles distant, and we did not meet a soul as we jogged along in our springless carts over a road that was now a mere track. Suddenly a halt was called from behind, and a panic spread down the line. The women's faces blanched, but they said nothing; the one prominent thought was "Cossacks." We passed the word along to the leading cart to stop, and waited breathlessly. We were now so deeply buried in the wood that the last cart was not visible, for we had added to our procession by our guide and his wife in one vehicle, and by a large cart full of provisions, which we were taking to the band. The cause of our stoppage was quickly explained —we were waiting for a further accession to our party, which appeared in the forms of an old gentleman and his two sons, who were going to join the band as insurgents, and who had stumbled on us while endeavouring to find the way. After some little parley between them and our guide, who wished apparently to be quite satisfied as to their real character, he told them to fall in behind with their cart, and we once more went on threading our way between the trees, not a little relieved at finding the interruption to our progress did not arise from any more serious cause. Suddenly, on emerging from a thicket, we came upon a mounted picket, who halted us. It consisted of two mere boys, neither of them twenty years old, each armed with rifle, sword, and pistol, and on excellent horses. The well-known face of our guide was a guarantee of our good faith, but still we were not allowed to proceed till the band was informed of our proximity, and one of them galloped off with the news. We had not waited a quarter of an hour before a dozen mounted men came dashing through the woods towards us. They seemed scarcely able to restrain their high-mettled horses, which were all in first-rate condition, and would have been a credit to Rotten Row. With little flags waving from their lances, and tricoloured ribbons fluttering from their square fur caps, with long jack-boots and massive spurs, and broad belts garnished with revolvers, and swords jingling from their sides, they came on us as suddenly from the depths of the woods as if they had been waiting in the side-scene of a play to come upon the stage with due *éclat*. The whole effect was most theatrical; but at the moment we felt its thrilling reality, and some of the women burst into tears.

Under the guidance of these cavaliers we penetrated still further into the gloomy recesses of the forest, until at last the way became too intricate for the waggons, and we walked to what, by a figure of speech, might be called the camp, but which consisted merely of a number of horses tethered to trees, and a number of men grouped round them. There was not a sign of a tent, or even of a "lean-to" of branches and leaves to shelter the men from the weather. One waggon, loaded with bundles and greatcoats, formed the *impedimenta* of the band, which was a very small one, but was composed of veteran guerillas, if men who had not been under a roof since the first day of the insurrection could be dignified by that title. The weather was now so warm and bright that they scorned the idea of sleeping under any kind of cover; and so used were they to the mode of life, that they ceased to feel its hardship. Both men and horses seemed in first-rate condition: the horses were the best which the estates of the neighbouring proprietors could furnish; the men were nearly all under twenty-five; the leader of the band, who was away on a reconnaissance, being exactly that age. A few were the sons of country gentlemen: one had been a railway official; two others employed in Government offices; many were the sons of shopkeepers; some students; and others domestic servants: but they all lived together on terms of perfect friendship and equality, and seemed to enjoy the wild adventurous life. One of them, who spoke French admirably, told me that he was a student only nineteen years of age; he had left Warsaw on the famous 22d of January, and had been in the woods ever since. He considered that three months of incessant skirmishing had formed him into an experienced warrior. His arms consisted of a bran-new Dean and Adams revolver, a very fair carbine, and a sword. "I slept in a house the other night," he said, "and felt almost stifled; and I shall be quite sorry when the war is over, and puts an end to this free life in the woods. I have not been a day ill except when I received a trifling wound. We sing and sleep in the daytime, and gallop about the country at night. I have, moreover, already killed six Russians, and expect to exchange my carbine for a new rifle, as I am getting such a good shot that I am to be allowed one." When I contrasted the melancholy groups in the market-places of Warsaw and Cracow with this jolly band of Robin Hoods, I did not doubt who had the best of it. These men, from having been all their lives accustomed to a life of repression and surveillance, revel in their newly-found freedom. To be sure, they can only enjoy it under difficulties; but the ground they stand on is their own, and with fleet horses to ride, and impenetrable woods to hide in, they run but little risk except from their own rashness or negligence. They change about from day to day; if the weather is very inclement, they appropriate barns, make leaf huts, or sleep under the lee of hay-stacks; but generally they keep moving at night, and in the daytime make roaring fires, and comfort themselves with warmth and tobacco. They live on the fat of the land, and are never at a loss for supplies: this is the great advantage of a small band. The chief had limited his number to forty, and upon no pretext whatever would he add another to it, although he was most urgently pressed to do so.

Generally the neighbouring gentlemen and farmers are only too glad to furnish the little troop with provisions; but if they run short, they pay a nocturnal visit to a proprietor, from whom they take as much forage as they want, and with whom, *bon gré mal gré*, they regale themselves till the small hours, when each man, filling his haversack with the good things of this life, and loading his nag with fodder, trots back to his nest in the woods, leaving with their late host an order on the National Government to repay "Mr Soandsosky" for food furnished to the band commanded by "Suchanonesky." This order "Soandsosky" most carefully conceals, as, if it is ever found among his papers, his property is inevitably confiscated by the Russian Government. On the occasion of my visit, three of my companions were country gentlemen of the neighbourhood, each of whom pulled out his pocket-book and wrote an order for a supply of forage and provisions, to be obeyed by the servants in the event of "Suchanonesky" or any of his band visiting his house during the absence of the master. Almost every day the band changes its *habitat*, which, as they have nothing to carry, is a very simple proceeding. As the wood in which they live is about eighty miles long by twenty broad, and as they know every nook and corner in it, there is not much chance of their ever being caught by the numerous Russian garrisons which are posted in the vicinity, and which they amuse themselves by annoying at night. My observation of this band proved to demonstration the erroneous principle upon which the war had been conducted by the insurgents in most parts of the country hitherto. Instead of multiplying, to an indefinite extent, these small cavalry bands, they would collect great masses of men together, of whom scythemen are the least adapted to the style of warfare they wish to wage. In a flat country of woods and plains, it is perfectly clear that a weapon which can only be used by a man on foot at close quarters, is about the worst which could possibly be devised for undisciplined men to wield against regular troops. It is true that a great difficulty has existed in procuring rifles; but it would have been better to have fewer and smaller bands well armed, than to waste unnecessarily the best blood in the country. With a good horse and a good rifle a man is more or less independent, and may act singly or in company as his fancy dictates; but men on foot must act together, and have no means of escape from Cossacks. In a country so admirably adapted for cavalry, and where horses are so abundant, it is surprising that more bands formed on the principle of the one I was now visiting should not have been formed: so far as I could learn, it was the only one of the sort which existed. Many were the feats of prowess which its members had performed singly. Upon one occasion two of them had encountered five Cossacks, who immediately gave chase. As the Cossacks are mounted on ponies, the insurgents would have had no difficulty in escaping; but this was not their object: they reined in, and tempted their pursuers to discharge their five carbines at them; then, before they could reload, they wheeled round, and shot the whole five with their revolvers. I found a good many of the band spoke French, and our visit was quite an episode in the routine of their daily life. They clustered round, showed me their arms, and seemed delighted at the courage which the women had displayed in visiting them, and in the interest manifested by a foreigner in their proceedings. Meanwhile the contents of the commissariat waggon we had brought with us were spread upon the ground, and the more hungry portion of the community began to discuss them; others, however, declared that our company was so much more to their taste than food, that they devoted themselves to us instead of to the cold beef and large jars of pickled cucumbers which their less sentimental comrades were devouring.

When they had concluded their repast, they grouped themselves in an open space among the tall trees, and "the lofty aisles of the dim woods rang," as, inspired with patriotic ardour, they burst out with the magnificent chant which so well conveys the mournful meaning of the words of the national anthem—"Boje cos Polske".—when all joined in the grand prayer to God which forms the swelling chorus, and the men, with swords drawn, uplifted their arms in supplication; then tears streamed down the cheeks of the women as they sang, for they remembered their sisters slain on their knees in the churches at Warsaw for doing the same, and bloody memories crowded on them, as, with voices trembling from emotion, they besought, in solemn strains, the mercy of the Most High.

The scene was so full of dramatic effect that I scarcely believed in its reality till I remembered the existence of six thousand Russian soldiers in the immediate neighbourhood, who were thirsting for the blood of this little band of men and women. There was something practical in this consideration calculated to captivate a mind too prosaic to be stirred by theatrical representations; for I confess I find it generally more easy to delude myself by believing in the sham of a reality than in the reality of a sham. However, upon this occasion he must have been a most uncompromising stoic who was not touched and impressed. Those bronzed and weather-beaten features, and those wet cheeks, told their own tale; and as, with each succeeding verse, the enthusiasm of the singers rose, and their countenances glowed with the fervour of their emotion, and men who, tired with their night-forays, were lying listlessly on the ground, unable to restrain themselves, sprang to their feet and joined, and every voice trembled and every pulse throbbed, I felt that patriotism was a sentiment in which one could believe—not merely as an abstract principle, but as the most absorbing passion which could stir the human breast. I soon after had a proof of the devoted self-sacrifice to which it gives rise. The old gentleman who, with his two sons, had joined our *cortège*, stepped forward when the anthem was finished, and in broken accents consigned the young men to their country's cause. "I devoutly hope," he said, "that it may please God to spare at least one of my sons to my declining years, but rather a thousand times that both should perish than that either should venture to appear before me while the battles of his country still remained to be fought." Then with trembling hands he drew them each to his breast, and, straining them in a last embrace, turned abruptly away, and was no more seen till we returned to the waggons. I no longer wondered that deeds of heroism should be performed by men thus solemnly consecrated to their country's cause. Usually before leaving home they receive the benediction of their priest, then the blessings and injunctions of parents; and now, under the greenwood tree, the prayers and the tears of women, and the hearty welcome of their new comrades, conspired to impress them with the determination to do or die. Under such circumstances, even if there were the will, it would be difficult to shirk. With a keenly imaginative people, it may be conceived how stimulating to enterprise is the romantic character which attaches to this mode of life, and the auspices under which they adopt it. Many of them are accompanied by their wives or by their *fiancées* to the camps—some bands are led by priests, who, with the emblem of their faith uplifted, are ever to be found in the post of danger. With the band I was now visiting, a young amazon in male attire had done good service. She was reported pretty, an excellent shot and horsewoman; but as she was absent with the leader on a reconnaissance, I unfortunately lost the opportunity of making her acquaintance. But it is in homes, in hospitals, in prisons, and in hiding-places, that the women of Poland have served the cause. They stir up the ardour of the men round their own firesides; they fan the martial ardour of their own husbands, lovers, sons, or brothers; they watch over beds where men unknown to them, except as wounded in their country's cause, groan and die. All the tenderness of the women, combined with intense sympathy for the cause, and an inextinguishable patriotism, stimulate them to acts of unwearying devotion and self-sacrifice. For hours do they stand in all weathers in the prison-yards, waiting for permission to visit prisoners in their cells, and to minister to them, like angels of mercy. Wherever a patriot is in distress, hunted, or hiding, or sick, women are the first to come to his rescue; their ready wit and instinctive tact are invaluable; and it may safely be said that without their encouragement the movement never would have begun, and without their devotion and co-operation it could never have lasted as it did. Who are the most courageous and intelligent spies? who are the surest messengers with important news? on whom do the National Government most surely rely for many a delicate negotiation? whose fertile brains devise new combinations for strong arms to carry out? —the women of Poland. Therefore it is that they are considered worthy of being flogged by the Russian authorities. Therefore it is that young girls of eighteen have already been shot by the orders of Russian officers, and that they are imprisoned and exiled. They are a power not to be despised, and certainly not to be intimidated, now that, like tigresses robbed of their whelps, they are pushed to the extremity of frenzy and despair.

When I saw the ladies who had accompanied us to the camp, each surrounded by a group of insurgents, eagerly narrating their achievements, or asking for news of home, and heard words of encouragement and approval drop from pretty lips into the ears of men so seldom brought into contact now with such a grateful and softening influence, I thought that these well-born women had not incurred the risk in vain, and that long after our departure the memory of our visit would remain a bright speck in the hard lives of our entertainers. When at last we thought it time to move, nearly the whole band accompanied us, not merely to the waggons, but they insisted upon escorting us to the edge of the wood. Nothing but a plain four miles broad then divided us from a Russian army; so we thought they had pushed politeness to its utmost limits consistent with prudence; and with many warm hand-shakings and expressions of gratitude on their part, and good wishes for their success on ours, we left them drawn up in line, and looking after us for a moment with longing eyes before they slowly wheeled round and disappeared in the forest.

Our journey home was even more exciting than the morning one had been. The chances of meeting Cossacks were considerably increased; and we had so much to say about the band that our attention was a good deal distracted.

On our arrival my host showed me where arms were secreted in the establishment, in localities which had hitherto defied the most minute examination by the Russian soldiery, who had already favoured him with sundry nocturnal visits. This habit might have been attended with results most inconvenient to the whole party, had we been favoured with a domiciliary visit an hour or two later. We were all seated at dinner, discussing the events of the day, when suddenly the clattering of horses' hoofs and the jingling of swords were heard outside the window, as the dining-room was on the ground-floor. There was an instant commotion, not unmingled with alarm. Our guilty consciences pictured ferocious Cossacks surrounding the mansion, as they had already done in so many instances; and we felt that we had given them some excuse. I fumbled in my pocket for my passport, to display in case of necessity; though, as I had already seen a man, in the person of Mr Finkenstein, who received thirty-three wounds after he had shown his British passport, and had not been in an insurgent camp, I did not feel much confidence in its protection. The cold touch of my revolver in the same pocket afforded me more satisfaction, though the fact of a weapon of any kind being found upon the person is considered proof presumptive that its possessor is an insurgent, and warrants his instant execution. Some of us ran to the hall, and there, sure enough, were three men bristling with arms; but to our intense relief they turned out to be the chief of the band we had visited in the morning, accompanied by his two aides-de-camp.

On his return to the band, he was so much touched and gratified by our visit, that he determined instantly to repay it; and although this was an honour so excessively compromising that we could willingly have dispensed with it, I was not sorry for the opportunity which it afforded me of making the personal acquaintance of a man of whom I only heard by reputation. After an immense deal of kissing on both cheeks, the chief apologised for having taken, in the dead of night, four of his best horses out of the stables of one of the gentlemen present, who immediately jumped up and embraced him again, saying, "My dear fellow, you're welcome to them all; the more robberies of that kind you make the better." And then they all laughed at the same thing having happened to a stingy and rather unpatriotic neighbour, whose stables had been altogether cleared out; for the insurgents appropriate property very much according to the sympathies of the owner. A selfish and unpopular skinflint they denude unmercifully; but a hearty good-natured patriot, who is doing all he can for the movement, they let off as easily as they can. A good deal has been said by persons, ignorant of the conditions under which the struggle was conducted, of the apparent apathy of the landed proprietary, who, except in very rare instances, did not take the field themselves. This was not from any indifference to the cause, but from the fact that the movement depended upon the wealth of the country for its resources; and as the property of any one taking an active share in hostilities would have been immediately confiscated, the National Government would have been deprived of its revenue, and the bands have lost those facilities for procuring supplies, concealing wounded, accumulating arms, &c., which they enjoyed. Every country-house was a harbour of refuge, and the proprietors who lived upon them could be of far more use to the insurgents in a variety of ways than if they merely helped to swell the number of a band. As it was, half the fighting population was unable to go into the woods for want of arms and ammunition. There was no lack of volunteers—quite the contrary. The leader, who took his place next me at dinner, when the excitement attendant upon his arrival had subsided, informed me that he refused as many as eight and ten applications every day of men anxious to join his band, some of whom were experienced men, and had been officers in other bands; but that he had decided upon not adding to his numbers, partly because he felt that a larger body of men would be unwieldy, and partly because he had neither the requisite arms nor ammunition. "Though," he said, slyly, "I did a good stroke of business to-day. I went down to the railway station, put on a paletot, and took thirty carbines out of a train under the eyes of a company of Russian soldiers, without their suspecting what I was about." I asked him how much ammunition he had got, and where he kept it. He said that it was buried in different parts of the wood, and that he had enough to last his present band three months. It is only natural, where collisions are of daily occurrence, with ever-varying results, that the composition of bands should be constantly changing. When a body of insurgents are hard pressed, or run out of ammunition, they disband entirely, and each man looks about for a leader that he likes, just as sailors choose their captains. Some of the men I conversed with in the wood had been in half-a-dozen bands, and had fought in every palatinate in the kingdom. The united ages of the leader and his two aides-de-camp did not amount to seventy years, and they had all the confidence and buoyancy of youth. There was evidently a refreshing novelty about sitting at a civilised table, and they did ample justice to the good things with which it was loaded; while they were apparently quite unconscious of our regarding them with feelings in which terror combined with a desire to make ourselves agreeable. Our poor hostess sat and did the honours white with anxiety. She would have infinitely preferred an open barrel of gunpowder on the table to her three dangerous guests, but no words escaped her lips except those which were kind and hospitable. At any moment we might expect a visit from Russians, and then every soul would have been slaughtered. There were already too many precedents to render our fate doubtful; but still we laughed over our wine, and sipped our coffee, as if we liked it; and indeed I was hearing so much that was curious and interesting from the chief, that I should have regretted anything that would have curtailed his visit. He had been educated at the Polish Military College, established by the Italian Government at Cuneo, and which has since been abolished. He spoke, therefore, very fair Italian and a little French, and was most intelligent in his observations, and in the ideas he had formed as to the mode of conducting the war. Some of them were eminently original; but they showed that he thought and acted on a principle which he understood—not a common quality among Polish insurgent leaders. We discussed a variety of stratagems and ruses which might be effectively practised upon an unsuspicious enemy. The Russians have an intense dislike to nocturnal operations, in which my young friend especially delighted; and he related with satisfaction the numerous plans he had devised for keeping them awake. Not that he spoke with any excitability or swagger: his tone was calm and measured, his eye deep and thoughtful. He impressed me at once as a man of great force and individuality of character; and I afterwards understood that he possessed the most complete ascendancy over his band, especially since he had shot one or two for breach of discipline.

The glance of his eye was enough to make an aide-de-camp jump, and I was rather amused to see it; for he was descanting at the time on the democratic constitution of his band. "I am only the leader in the field; we are all really upon an equality. Only some one must direct, otherwise we dislike all distinctions of rank." A Garibaldian shirt corresponded to all these opinions; a brace of revolvers, jack-boots, spurs, braided trousers, a handkerchief loosely knotted round his neck, and a coquettish square Polish cap on a beautifully shaped head, completed a very picturesque attire; and although there was nothing foppish about his dress, it was evident that he had rummaged the one waggon containing the clothing of the band before he presented himself to the ladies. But he became as timid as a girl, notwithstanding, when any of them spoke to him; and he made a complete conquest of one enthusiastic young lady—principally, I think, by blushing and looking down whenever she addressed him. Handsome, dashing, brave, and gentle, with eyes that flashed now and then with subdued fire, a tender voice, and only twenty-five, no wonder he was irresistible, and all the more so from seeming utterly unconscious of his personal attractions. His aides-de-camp, neither of whom were troubled with bashfulness, and one of whom was attired in all the elegancies of the camp, had not a chance with their quiet leader. They laughed and chatted, while he rarely smiled; but when he spoke all listened, and what he said was always worth listening to. His whole soul was absorbed in his occupation; the admiring glances of women, and the complimentary phrases of the men, were alike unheeded. He made me describe how Indians fight, how Caffres fight, how Chinamen fight; we discussed guerilla warfare under every phase as practised in different countries, and I saw he was making mental memoranda for future use. He assured me that he felt that, if any mishap befell either himself or his band, it would be their own fault. With fleet horses, and an extensive forest to hide in, he could defy the whole Russian army; and, in his opinion, the whole insurgent forces should be mounted and equipped upon the principle he had adopted. In each district there might be ten or twelve such bands, under the control of a general-in-chief, but each acting independently, except when some combined operation rendered union necessary. All the insurgent bands were of course under the direct control of the National Government, which appointed the local, civil, and military authorities throughout the country. They reported officially upon the strength of the bands, the nature of the operations which are to be undertaken, and the extent of war material available. The leader was at liberty to act according as circumstances might direct, but he only held his position at the pleasure of the National Government. My informant told me that he had great difficulty in getting permission from Warsaw to carry out the formation of his band on his own system: that in the first instance they had pressed upon him the leadership of a band of two hundred men, half of whom were Kossinieri; but that he had refused to take any command except as organised by himself. Upon every occasion where serious disaster had befallen the national arms, it was to be traced to the same cause, the massing together of too many undisciplined men.

It was late before we brought our interesting discussion to a close, and my hostess heaved a sigh of relief as her guests rose to take their departure. Embracing each other as men only do where there is small chance of their ever meeting again, all the gentlemen present bade adieu to the three insurgents, whose fiery steeds seemed impatient for the midnight gallop which was to take their masters to roost among the trees. I could not help congratulating myself upon the prospect of a comfortable bed. It seemed cruel to turn out of a luxurious country-house and go to sleep in a wood without even the covering of a tent; and yet I doubt whether any of the three would have changed their mode of life for any that could have been suggested to them. We all grouped round the door to wave our farewells as they dashed off into the darkness, the women heaping blessings upon their heads, and offering up prayers for their safety.

Next morning, as I crossed the yard to breakfast, I saw a poor woman sitting crying in the porch. I inquired of my host, who was cross-questioning her, what her distress arose from. She said that about midnight three insurgents had come to the door of her cottage and woke herself and her husband; that he had got out of bed, when he was immediately seized, carried off between them to the edge of the wood, and then and there hung. And she added, weeping bitterly, "I know he must have done something very wrong to deserve it, or they never would have hung him." I was rather shocked at this piece of retributive justice, so promptly executed by my three young friends of the night before. It appeared that, on their way back to camp after dining with us, they received undoubted information that the proceedings of the day had been reported to the Russians by this peasant, who was in the employ of my host, and had long been mistrusted by him; and as the execution of spies is an essential condition to the safety of every one connected with the movement, the disagreeable necessity of hanging them is forced upon the insurgents against their inclination. In fact, the story was not likely to make my host feel very comfortable. True, the man was hung, and could not give evidence against him; but we had done a good many compromising things during the last twenty-four hours, known to numbers of people, and it was not reassuring to feel that the Russians had been made aware of them. I began to think it quite time for the carriage to appear which was to carry me away from a locality where I had been treated with such unbounded confidence and hospitality, but which was getting rather too warm to be pleasant. It seemed ungrateful to get all one could out of people, and then to desert them; but they said I had seen everything, and that it would be folly to stay longer in the country—"unless, indeed," said one gentleman, "you would like to take your chances with me, and drive into Lithuania in my carriage, visiting camps *en route*." The proposal was tempting; but I hardly think it was really expected that I should accept it, the more especially as he never drove into Lithuania at all, but went peaceably back to his wife in Warsaw. So I contented myself with a twenty-mile drive in his company, parting from my late host with many cordial expressions of goodwill and mutual kind wishes.

On arriving at the country mansion of my next host, the first intelligence which greeted us was another case of hanging. It seemed that his footman had been campaigning for a week with the insurgents, and had returned home for a rest, preparatory to starting off afresh. One of the farm-labourers, who bore him a grudge, informed the Russians in the neighbourhood of the circumstance, and he was made prisoner in the night by a patrol, and walked off to be executed. A few members of the band we had visited in the wood, reconnoitring close by at the time, on hearing of this, at once retaliated on the informer, who was at the moment swinging from the branch of a tree in a wood close by.

Incidents of this tragical nature were constantly happening. My host deeply lamented the loss of his domestic servant, but did not the least seem to regret the fate which had overtaken the peasant, " who," he said, "richly merited it." The insurgents had also taken the opportunity of abstracting two of his best horses, at which he only laughed. We now debated the possibility of witnessing a skirmish, reported to be going on in the neighbourhood between a band of 700 insurgents, of whom 200 were peasants, and the Russian troops. When we reached the railway, we found a train full of the latter hastening to the scene of action. But on approaching it ourselves matters did not look propitious: inquisitive Poles, not wanting in daring, had found the vicinity of the fighting too dangerous for spectators to remain. There was no alternative between taking an active part with the insurgents and keeping out of the way altogether. Every Russian soldier we saw looked at us with suspicion. The platform of the station at which they alighted to march down to the fighting was crowded with scowling, ill-favoured-looking men, who only wanted an excuse to be let loose on society; and the whole country within a radius of five miles of the scene of action was deserted. Moreover, the Russians were between us and the insurgents, and anybody travelling towards the latter would be almost certainly arrested; so we contented ourselves with picking up scraps of news. My friend determined to remain in the little country town to hear the result before returning to Warsaw; but as every stranger in it was suspected, and the whole neighbourhood had become more or less informed of my proceedings, the notoriety might prove inconvenient, as an Englishman was naturally an object of curiosity: so, as I was near the frontier at any rate, I thought the wiser course would be to cross it while it was yet time, and make my final exit from Poland. Every guard and conductor on the line knew where I had been, and was overwhelmingly civil in consequence: a ticket was considered a superfluity, the examination of luggage a solemn sham.

My passport might have been a piece of waste paper. Had I not been to a camp? was I not a well-wisher to Poland? was not that passport and railway-ticket enough? And to avoid a shower of benedictions, and the most profuse expressions of gratitude for having ever taken the trouble to come to their country, I left it a wiser and a sadder man than when I had crossed the frontier from Galicia, scarce a fortnight before.

CHAPTER XVI.

TWENTY-FOUR HOURS IN VOLHYNIA.

FOR the six months which followed my visit to Poland during the insurrection, I watched its progress with a keen and unflagging interest. I heard that one friend, with whom I had been most intimate, had been arrested and placed *au secret* in a cell, where all access was denied to him; that the daring young leader of the band I had visited, after performing many feats of valour, which were chronicled in some of the papers, had been captured and shot by a file of Russian soldiery; that the chief of the band of 700, who were successful in the fight I did not see, had been accused by his men of treachery, and was in confinement by the orders of the National Government, no one knew where, and was to be tried by court-martial, no one knew when; that the venerable archbishop who had discussed with me in Warsaw the prospect of the insurrection in broken and despondent tones, had been exiled to Siberia; that women whom I had met were in prison; and that the list of men whose acquaintance I had made or whose names were familiar to me, who had been shot, was daily increasing,—but that, in spite of all this, the Poles were still sanguine of intervention in their favour on the part either of France or of England, or of both jointly. The only intervention they craved was protection for the introduction of arms and the munitions of war, either by the Baltic or across the Austrian frontier. For the resistance which they had offered to the Russian troops for nearly a year, armed only with scythes, and with rifles smuggled into the country, had convinced them that they only needed artillery, and a sufficient supply of ammunition, to achieve their own freedom. Meantime the efforts of the insurgents had latterly been directed mainly towards spreading the flame of revolt into Ruthenia, and the various rumours I heard of the condition of that part of Russia induced me in the autumn of the same year to make a trip in that direction.

My travelling companion upon this occasion was the Hon. Evelyn Ashley. Our intention was to traverse the Russian province of Volhynia as far as Kamienetz Podolsky, as the accounts which were published with reference to the condition of that part of the country were the most conflicting, the Poles maintaining that the elements of insurrection existed abundantly, and only required encouragement to blaze forth; the Russians, on the other hand, declaring that the province was profoundly tranquil, and that, with the exception of a few landed proprietors, the loyalty of the population was to be thoroughly counted upon. That the Poles were sincere in believing in the possibility of spreading the revolt into this part of the Russian dominions, is sufficiently demonstrated by the fact that they organised a large band under Wysocki for the purpose of invading it; while the disaster which overwhelmed the expedition at its outset strengthened the public conviction in favour of the correctness of the Russian statements on the subject. In this latter case, however, it would scarcely seem that the internal condition of the province warranted the extreme measures resorted to by the Russians to maintain a tranquillity which, according to their own assertions, was not in danger; and I was anxious to judge for myself whether the charges of cruelty brought against the Russian administration were true, so far as they applied to Volhynia, and to what extent the population sympathised in the national movement. As the scene of our projected expedition was beyond railways, or even the appliances of posting in civilised countries, it became necessary to invest in a carriage at Lemberg; and we employed two mornings in investigating the mysterious workings of the Jewish mind in the matter of bargain and sale. It was only after two days of patient, and I may say conscientious, intrigue, and after having explored the recesses of almost every coach-house in Lemberg, that we ultimately purchased, for the sum of £9, an excellent roomy conveyance, with C springs and strong axles, in which we journeyed for more than a month—traversing upwards of a thousand miles, and never once having to do more than tighten the screws. The Jew who ultimately effected this bargain for us received a tenth of the sum as his commission. It took us a night to post from Lemberg to Brody, a Jew-inhabited town, containing the usual square, with arcades all round, and arcades forming a market-place in the centre, where only this one class of the population buzz and swarm, and almost forcibly drag you into odoriferous corners to buy things you don't want; and where the women, with greasy plaits of false hair, which last them a lifetime, twined round their heads, try to persuade you, with soft glances, to leave some of your riches on their counter. As we were both ignorant of Russian, we had procured a servant at Lemberg, a snub-nosed individual, who gave a somewhat indistinct account of his former life, was vague as to his nationality, and incoherent in his general conversation. However, we were obliged to close with him at the last moment for want of a better; and with this questionable addition to our party we started about ten o'clock one fine autumn morning for the Russian frontier; four little rats of ponies dragged us painfully across the sandy plain, which extends eastward, and which near the frontier is covered with a dense pine forest. Here the deep sand forces us to walk, and our coachman explains to us that in these extensive woods the ill-fated expedition of Wysocki collected prior to their attack upon Radziviloff. Emerging from their dark recesses, we debouch upon a plain which was the scene of the disaster. But first we are detained at the Austrian frontier, and go through the necessary passport formalities; a mile beyond it is the first Russian picket, where an ill-looking Mongol is keeping guard over a sentry-box made of the boughs of trees: in the distance a group of Cossacks, with long lances and shaggy ponies, are struggling over the plain towards the town of Radziviloff, now visible in the distance. In crossing this piece of country the Poles suffered severely from the Russian artillery, but they were not finally checked, as we were, at the barrier. This is placed on a narrow strip of land which divides a marshy pond from a reedy lake—a dismal swamp extending indefinitely round the position, and rendering it in every respect one most undesirable to attack, and easy to defend.

We were detained for some time outside the high gate which, flanked by stiff palisades and guarded by a couple of sentries, barred our further progress; and if we could only have foreseen the annoyance to which we were to be exposed upon the other side, we should not have been so anxious to pass through. However, we waited patiently, until, at the expiration of an hour, we received permission to drive on, when the gates were instantly closed behind us, and we found ourselves impounded in an enclosure, the exit from which was also a guarded gate, while there was just room on the causeway for a custom-house and guard-room. We were instantly surrounded by half-a-dozen officials, and our luggage was soon ranged in the verandah for inspection, and became a centre of attraction for other wayfarers, impounded like ourselves, waiting for their passports, and who were glad of the distraction which the examination of our effects afforded. These were, for the most part, Jews or peasants—the former especially swarmed here as elsewhere. Meanwhile the carriage was being minutely examined, the pockets and lining were carefully inspected, and then the attention of the authorities was concentrated upon ourselves. Just as the operation was beginning, however, our feelings received a sudden shock by the announcement that our servant was found to be a compromised person, if not an actual insurgent—that his name was down in the police records, that he was a Russian subject, and that we should, in all probability, be deprived of his services, after having enjoyed them only a few hours. In vain did he protest that they must have mistaken him for somebody else; his forbidding countenance seemed to give the lie to his assertions; and we felt that his connection with us threw a serious doubt over the respectability of his masters. All this time our clothes were being taken out of our portmanteaus, and, after being separately examined, thrown in a pile in the yard. The shirts were carefully shaken out, the lining of the coats was felt; a piece of old newspaper, in which boots had been wrapped up, was laid on one side for further inspection; a very harmless map of the country, a 'Bradshaw's Railway Guide,' a French novel, and half a sheet of note-paper, which was written over, and which I had accidentally left in my blotting-book, were all placed together as objects of suspicion. Still we were sanguine as to the ultimate result, when suddenly a breast-pin—which I had bought some months previously, on account of its antique form, at Cracow—was seized upon triumphantly. I could not deny that the device was a Polish eagle; and when I offered to present it to the inspector as a proof of the little value I placed upon it, he shrank back with horror. From this moment the chain of evidence against us was complete: a rebel servant, a map, a breast-pin, and a 'Bradshaw.' Our treacherous intentions were indeed made so clear by these last three articles that the servant was no longer necessary, and the head official frankly told us that it was all a mistake, and that he was not known to them at all. It was evident that they had begun with securing something fatal against us, in case they should fail in seizing anything really dangerous; but having got the breast-pin, it was no longer necessary to assert that we had an insurgent for a domestic. Our fate was already sealed; still our ordeal was not ended. Leaving our raiment piled outside, we were now each ushered separately into a small room, and, accompanied by an inspector and a searcher, were submitted to a close personal examination. Every pocket was turned out, our arms and legs carefully felt, strange hands dexterously explored hidden recesses under our waistcoats and between our shoulders; but the only objects found in my pocket were a metallic note-book, and a note containing a few simple lines of introduction to a gentleman in Volhynia who had never taken part in the movement, and was then residing at large on his property. With these trophies added to the list, the inspector took his final leave, and we returned to sit in our carriage and await the result. The process above described had already lasted three hours, and time wore on without any prospect of release. Our only amusement was watching the inspection of fresh passengers, as others had watched us. We saw sacks of produce prodded with iron rods, and an admonitory prod given to the owner as a finish; we saw one male stripped after another, for the common herd were not treated as we were to a private room, but made to undress unceremoniously in the road; and we saw females subjected to examination in public—not, indeed, to the extent of undressing, but of a personal inspection too minute to be pleasant, while every article of their wearing apparel was shaken out as ours had been for the benefit of the bystanders. And we saw Jews kicked and cuffed more heartily than usually falls even to their lot;

but they drive a thriving traffic on these frontiers in times too trying for any other merchant; and if they receive abundance of kicks, they make halfpence to an extent which fully compensates them, and thus reverse the old proverb. But even these scenes after a time become monotonous, and the feeling of indignation they occasionally roused was not calculated to allay our growing impatience. We had arrived at the frontier at midday, and had now been just eight hours confined to our carriage. We could hear nothing as to our fate; the evening was rapidly closing in; it was twelve hours since we had eaten a light breakfast; and what with hunger, vexation, and uncertainty, the stock of philosophy which had supported us through the trials of the day was beginning to be exhausted. Then we were objects of derision, curiosity, or compassion to the crowd, according to the temperament of the individuals who composed it. The soldiers grinned at us in evident amusement at our predicament, until we came to hate them separately and collectively. I can even now recall to my recollection the repulsive lineaments of their respective Tartar physiognomies. The *employés* looked at us with curiosity, wondering what on earth induced two Englishmen to place themselves voluntarily in their clutches, a sentiment in which I began equally to share: the Christian passengers felt for us probably as much compassion as we did for them; while the Jews vainly strove to hit upon some device by which we might be turned to pecuniary account.

At last came a message from the general commanding in chief, to the effect that he would be glad to see us. The long-closed portals opened wide to let us through, and we found ourselves in the broad muddy streets of the straggling Russian town. Upon reaching the General's residence, we were given to understand by an aide-de-camp that the eight hours' delay had been caused by a deliberation on the part of General Kreuter as to whether, considering our evidently dangerous character, he could permit us to enter the country, and that he had reluctantly been compelled to decide against our admission. As this seemed scarcely warranted by the objects found in our luggage, we asked permission to see his Excellency, who shortly afterwards appeared himself, and informed us that the only concession he could make in our favour was to send us to Kief, the seat of government, to which city the breast-pin, the piece of old newspaper, the 'Bradshaw,' the sheet of note-paper, the map, the French novel, and the metallic note-book would be safely forwarded, and there delivered to us, if in the opinion of General Annenkoff, the Governor, we deserved to have them back. We now began to suspect the real cause of the delay. It was evident that General Kreuter and General Annenkoff had been in hot telegraphic communication on our account, and that the result was the alternative now presented to us, of proceeding to Kief or returning to Austria. As Kief was distant about four days' journey in exactly the opposite direction to that in which we wished to go, we declined the opportunity afforded to us of seeing this part of Russia, and requested to know exactly the reason of our not being allowed to go to Kamienetz. Even the General could hardly venture to find in the confiscated articles alone a sufficient cause for our prohibition, so he added to it a paternal solicitude for our safety. The country, he said, was in such a disturbed condition that he could not answer for our safety. As at this time the St Petersburg journals were insisting that Volhynia was profoundly tranquil, we were rather surprised to find the assertions of the Poles to the contrary thus strongly corroborated by so good an authority—at the same time, we expressed our willingness to incur the risk. It did indeed seem curious, if, as was assumed, we were dangerous Polish emissaries, that our safety should be a matter of much concern to the Russians; while it was evident that in that character the only thing we had to fear was from their own soldiery, who, if they murdered two unarmed travellers, would fully justify the reports which were current of their cruelty. However, we did not think it expedient to submit these arguments; probably the order, and not the logic, had been transmitted by telegraph, and both we and the General had to obey it: indeed, we had no reason to complain of the latter, who had treated us with much civility, and most likely exceeded his instructions when he good-naturedly gave us permission to pass the night in the village. It was now late, and we were famishing: as usual, we had recourse to a Jew in our extremity, who possessed a miserable cottage, which he called an inn, and where at least we found tough meat and dirty mattresses. Our Brody driver, who had been in a state of revolt all day, was soothed by a large gratuity; and the wretched nags which had shared our misery were at last detached from the carriage in which they had spent twelve hours without food. Finally, under the benign influence of a Russian somovar and tobacco, we consoled ourselves for the fatigues and disappointments of the day.

We employed our first hour of the following morning in strolling about the village. There was not much to be seen—low houses in ragged gardens, or rather waste plots of ground, detached from each other and separated by walls from the streets, which are overshadowed by avenues of trees, and in winter are knee-deep in mud, that is exchanged for dust in summer. The principal element in the population seemed to be military; soldiers were loitering in every direction, as it was rumoured that another expedition was destined to cross the frontier in the neighbourhood; troops were massed here in large quantities, and all the necessary dispositions made to give the insurgents a warm reception. I afterwards heard that an attempt was subsequently made to cross the frontier higher up, which had resulted in failure. The streets of Radziviloff had been the scene of bloody fighting a few weeks prior to our visit, in consequence of the ill-judged attempts on the part of Wysocki and the leaders of the expedition to take possession of the town. Not warned by the fatal disaster of Miechow, which cost the lives of so many brave men, the Poles seemed to think that the capture of a town was a profitable military operation. As the Russians were nearly always superior in numbers, they only needed the advantageous position afforded by the streets of a town to render the chances of their assailants hopeless; and it did not require a military eye to see that Radziviloff might be successfully defended against a much larger force than the Poles could possibly bring against it. On our return to our humble abode, we found a Polish gentleman who had arrived for the purpose of paying his contribution into the coffers of the Russian Government, for the suppression of the rebellion in which he sympathised. He was afraid to be seen speaking to us; indeed, we had already found, on the previous evening, that we were spurned by one or two of the "respectable" inhabitants; but this poor man would have been only too glad to pour out his woes to us had he dared, for he soon saw that we were to be trusted; but he hurried away after giving vent to a curse and a groan, saying he had already lingered in our company too long.

We were by this time more anxious to leave Russia than we had been to enter it; indeed, in the course of several visits to that country, I have invariably found this to be the case. The only inconvenience is, that instead of being glad to get rid of one, the officials make as many difficulties in letting you out as they do in letting you in. We had given up our passports on the previous morning, and had never seen them since, and of course we could not leave the country until they had been returned to us. So we found ourselves again sitting disconsolately in our carriage between the wooden gates. The real object of this detention was to extort a heavy bribe, without which, we were assured, we should never get our passports: indeed, one of the minor *employés*, taking compassion upon us, informed us in an undertone that if we wished to get our passports back we must make it worth the Director's while to give them up. If our informant expected a fee for this piece of intelligence, he was disappointed; and the rapid transition from silkiness to sulkiness which his manner underwent when he found we were obdurate, warranted the suspicion. If we were to be treated to twenty-four hours of worry in Russia, we determined not to pay for the luxury as well. The only melancholy satisfaction remaining to us was the reflection that we had caused a great deal of trouble to everybody, and been a source of profit to no one. So we sat obstinately in our carriage, and the crowd of the day before stared and laughed and wondered. It was a mystery to the whole world of Radziviloff, *employés* included, that we should be too dangerous to be admitted into the country, and yet not dangerous enough to be imprisoned. It did not seem that the middle course of turning people back had ever yet been adopted at Radziviloff, and the speculations of the night before as to our character and purpose reached a much higher pitch in the morning. At last our patience was exhausted, and before either the guard or the officials suspected our design, we jumped out of the carriage, ran back through the wicket which led into the town, and hurried straight to the General's house, with the view of laying our complaints before him. Just as we reached the gate, the shout of a breathless official reached our ears; the sulky had again become the silky one. "Our passports were ready;" "what a hurry we were in!" "the Director was waiting to offer us every facility," &c. We found on our return that our rush towards the General's had produced quite a magical effect; there was *empressement* everywhere. One man handed us our passports, covered with Russian writing, another presented me with my breast-pin and letter of introduction, together with the metallic notebook. The map had been altogether confiscated, and forwarded to Kief as a glaring evidence of the deep-laid plot in which we had been implicated. As this map had been bought by my friend at Artaria's in Vienna, and chosen expressly because it was devoid of every political character, we may hope that the official mind of Kief was long intently absorbed in the futile attempt to discover the hidden significance which it might contain. But the most singular instance of aberration of intellect on the part of frontier functionaries which ever came under my notice, was to be found in the importance which they attached to the 'Bradshaw,' the French novel, and the piece of dirty old newspaper: these were carefully made into a packet, and intrusted to the charge of a mounted Cossack, who was to accompany us to the Austrian frontier. On no account would they trust these dangerous books in the carriage with us. We even offered to leave 'Bradshaw' behind us as a token of our friendship, on condition that they would read it; but, seeing that we had determined not to corrupt them with money, they became incorruptible when it came to taking a literary present, and conscientiously insisted upon returning us that valuable work. Thus, after having spent exactly twenty-four hours in Volhynia, the greater part of the time between two gates, we bade a final farewell to the provinces of Russian Poland, and careered over the plain towards Brody, preceded always by a ferocious-looking Cossack carrying 'Bradshaw.' On arriving at the Austrian frontier, he presented it to us with great form and ceremony, as if he was restoring us our swords, of which, after an unsuccessful combat with an honourable enemy, we had been temporarily deprived; while we, once more armed with our Railway Guide, bade him a reckless and defiant adieu, and hugged to our grateful bosoms that true evidence of an enlightened country in an advanced state of civilisation. In the meantime we had a month's journey with post-horses to look forward to, before we were again likely to hear the familiar scream of the locomotive.

I think it likely that the real cause of our arrest on this occasion was the result of an episode which had occurred to me in Cracow in the spring. I received a peremptory summons one morning to present myself at the police office, and my heart throbbed with the beating of a guilty conscience, for to oblige a lady I had so far compromised myself as to be the means of secretly conveying a note to a prisoner to whom she was attached; but how could I have been inhuman enough to resist the pleading voice of so charming a creature? Now I thought it just possible that this correspondence might have been discovered, and that, instead of conveying the expression of a tender sentiment, it might have had some deep political significance. Patriotic young Polish ladies were capable of anything in their country's cause at that time. So with inward trembling, but with an outwardly defiant attitude, I appeared before the Herr Inspector. I was relieved to find that he was a feeble-looking old man, with large goggle spectacles. After solemnly considering me from head to foot, he opened a large book, and with solemn impressiveness asked me where I was born.

"Am Cap der guter Hoffnung," I answered flippantly. The idea of any one having been born at the Cape of Good Hope was so amazing, that he ejaculated, Herr Ye? and took off his spectacles in his astonishment, on which a bright idea suddenly flashed upon me, for it was evident that my interrogator was an impressionable and somewhat simple person. After my nationality had been established, he questioned me as to whether I was married.

" *Vier*," I promptly replied, holding up four fingers.

" Is one alive now ? " he asked.

" Oh, they are all alive."

" Impossible," he said; " nobody is allowed more than one wife at a time."

" Oh, pardon me, Mohammedans are allowed four, and I am a Mohammedan naturally; being born at the Cape of Good Hope, you know I must be;" and I went off at score in abominable German in an attempt to explain to him the merits of the Moslem faith. He was evidently rapidly coming to the conclusion that I was mad, which was the one I was anxious he should arrive at.

" What are you doing here ? " he interrupted impatiently. " We have reason to think you are meddling with politics."

" Reason to think ! " I exclaimed, " why, I am the heart and soul of the movement; there would have been no Polish insurrection but for me." I then went on in a rambling manner to discourse upon my own importance, during which I observed him writing.

" What are you writing ? " I inquired.

" I am saying that you came to Cracow to see the antiquities."

To this I vehemently objected, adhering strongly to my political motives; but he would not listen, and benevolently waved me out of the room as a hopeless and harmless lunatic.

I left the day after for Warsaw; but as the Russian and Austrian police were in close relations, it is not impossible that this incident, taken in conjunction with my visit to the insurgent band, may both have come to the knowledge of the Russian police, and that my name was inscribed in their books as being not so harmless as the Cracow inspector had imagined.

It is a long day's journey from Brody to Tarnopol; the road first ascends a range of wooded hills, on the summit of which stands the old castle of Podhorsce, commanding a magnificent view, and full of old armour and relics of the middle ages. Then, winding down through romantic glens, it debouches on the undulating corn-country which extends in uniform monotony all the way to the Black Sea. There is nothing, in a picturesque point of view, to interest the traveller as he journeys over these boundless steppes; but he will be struck with amazement at their vast cereal resources, which the railway, since completed, has done so much to develop. Tarnopol is a dull dirty town, with a large central square, and a population of about 20,000 inhabitants; of which 8000 are Poles, 2000 foreigners, and the rest Jews. It was only interesting in a political point of view, from the fact that a large expedition was supposed to be collecting in the neighbourhood for the purpose of crossing the Russian frontier, distant about twenty miles. As, however, this rumour was in everybody's mouth, and even the waiter of the hotel gave us confidential information on the subject, we did not think that a project, if it really existed, which was already so public, was ever likely to be put into execution; and, in fact, we have never afterwards heard of the operations of any band from this quarter. It is possible that, had we tried, we should have been more fortunate in an attempt to penetrate into Volhynia from this point; but we were satisfied with the experiences I have already recounted, and contented ourselves with obtaining information with reference to the state of the province from Poles who had just left it, or who owned property in it. It would seem that the danger to which, probably, General Kreuter alluded, and which we had to fear in travelling through the country, consisted in the chance of meeting with armed bands of peasants, invested by the Russian Government with the functions of police, which they exercised much to the benefit of their own pockets and the detriment of peaceable wayfarers. While all the landed proprietary of the province are Poles, the peasantry are for the most part Ruthenian, who had no sympathy with the movement; and who, although by no means attached to the Russian Government, had been easily bribed by the latter, by the prospect of plunder, to side with it. It is only due to the peasantry to say that in many instances they had resisted every temptation, and remained faithful to their masters. One of our motives for visiting the country just at this period was a desire to be present at some of the sales of sequestrated property, which were taking place daily. These sales were expressly arranged for the benefit of the peasantry. One of my friends, for instance, who was a Galician as well as a Volhynian proprietor, was called upon to pay to the Russian Government a sum equal to £8000 for the suppression of the rebellion. As he had carefully abstained from taking part in the movement, the amount of this tax in itself was sufficiently onerous; but lest he should be in a condition to procure that sum at short notice, he was only allowed three days to raise it; and as he was not resident in Volhynia, it was manifestly impossible for him to make the necessary arrangements. In default of prompt payment, the live stock of the proprietor was put up to auction among the peasants, who were thus enabled to purchase their masters' horses at a shilling a-piece; and merino sheep have been known to sell for as little as three-halfpence each. In other words, the peasantry receive a present of their masters' stock, while he is deprived of the means of getting in his crop or working his land, and is still obliged to pay the difference between the trifling amount which his property has realised, and the sum originally demanded by the Government. We heard, however, that the peasantry were becoming unmanageable and independent in their bearing towards the Government which has thus spoiled them, and complained of being obliged to pay to the Government the tax properly due to the proprietor, in compensation for the land which was originally his, and had by a recent arrangement been transferred to the peasant. Having paid only a nominal sum for their cattle, they now wanted to get the land for nothing as well; and it was some consolation to the proprietor, who had been robbed of both, to see the thieves fall out. The position of a country gentleman in these provinces was in fact becoming intolerable: not allowed to leave the country, he was constantly subjected to the suspicion of the Government while he remained in it, and too often found himself at last an unwilling occupant of a dismal cell, or one of a melancholy *cortège* on its way to Siberia. Those who were fortunate enough to procure passports at the commencement of the movement fled the country; those who were left, were in most instances arrested, so that scarcely a property remained tenanted. Any who had been discreet or lucky enough to be left at liberty had been called upon, on the one hand by the Russian, and on the other by the Polish National Government, to pay heavy contributions. In both instances the payment was compulsory, while the constant presence of armed bands of disorderly peasants, or of Cossacks, rendered daily life unsafe. One gentleman, who had been most fortunately circumstanced throughout in comparison with many of his compatriots, assured me that the movement had already been a clear loss to him of £25,000; and that, in the event of its lasting through another year, he would be a sufferer to a still greater amount.

From Tarnopol we posted through to Jassy, travelling only by day, and enabled by our method of locomotion to come into closer contact with the population which inhabits the comparatively little known districts of the Bukovine and Moldavia that we traversed, than is possible now that one is whirled by railway, with no other variety than a different station and stationmaster. This consideration was very forcibly impressed upon my mind five years ago, when I again had occasion to visit Brody, this time as the emissary of the Mansion House Committee, for the purpose of distributing relief to some 15,000 distressed Russian refugee Jews, who had taken refuge there in a starving condition, and when my experiences, had I time to narrate them here, were as painful as they were novel and interesting. I then made the journey from Brody to Jassy by rail; and so intensely wrought up were the expectations of the much-suffering race, who form the largest proportion of the population of this part of Europe, that at every station they were assembled in crowds with petitions to be transported to Palestine, the conviction apparently having taken possession of their minds that the time appointed for their return to the land of their ancestors had arrived, and that I was to be their Moses on the occasion.

The nineteen years which elapsed between my two visits to Jassy had worked a great change in this latter town, which on the first occasion still retained many of its Eastern characteristics, and was, in comparison to what it is now, in a condition of relative barbarism. From a mere tourist point of view, it was, however, far more interesting; and during our stay in it for a week, we had abundant opportunity of testing its peculiar social characteristics and attractions. One night at the opera, in the box of a friend, much to our surprise, we met a nun, a very charming person, to whom we were introduced, and who explained that she was on three weeks' leave from her convent, which was situated in a valley of the Carpathian mountains. She further explained that it was the custom in Moldavia for nuns to invite their gentlemen friends to pay them visits in their nunneries. She hoped we would accept her invitation to pay Agapia, which was the name of her nunnery, a visit, and spend there as many days as we liked. She only regretted her own unavoidable absence. There was a refreshing novelty about such an invitation which it was quite impossible to resist. We were assured by those who knew all about it, that we should find the scenery most attractive, the hospitality unbounded, and that on the way we should have an opportunity of visiting a most interesting monastery called Nyamptz, while some kind friends offered us letters of introduction to another convent, by name Veratica; and so it came about that, instead of looking for bands of Polish insurgents in the Ruthenian provinces of Russia, we found ourselves bound on a tour of visits to Greek monasteries and convents in the wild Moldavian valleys of the Carpathian Mountains. We soon made our preparations to post to Nyamptz, two of our Jassy friends kindly volunteering to accompany us to that monastery, and do the honours of the establishment.

CHAPTER XVII.

A VISIT TO THE CONVENTS OF MOLDAVIA.

IT was ten o'clock at night before we had bidden our last adieux and galloped out of Jassy. I say galloped advisedly, for we were in two light open carriages and four, and Moldavian postilions have no notion of letting the grass grow under their wheels. Indeed, it is to be regretted it does not, for one would be spared the dust. It does not, however, produce the slightest effect upon the picturesque-looking ruffian who, riding one horse, does nothing but yell and crack his whip over the other three; and whose chief object seems to be, not only to make as much dust as possible himself, but to keep well in the cloud caused by the carriage ahead. Anyhow, it is exhilarating to whisk through the crisp night air, *ventre à terre*, even though one is half choked. When day broke, Jassy was sixty miles off. We had been dreamily conscious of having changed horses occasionally, and of having undergone violent jolting, and now we felt the need of something warm. A Moldavian post-house is generally a thatched hut, the inside of which consists of a large fireplace, big enough to dine in as well as to cook one's dinner; and at this early hour the family was lying about asleep promiscuously. However, they gave us hot water and milk, and wondered intensely at such singular specimens of humanity as we seemed to them. Then we descended into the pretty valley of the Moldava, and, crossing that stream, entered the town of Nyamptz just as a heavy shower of rain came down to turn the dust into mud all over our bodies. Nyamptz is prettily situated at the foot of the lowest spurs of the Carpathians, on the river of the same name. Our intended visit had been notified to the sub-prefect from Jassy, and we found that worthy waiting, in the most obsequious attitude, for our arrival. The whole town was in a fever of excitement at the unwonted event of a visit from distinguished strangers, and any one who was in an official position cringed and crawled about us after the manner of Neapolitan *impiegnati*, in the hope that we might possess influence and use it to their advantage. Nothing would induce them to leave us alone. Not only would they stand over us while at breakfast, but insisted upon accompanying us to the convents, attended by a mounted escort. The standard of intelligence of these gentry may be judged of by the answer which the chief official gave when we asked him what o'clock it was? With the utmost *naïveté* he informed us, that the only people who knew the time were the Jews; and as it was a Jew's holiday, and they were all in their houses, it was not possible for him to let us know what the hour was. He was extremely proud of two schools, however — one containing one hundred boys, and the other sixty girls — of which this town of 8000 inhabitants could boast;

but his statistical knowledge in other respects was limited.

The whole population turned out to see the *cortège* as we drove away. Half-a-dozen imposing horsemen, in a sort of janissary uniform, and with immense swagger, led the way; then followed sundry carriages and carts full of officials, and then ourselves, with postilions very highly decorated for the occasion. We might have been Garibaldi, so humbly did the people bow before us, and with such gracious dignity did we return their salutes. Whether they supposed we had come to annex them, or whether they were simply overawed by the majesty of our appearance, must for ever remain a mystery; certain it is, we acted royalty all the way down the long street, and bowed ourselves into the ford of the river, and away into the happy valley beyond, at the head of which the monastery of Nyamptz is situated. Here we had nothing to do but revel in the glorious scenery, doubly refreshing after the monotony to which for some weeks past we had been doomed. Swelling hills, rising into blue mountains in the distance, but near us covered with oak and maple woods, bright with the fiery tints of autumn; green meadows and fields of melons and Indian corn; cottages half concealed by orchards, from which smoke curled languidly in the humid air, for the rain had ceased, and left a fresh soft feeling, delightful after long days of blazing sun; a precipice rising abruptly from the river-bed, and the crumbling ruins of the once extensive Castle of Nyamptz perched on its dizzy edge,—these were sights that made our drive along the grassy track up the valley a perfect luxury; and when at last it narrowed, and we dived into a wood, and came out of a green glade upon a massive straggling pile of white buildings, with tin cupolas glittering in a sudden gleam of sunshine, we thought that these Nyamptz monks had not denied themselves the most exhaustless of all pleasurable emotions— the enjoyment of nature under its fairest aspect. Five members of the committee of direction were standing upon the verandah of the superior's house as we drove up, and, in the absence of that dignitary, the dean, a man with meek brown eyes, a gentle smile, and an auburn beard, did the honours. Service was going on, so we were delayed till it was over, and regaled with the invariable preserve and water, which is the first form of Moldavian hospitality. Whether the sweetmeats are an excuse for the water, or the water for the sweetmeats, or both for the cigarettes which immediately follow, is a subject open to discussion; but when conversation is apt to flag from ignorance of the language on both sides, sweetmeats and water create a diversion, and rolling cigarettes and making profuse apologies for wanting a light, help to make the visit go off. As none of our hosts could speak anything but Moldavian, we were dependent entirely upon one of our companions from Jassy to interpret, and the whole committee seemed to think it necessary to sit in solemn silence, and inspect us while the dean answered our questions. At last the superior, a heavy, unamiable-looking man, with an iron-grey beard, appeared, and listened while our letter of introduction was read aloud to him, his own literary acquirements being of the most meagre description; then we ate more jam together, and he led the way to show us over the establishment. Scarcely three months had elapsed since a large part of the building had been burnt down; the consequence was, that a great deal of carpentering and rebuilding was going on in all directions. Unfortunately the library had been destroyed, and, besides the books, much of the picturesque effect of the monastery had been lost. In the centre of the principal courtyard stands the church, untouched by the fire, and upwards of four hundred years old. We went up a narrow stair, heavy with the fumes of incense, where a large collection of jewellery and ornaments, the gifts of devoted women, were displayed before us. Enormous Bibles covered with jewels, and ponderous with gold and silver decorations, were pulled out, and the quaint MS. and illuminated parchments turned over for our inspection. The oldest Bible was one in Bulgarian MS., dating from the middle of the fifteenth century. Then we were taken to another smaller church, and there, with great form and ceremony, our cicerones exhibited their principal curiosity, a priest's robe worked by the hands of the Empress Catharine herself, and presented to the monastery. There were until quite lately nine hundred monks in the monastery of Nyamptz; but the intrigues of a much-abused priest, called Vernouf, caused a secession of more than two hundred, who have joined the affiliated monasteries. The merits of this quarrel were too complicated for me to understand; moreover, I had no opportunity of hearing Vernouf's side of it. The result has been a deplorable split. Nyamptz itself, as the parent monastery, contains the largest number of monks. At the time of my visit there were four hundred and seventy in residence, but a good many get leave and take a turn in the world by way of a change. There are six smaller monasteries affiliated to Nyamptz, containing between them seven hundred and sixty monks. They are all situated in neighbouring valleys. Surrounding the main building are grouped about three hundred little separate cottages, called, by a figure of speech, cells, but really charming little abodes, covered with honeysuckle and jasmine, and surrounded by flowers or vegetables, according to the æsthetic or material tendencies of the owner. Almost every monk has thus his own little abode, with a neat wooden palisading round it, high enough to prevent curious eyes from prying, and enclosing a good garden; besides which, he can cultivate the neighbouring land to any extent he likes. This village of scattered cottages, with neat lanes leading between them, adds indescribably to the charm of the scene. We inspected the hospital, which was very clean and admirably kept; also a madhouse, which contained sixty patients, chiefly epileptic. Then they showed us the lock-up for refractory monks, four of whom were at that moment expiating their sins on bread and water. By a new law no monk is allowed to take the vows till he is fifty; formerly there was no such restriction, and several of the monks at Nyamptz were young men. We were informed that there were upwards of a hundred who were more than a hundred years of age, and I certainly observed some very patriarchal specimens. The revenues of Nyamptz amounted nominally to a sum equal to about £20,000 a-year. Prince Couza had, however, appropriated the greater portion of this sum, and made an allowance to each monk of three piastres a-day, and two hundred and fifty ducats a-year for his clothes. With this arrangement they seemed perfectly satisfied. To account for what appears an anomaly, it would be necessary to enter upon the question of the dedicated convents, which, however, is too dry and complicated to discuss here.

We had not time to linger long at the monastery of Nyamptz, though we were hospitably pressed by the superior to stay there for as many days as we chose. Among the monks who had done the honours was a fair-haired intelligent man of about forty, who had passed many years of his life in wandering over the world. He had made a pilgrimage to Mount Sinai, and visited the Greek monasteries in Turkey and the East generally. Then, obtaining a dispensation of two years for the benefit of his health, he travelled through Europe, and, doffing the long serge robe which he wore now as a monk, and which became him as a pilgrim, had visited, as a layman, most of the capitals of Europe; had *flânéd* upon the boulevards in Paris; had sat upon iron chairs in Rotten Row; and had even pushed his explorations as far as Cremorne. The consequence was that he was a thorough man of the world. He spoke French perfectly; was extremely tolerant in his religious opinions, and enlightened in his political and theological views. There were few subjects he could not converse upon, and I was never tired of listening to the singular experiences of his adventurous life. When, therefore, the superior attached him to us as guide, philosopher, and friend, during our monastic and conventual tour, we were well satisfied with so agreeable and intelligent a companion, and put him bodkin in our open carriage with pleasure. We got rid of our officious friends from Nyamptz here, and, furnished with eight horses by the monastery, we spun in our light carriage over grassy glades or along the beds of mountain-torrents with equal indifference. The wild post-boys never looked to see whether we were jolting about on our seats, like peas on a frying-pan—little recked they how our springs liked it—away we went, now through fiery-leaved oak woods, now along dark valleys, where dense pine forests gave warning of a higher elevation, deeper and farther into the wild Carpathians, till, as the shades of evening were drawing in, we took the steep pitch of hill at a gallop, on the top of which is situated the monastery of Seku, and dashed through the old archway into a court-yard, where a group of monks gazed open-mouthed at the unexpected apparition. Since leaving Nyamptz we had not met a soul, and we felt that Seku, buried in its narrow valley, with only a rough track to the monastery, and no road beyond, with high pine-clad hills all round, and only one outlet to the world, was indeed a retreat so secluded, that we deserved some credit for having found it.

Seku is one of the affiliated monasteries, and only contains 250 monks; unlike Nyamptz, the monks do not live in cottages apart, except in a few instances. A large courtyard, enclosed by a double-storeyed range of buildings with two galleries, and the dormitory doors opening on to them, furnish accommodation to the monks; and in the centre, as usual, surmounted with tin cupolas, and highly ornamented within, is the church. The great curiosity here was a magnificent piece of gold embroidery presented by the foundress of the monastery 250 years ago; besides were many quaint old MSS. on vellum, gorgeously bound, and the usual collection of jewels and altar ornaments, all stored away in old presses, and each produced in due form for our inspection—a crowd of admiring monks examining us the while more narrowly than we examined their ecclesiastical treasures. To me the romantic situation of this monastery, the utter silence of the scene, as darkness fell upon the sombre hillsides, and only the distant murmur of the mountain torrent broke the stillness, was more impressive than the wealth of "the foundation." It recalled to my mind a similar scene in the remote valleys of the Province of Kiang-su in China, where I had been the guest of Buddhist monks; nor to the uninitiated in the externals of their respective theologies was there any difference to be seen between my former hosts and those I was now visiting. The same courtyards and sacred edifices in the middle, heavy with the perfume of incense; the same presses stored with ornaments; richly decorated altars and monster candles; above all, the same lazy groups of long-robed brothers, who chose the most out-of-the-way corner of the world they could find to live in and do nothing. Inasmuch as many of the Moldavian monks cannot read, and none of them, with one or two exceptions, know any other language than Moldavian, they have not even the excuse of study to justify their life of utter sloth. With the Buddhist, it is more or less conducive to that state of "Nirvana," which it is the object of his ambition in this life and the next to attain. But the Greek monk attains it in spite of himself. To all intents and purposes he is as much buried, and as utterly useless to the world at large shut up in this valley, as if he were actually under the sod. Nor can one discover any palpable difference between religions which produce such exactly similar results. It is true that the Greek monks appear to wash more than the Buddhist, and never cut their hair, instead of shaving their heads; otherwise the cut of the robe is exactly the same, only in China it is either yellow or lavender, here it is a reddish brown. The service in a Buddhist place of worship is intoned in the same key as here, nor do the priests seem to attend more to what they are saying among the Greeks than among the Buddhists; but it is performed more constantly among the latter, and of course the divinities invoked go under other names. To the ignorant and impartial spectator these are the only observable points of distinction between the two establishments.

Altogether we were not captivated by anything we saw at Seku except its position, and resisted the invitation of the monks to pass the night there. A bright full moon tempted us to drive on to Agapia, and for two hours we tore along at the usual pace, regardless of no roads, and the uncertain light which, even when they existed, made them difficult to find. At last, like a fairy scene, the convent of Agapia burst upon our delighted gaze. Never, during a long and varied course of travel, have I felt more thoroughly rewarded for undertaking a journey, than I did when this novel and unexpected picture was presented to me. The glittering spires and cupolas of the churches seemed to rise like monuments of burnished silver out of the dark pine-woods. Hundreds of little cottages, in close proximity to each other, clung to the hillside, the white walls gleaming out amid the foliage; the convent itself, a massive irregular pile of building, with its great archway facing us, and looming large in the moonlight, was lighted up at every window; and dark female figures fluttered along balconies, as the bells on our horses gave warning of our approach. Our visit had been already notified by the metropolitan, so the whole place was on the *qui vive;* at all cottage windows white faces, half shrouded in the nun's hood, peered curiously out—till we felt guilty of the perturbation and excitement which our unusual visit was likely to cause among the fair devotees, who were supposed to have retired from the world expressly to avoid such disturbing influences. Our postilions, who belonged to Nyamptz, knew the right door at which to draw up inside the court, and here, grouped at the foot of the staircase, were five or six elderly nuns waiting to receive us. Our travelled monk presented us, and, after kissing the hand of each, we ascended by an outside staircase to the wooden corridors which ran all round the interior of the court, and upon which opened the rooms set apart for our accommodation. Both in the monasteries and convents the stranger has the right to claim three days' hospitality; so in all the establishments there are regular guests' rooms, and not unfrequently the natives of the country take advantage of the privilege to spend months in making a tour of visits, staying in each until even the good nature of the monks or nuns is exhausted. There was therefore nothing unusual in the fact of our visit; the interest lay in the circumstance of our being foreigners and Englishmen. Few of the nuns had ever seen specimens of a race of which they had heard a great deal; and even the middle-aged ladies who were now waiting upon us, examined us as narrowly as good breeding would permit. It was useless to explain that our object in visiting these secluded valleys was sheer curiosity. They were firmly persuaded that we were Commissioners sent by England to make inquiries into the confiscation of ecclesiastical property by Prince Couza, which was at that time agitating the whole country, and causing great dissension among the protecting Powers. As we naturally wished to understand the question for its own sake, our incessant queries, and the interest we showed in it, only confirmed their suspicions and increased their respect. Indeed, we found our greatness inconvenient upon several occasions, though it was not without its advantages. In the first place, the most elaborate arrangements had been made for our reception. The table in the large dining-room groaned under an extensive assortment of the good things of this life. Everything was scrupulously clean, and the dinner, for which our long drive had prepared us, admirably well cooked. All round the room were broad soft divans, and in the next room, in which we were to sleep, luxurious beds with fine linen had been made up. There was an air of abundance and comfort truly refreshing, and the gentle attendants who waited upon us, anticipating every wish, and sparing themselves no pains or trouble to please us, imparted to their hospitality a charm all its own. While we were doing ample justice to the viands they had prepared for us, they sat in a row on the opposite divan, applauding our appetites, and conversing with us by means of our friend the travelled monk and one of the gentlemen who had accompanied us from Jassy. We discovered that they were the committee of direction for the affairs of the convent, and we were promised an interview with the lady superior on the following day. They were all members of the best families of Moldavia, and had been dedicated to the conventual life from their earliest childhood, whether they liked it or not. At the age of five they had been put to school in the convent, and when they reached eighteen had been compelled to take the veil; so that, except when they obtained leave for a month or two to go and see their friends, they had never known any other existence than that which we now saw them leading—had never had any other excitement than that caused by the admission of a new sister, the arrival of relatives or travellers, a dissension among themselves, or a metropolitan visitation. To them the lovely valley at the head of which the convent was situated, had been the whole world from their earliest infancy. If they were not so strict as those nuns who retire to convents because they are disgusted with the world, it was because they scarcely knew what the world meant. They were all still artless children, happy, pleased, and natural; there were no downcast eyes or gloomy penitential expression. They were as delighted to see us as children would be with a new toy, and we had not been an hour in their company before we felt thoroughly at home. Unfortunately there was only one of them who could talk a little French; and another, but she was not a lady director, who spoke German. Presently appeared—the last of the committee, whom we had not yet seen—a beautiful woman, in the prime of womanhood, with the softest eyes, the sweetest smile, the gentlest and at the same time most distinguished manner—a border of pale yellow round her hood, which was coquettishly arranged, and a slight expansion in the skirt of her reddish-brown serge robe, indicated a tendency towards a cap and crinoline, and accounted for the slight delay in her arrival. After we had satisfied the cravings of nature, they took us out to the upper balconies to look over the convent by moonlight. If the scene had seemed unreal when we first came upon it, the magic panorama upon which we now gazed was still more enchanting. All round us dark woods—at our feet, and half concealed in their recesses, three hundred and fifty little separate cottages, each with its balcony, its shingle roof, its white walls, and its overhanging foliage. Now all the lights were extinguished, and the most profound stillness reigned—not even the barking of a dog was to be heard. Except ourselves, there was not a man within two hours' walk of where four hundred women were sleeping among the trees of their own quiet valley. The moon was at the full, and poured floods of light into every nook and corner—into the courtyard, with its quaint, old, carved wooden balconies—into the long narrow windows of the church, throwing silver rays into its gloomy recesses—doubtless falling softly upon the face of many a sleeping nun, as it did upon the river that gleamed and shimmered in its light under the black shadow of the steep mountain-side.

Though the day had been a long and tiring one, and it was now late, we lingered long upon these balconies, walking all round them, and finding, as each corner that we turned disclosed a new picture, fresh inducement to remain. The nuns, amused at our enthusiasm, asked us if we could continue to enjoy the view until it was time for the midnight service; and on our professing our readiness to remain up in spite of our heavy eyelids, they most considerately promised to have prayers half an hour earlier for our especial benefit; so at half-past eleven the absolute stillness was suddenly broken. First an old nun with a lantern flitted like a black spectre from door to door, and chanted the *réveille* at each in a voice loud and harsh enough to wake the soundest sleeper. She looked like an old witch hobbling silently and rapidly on her rounds, and bursting out periodically with the same nasal refrain, holding her lamp the while high above her head. As we were watching the operations of this old creature, we were startled by a sound resembling the taps of a very powerful and rather musical woodpecker. First shrill and sharp, rising to a high key, then with a dull and muffled sound, tap, tap, tap, came from the quadrangle below us; then a rattle so quick that I imagined it must be somebody playing on a wooden drum. The cadence was wild, but not irregular; and the effect of the roll dying away until it was scarcely audible, and then breaking out at its full strength, was most peculiar. Watching and wondering, the mystery was solved by the appearance of a stately nun stepping out from the dark shadows of the church, and bearing upon her shoulders what seemed in the uncertain light a long white plank. This she poised in a peculiar way, and with a short stick tapped a tune upon it. On the following morning I examined the apparatus, and found the board about twelve feet long, extremely thin and light, and pierced from the centre towards the extremities with a series of holes gradually increasing in size, so that it was really a musical plank, and, in the hands of an experienced player, could be made to convey the idea of a tune; but the chief feature of the performance was the tremendous noise it made. What between the old woman screaming her waking chant, and two nuns walking about the court tapping musical planks, there was no fear of any sleeping sister remaining unaware that her prayer-time had arrived; and, sure enough, a very few minutes elapsed before, from all corners, they came tripping, or rather gliding, like dark ghosts, to the church-door. They must sleep in their dress, or else have acquired the art of making a toilet as rapid as that of an undergraduate late for chapel, so speedily did they obey the summons. It was now time for us to follow. The old woman and the plank were still, and the swelling tones of a sacred chant warned us that the service had commenced. Modestly, and with downcast eyes, did we pass between two motionless rows of fair worshippers, until we reached the place of honour among the elder sisters. Here, in a little carpeted niche, we stood meekly—the only men—and listened to the women's voices repeating in high monotonous key the perpetual refrain. By degrees we acquired courage, and were rewarded for our boldness in looking up by detecting stolen glances shot at us from every quarter. The principal performer of the service was a lovely girl, apparently of eighteen or nineteen, who was standing in a group of young sisters when we came in, and whose turn it seemed to be to officiate, for she slipped out of her corner and donned over her hood a sort of surplice, then advancing to the desk in the middle of the church, she opened the massive ornamented volume before her, and went off at score. I could not have imagined that those ruby lips could have moved with such extraordinary rapidity, that the exquisitely chiselled nose should prove an organ for conveying the shrillest and most unpleasant sounds at a pace which was quite electrifying. Whenever the moment for a response came, the chorus "cut in" with something "Gospodin," as if the whole thing was being done for a wager. She never paused nor flagged in her harsh nasal rattle of Moldavian prayer, worked up now and then to a shrill invocation, and varied with prostrations, the extinction and lighting of candles, and full choruses. An hour seemed to pass, nevertheless, like a few moments. There was something fascinating in watching these fair devotees managing all their own matters without male interference; and I could conceive from the scene before me what that might be so well imagined by Tennyson. Those

"Prudes for proctors, dowagers for deans,
And sweet girl-graduates in their golden hair,"

only needed to be transported to a wild Carpathian valley to realise the poetic fancy.

I should remark, however, that there is one priest in Agapia who officiates at Mass, and who is a married man. Notwithstanding the rumour which had got abroad that we were to be present, there was a smaller congregation than I expected; but I was assured that some of the nuns were performing service in another church, and the rest saying their prayers at home. This last I take to be the most common practice; for on subsequent occasions, on dropping incidentally in for service, I have found no audience at all; the officiating nuns make up a little congregation in themselves, as there must be a certain number for the church and a certain number to read in turn. It was one o'clock in the morning before I sought my divan bed, after one of the most novel and interesting day's experiences I ever remember to have passed. Nothing but downright fatigue would have enabled me to sleep with so many quaint sights and sounds dancing before my eyes and ringing in my ears; but our time was short, and there was much to be seen, so we slept as fast as possible, and were up in time for matins at six o'clock. Here we saw a number of new nuns, with some of whom we made acquaintance; but the absence of any common language was a terrible drawback to our intercourse. Never having received an education to fit them for society, they knew no language but Moldavian; and though we applied ourselves to the acquirement of that tongue under their tuition with the utmost diligence, our time was too short to make progress.

After matins, we paid a visit to the lady superior, a dear old lady, who gave us sweetmeats and cigarettes, and kissed our foreheads when we were presented and when we took leave. She was very anxious that we should prolong our stay for as many weeks as we liked, and was quite hurt when we told her how hurried our visit must necessarily be. Anxious to carry away a memento of the place, we prevailed upon her to give us an old-fashioned daguerreotype of the convent, which was fading rapidly, and which we promised to have photographed in England and send her back. Most unfortunately, some weeks afterwards, the portmanteau containing it was cut off the back of our carriage by thieves in the night, and we proved, to our regret, unavoidably faithless.

We now went on a round of visits, and were delighted with the charming little cottages, each in its own garden, and containing one or two fair occupants, sometimes a young girl quite by herself. The rich ones are waited upon by the needy sisters, but at Veratica, which we afterwards visited, there was a much greater profusion of wealth than here. Some of our friends proposed a picnic for the afternoon, and we started off, a merry party of eight or ten, on foot for a romantic rock in the woods, from the summit of which a magnificent view was obtained of the valley and convent. After a regular scramble, we were rewarded for our exertions by finding that our kind hosts had sent on a hamper with sundry delicacies—that hot coffee was prepared, and a brisk fire ready for the emergencies of our repast.

So we chatted and refreshed, and were smoking tranquilly, when, to my astonishment, I observed some of the ladies engaged in dragging dead branches to the base of a lofty pine-tree, and piling them round it. On inquiring the reason of this proceeding, they informed us that it was great fun burning a pine-tree, and assured us, if we had never seen it, that we should enjoy the spectacle. We suggested the possibility of the whole forest catching fire; but they said they had chosen an isolated tree, and that even if it did run along the hillside, what would that matter—pine-trees were cheap in the Carpathians. So we heaped up branches round the old forest giant, and doomed him to a splendid but lingering death. Then we threw blazing logs into the dry mass, and the flame leaped crackling up to the highest branches. Our fair companions clapped their hands with delight as the fire roared and darted out angry forks of flame with each fresh gust of wind, and a spiral column of dense smoke burst in jets from the top, and, spreading like a pall over the grave of the dying patriarch, gave notice far and wide of the sacrilege which was being perpetrated.

The term employed in addressing our companions was always Mika (mother); and there was something quaint, considering the age of some of them, in bestowing the appellation. Nevertheless, it was pleasant to be called "Son," even by a girl of nineteen, and gave one the impression of having inspired an affectionate interest. From our present elevated position the convent appeared to great advantage. Instead of the gaunt solitary building usual on such occasions, the large collection of little cottages, prettily distributed and divided by the neatest of fences, clustered round the convent like chickens round a hen. Instead of a barred doorway with a "grille," and a stern "janitress," the fair occupants were free to roam about the valley where they pleased and with whom they pleased. Instead of lugubrious countenances and an air of general mortification in dress and manner, there were laughing merry faces, and numerous innovations upon strict conventual costume, of which the most serious was crinoline. Only a few weeks before our visit, the metropolitan had made a tour of inspection, and confiscated every "cage" he could lay his hands on. Still there was abundant evidence that some had escaped the sweeping measure. Where were there ever such "cells" as the lovely little boudoirs to be found in some of these cottages? Alas! the palmy days of the convents have gone by. Before long there will be a railway-station within two hours' drive of Agapia; and a recent order has been passed prohibiting any religiously minded young person from being compelled by her parents to take the veil until she is forty-five. This is practically putting an end to the system of convents altogether—as old maids don't exist in the Principalities —happy land!—and widows are extremely rare. The only chance of catching a nun is to get her quite young, when she is a trouble to her family; now they can no longer be turned into *religieuses* as of old; and as infanticide is not in vogue in these parts, as in China, their prospects are extremely questionable. Under the old system, what between having plenty of visitors from Jassy during the summer, and getting leave to spend a little of the season in the gay capital themselves in winter, they make life pass pleasantly enough. I have more than once met in society at Jassy "recluses" from these establishments, only to be distinguished by their hoods, as they wear silk and crinoline when they are on leave, and doff the hood if they go to the theatre or any evening entertainments. If fact, they hold much the same position in society that the Chanoinesses used to do in France— except that in their case, unlike these latter, matrimony is of course impossible. Perhaps that is no great drawback, seeing that they enjoy all the freedom of married women, without any of the cares and responsibilities.

As the most touching memento we could take from Agapia, we obtained from the nuns enough of the serge they weave and wear themselves to make us a shooting-suit apiece, and then with heavy hearts swallowed our last meal under the same anxious superintendence as ever, and awaited the summons to our vehicles. Although our visit had not been long, we had made many friends, who all assembled to bid us adieu. The form of parting salutation is touching, and when extended along a row of nuns, produces a singular effect. We reverently kissed their hands, and they bent over and kissed our heads. It is easy to conceive how strong was the temptation to linger before this one, to hurry past another—how difficult to collect one's ideas in the confusion of such a moment, for a strict sense of propriety prevented any outward manifestation of partiality. Persons who have never known before what it is to have a great many pairs of lips, some fresh and ruddy, others old and wrinkled, pressed in rapid succession upon their foreheads, will be conscious of a sensation of numbness in the scalp at last, arising probably from a conflict of emotions; nor, if the head be bald as mine was, will it be possible to prevent its becoming red. But why dwell upon such harrowing details? We found the goodwill of our fair entertainers extended itself to our equipages. Each carriage was furnished with nine horses belonging to the convent, and three gipsy postilions of wild and uncouth aspect and somewhat ragged attire. Then with loud cries and sharp whip-crackings we dashed out of the convent-yard, and all the bells burst forth with a merry peal, and we frantically waved our hats as we passed by well-known balconies and under the windows of the charming cottage where the dear old lady superior stood kissing her hand to us in final adieu. Our gipsy riders and their ragged team did not allow us much time to collect our scattered faculties. They evidently were impressed with a great idea of our importance, and thought that exactly in proportion as we were great ought our movements to be rapid; so we flew down the beds of mountain torrents, between lofty wooded hills, and finally emerged from the mountains on to the undulating rich country, which stretched away to the plains we had originally traversed.

We were bound to Veratica, another convent not so prettily situated, but even more celebrated than the last On the way we passed several villages and a good deal of land, producing Indian corn, melons, and grain, and towards evening reached our destination—a larger collection of cottages than at Agapia, only placed not in a *cul de sac*, but on the slope of a hill commanding an extensive prospect over the lowlands of Moldavia, and altogether comparatively in the world. A village almost at the gates of the convent dispelled the delusion of complete isolation, and of seclusion so striking as at Agapia; and when the atmosphere was clear, even the town of Nyamptz was visible in the far distance, to remind us of the busy haunts of men. Here there was no conventual building at all as at Agapia, where a certain small proportion of nuns lived in the convent, properly so called. All the nuns of Veratica lived in their own cottages, of which there were upwards of four hundred. It is true that some of them were ranged in the form of a square, in the centre of which was a church, and which was entered under an archway; but the general aspect of the place reminded me of some of the mission establishments I had seen in India. There were no less than four churches in Veratica for the benefit of six hundred resident nuns, who never seemed to me to attend them; and there was a school for girls, presided over by the prettiest woman in the convent. There was every indication of greater wealth and *luxe* here than at the establishment we had just left; and we were put up, not in any suite of apartments destined to strangers, but by one of the principal nuns, to whom we had a letter of introduction, and who in the kindest way gave up half her house to us. Nor would it have been possible to conceive anything more perfect and artistic than the taste with which her little abode was arranged. Half-a-dozen really good pictures, picked up in Italy by some one who knew what he was about, and others from Paris, a piano, a handsome Turkey carpet, heavy curtains of silk brocade, spring couches and arm-chairs richly covered, some valuable little bits of old China, a goodly sprinkling of small Parisian looking-glasses in ornamented frames, composed the furniture of the two "cells" to which my friend and I were doomed. These opened out upon a balcony in front, overlooking a flower-garden and the convent square; and here we used to sit and smoke cigarettes, for the fragrant weed is much in vogue among the recluses, and their tobacco was always unexceptionable. Our first duty was to call upon the lady superior, who received us as kindly as her sister at Agapia. She told us that she had entered the convent at the age of thirteen—she was now seventy; and except an occasional trip to Jassy, had passed the whole of her existence in religious exercises. She, as well as several of the committee of direction, were keen politicians, and discussed with eagerness and a great deal of knowledge of affairs, the intrigues of Prince Couza and the abuses of his government. Nor were they at all sparing in the epithets they applied to the chief of the State. As many of the ladies at Veratica were nearly connected with families who have wielded absolute power in one or other principality, they were entitled to speak with a certain amount of bitterness; and as they maintained a hot correspondence with their relations, some of whom are the wealthiest and most powerful *boyards*, their information was generally pretty accurate. The brother of my hostess held a very high official position; she herself was very wealthy; and besides her delightful little house, she had a carriage-and-pair, a lady's-maid who was not a nun, and dressed in the last Parisian fashion; a very excellent cook, as I have good reason to remember; and most attentive servants. Altogether it was quite clear that between Veratica and Agapia there was as great a difference as between Trinity College and Emmanuel, or Christchurch and Wadham. There was no doubt which was the most aristocratic, the most wealthy, and the most mundane of the two. Still I looked back with regret to the unsophisticated atmosphere of "the happy valley" of Agapia. How easy it is to be hypercritical on these occasions! How romantic and overwhelming in its novelty should we have found Veratica had we paid it our first visit! now there was something flat and vapid about it. There was not quite enough of the odour of sanctity in the air to suit our refined tastes. We felt as if we had almost got back to the world, and were sorely tempted to plunge into the wild valleys of the Bistritz, where convents nestle in unexplored recesses, approached by rock-cut steps overhung by glaciers, and where the occupants would really appreciate the visits of a stranger; where one may shoot chamois or catch trout, hunt bears or go picnics, sketch lovely scenery or learn Moldavian under pleasant auspices, scramble over mountain-passes, and generally find on the other side an ecclesiastical bed not yet confiscated by

Prince Couza; where the monks are all really "good fellows," and only too glad to put you up, and forward your views, whatever they may be, to the best of their ability; where letters can't reach you, and the cares of this life cannot penetrate; where comfort is combined with economy, and the only way of gliding back to the world is down the river on a raft.

Valley of Bistritz! if an inexorable fate — and the approach of winter—compelled me once to turn my back upon you, may the day yet come when I may take another siesta under the conventual shadow, and awake from a dream as pleasant as this last.

CHAPTER XVIII.

THE WAR IN SCHLESWIG-HOLSTEIN; THE BATTLE OF
MISSUNDE.

FROM Jassy we posted on to Bucharest, and after spending a few days at the City of Pleasure, and making acquaintance with Prince Couza, an adventurer whose corrupt rule was not long after brought to an end by a *coup d'état*, we crossed the Carpathians into Transylvania at Cronstadt, then drove on to Hermanstadt, and went on a sporting trip into the mountains. On our return, we presented the carriage which had served us so faithfully all the way from Lemberg to the landlord of our hotel, and took train to Pesth. Here Mr Ashley left me to return home, and I visited some old Hungarian friends, and so worked my way into Silesia. It was while staying at Primkenau, the country-seat of the late Duke of Augustenberg, that the news arrived of the death of the King of Denmark. This event let loose upon Europe the Schleswig-Holstein question, with all its complications, and called Prince Frederick, the eldest son of my host, from his retirement into a position of prominence; for, in the opinion of the best German jurists, he now, in consequence of his father's abdication of his rights, became the lawful heir to the duchies. The question was one which, under the circumstances, I was naturally induced to study, and in regard to which I could only come to one conclusion. As confessedly it was one which the British statesmen of the day considered beyond their comprehension, and as the British public never even tried to understand it, it was no wonder that our policy was mistaken throughout. When a question has more than two sides, the popular intelligence fails to grasp it. As most questions of foreign policy have generally three at least, and sometimes more, and as Ministers are compelled to adopt the popular view, if they wish to retain office, the foreign policy of England is usually characterised by a charming simplicity, not always conducive to the highest interests of the country. Fortunately on this occasion Ministers were saved, by the exercise of an authority higher than their own, from plunging the country into a futile and disastrous war. It is not necessary here, however, to recur to the political aspects of the question, which were ably and conclusively dealt with at the time in a pamphlet by Mr Morier (now Sir Robert Morier, our Ambassador at St Petersburg), and by Mr Kinglake in the House of Commons, while I contributed my quota in the public press.

It was at Gotha, under the auspices of the present Duke of Saxe-Coburg-Gotha, who was the first to recognise Duke Frederick as having succeeded to the duchies, that a decision was arrived at in regard to the policy to be pursued; and here were gathered many eminent patriots, who met in conclave—an assemblage which I was very glad to have an opportunity of joining.

It was as the result of these deliberations that upon the

last day but one of the year 1863 three strangers might have been observed by the inhabitants of Harburg embarking on board a little river steamer lying at the wharf with her steam up. But the inhabitants of Harburg observed nothing, for they are a phlegmatic commercial race, who do not trouble themselves with the concerns of other people; and although there was something unusual in these gentlemen taking a trip down the Elbe in a steamer chartered expressly for themselves in mid-winter, no curious questions were asked as to who they were, or where they were going. They were a very quiet, unpretending trio, with no display of luggage or attendants; and the captain of the steamer understood them to be public functionaries, employed in making an official tour of investigation upon the river. So he steamed unsuspiciously down to Gluckstadt through a stream already cumbered with blocks of ice; and his passengers went ashore in a little boat, and were met on the pier by one or two gentlemen who apparently had received notice of their intended arrival, and were there to meet them. Up to this moment the little town of Gluckstadt had been as quiet and indifferent to the approach of the steamer, as Harburg had been to its departure. It is true that the inhabitants had scarcely recovered the breath expended in cheering the entry of German troops upon the departure of the Danes, and shouting the Schleswig-Holstein anthem; but they knew no reason why they should regard the gentlemen walking along the pier with any unusual interest. Suddenly a sort of electric shock seemed to thrill through the town; people began frantically to run towards the marketplace; the three gentlemen found themselves surrounded by an enthusiastic and excited multitude, who could scarcely realise the fact that he whom they maintained to be their lawful sovereign had come to claim his own, and had been compelled, in order to avoid the traps laid for him by his enemies, thus to steal into the country. No one could visit Holstein at such a moment without catching the infection. Who can stand by and watch unmoved the progress of a game when the stake played for is a crown? Who can live in an atmosphere of shouting and cheering and wild excitement, and remain indifferent to the popular emotion? How is it possible to see a whole nation testifying its unanimous desire for some one thing upon which they have set their affections, and not join in "wishing they may get it"? It may be bad for them, or they may have no right to it; but when nearly a million of wills are all turned in the same direction, there is generally a good deal to be said in their favour. Whole nations are not unanimous without some cause. And although we may not always trust the wisdom of popular movements, and generally disapprove of the means they employ to achieve their ends, they deserve to be respected when they represent the aspirations of every class of society.

When I arrived at Kiel, the day after the Duke of Augustenburg had made his triumphant entry into the town, the Holsteiners were still giving vent to the redundancy of their enthusiasm. They had been passing from one phase of patriotic excitement to another. First of all, the sullen departure of the Danish garrisons put them in good spirits, and they chuckled inwardly as they watched the retiring regiments. Then almost before the last Danish soldier had disappeared, from every window fluttered the national banner. The whole town instantaneously broke out into rejoicing. The shops were shut, and the population gave themselves up with one consent to singing, upon all possible occasions and without intermission, "Schleswig-Holstein meer umschlungen." The Saxon and Hanoverian troops were welcomed as deliverers, and overwhelmed with civilities. Every Danish emblem disappeared; the word Köngliche was taken down from all the public buildings, and, with a levity characteristic of all popular emotion, the people of Kiel thought that their cause was won, that their anxieties were at an end, and that nothing more remained but for Duke Frederick to come and take possession of his own; so that when that Prince did unexpectedly make his appearance, the town went off into a new series of demonstrations; and as I entered it at eight o'clock in the evening, I found the streets illuminated by a torchlight procession. Five hundred waving torches cast a lurid glare upon the snow-clad houses and whitened streets; and when they all collected in front of the Bahnhoff's Hotel, at which the Duke had taken up his abode, and broke out into enthusiastic cheers, and bands played, and banners fluttered, and a venerable citizen, with a voice trembling from emotion, in a few touching words welcomed back to his own capital the Prince who had been in exile from it for fourteen years, it was difficult to deny the genuineness of the popular sentiment, or to remain an indifferent spectator to this development of it. The Duke, standing at a window, addressed the crowd, which, with eager upturned faces, were gazing upon and listening to him for the first time. To judge by the cheers at the conclusion of his speech, they were satisfied with their inspection, and dispersed, not to go to bed, but to parade the streets and lanes. It was the last night of the year, and there seemed something hopeful in the auspices under which 1864 was being ushered in. I adjourned, with a number of excited citizens, to a club or harmonia, as it was called; and here, under the influence of beer, and in an atmosphere of smoke, patriotic speeches were made, toasts proposed, and the old year satisfactorily disposed of. Little did the worthy citizens of Kiel then imagine that before many weeks were over all would be changed; that they would be taking down instead of putting up flags, ceasing to apostrophise "Schleswig-Holstein sea-embraced," and meeting in the harmonia not to congratulate but to condole with each other—to drink no longer to the health of Saxon and of Hanoverian, but confusion to the Austrian and the Prussian. However, they did right not to anticipate misfortunes. They took advantage of the bright sun to make what little hay they could, and every demonstration that could be imagined was made. Twenty-four fair maids of Kiel, dressed in white, with tricolor ribbons, came and tendered their homage to the Duke on behalf of the sex generally. A grand patriotic representation was given at the theatre, with a tableau emblematical of the inseparable union of Schleswig with Holstein; while deputations succeeded each other in unvaried succession, not merely from all parts of Holstein, but from Schleswig as well. One of the most interesting of these consisted of a procession of four hundred yeomen and small country proprietors, who rode into the town, and formed with military precision before the hotel.

It was impossible to look upon these sturdy agriculturists, and not see in them the type of the British farmer. Schleswig-Holstein is indeed the cradle of the Anglo-Saxon race; their oldest national songs were preserved, not in their own country, but in ours; and our chronicler, the Venerable Bede, furnishes the most authentic traditions of their early history. The language of the Frisen and the Angeln is full of words which are to be found, not in German, but in English; and both the rural and maritime populations of these provinces bear the strongest resemblance to our own.

It was exactly a month before the Austrian and Prussian armies crossed the Eider, that I found myself performing that historical operation at Rendsburg. Contrary to my expectation, I crossed it without opposition. It is true that, inasmuch as the Eider was frozen over from one end to the other, a solitary invader might enter Schleswig in spite of the whole Danish army; and so probably they made a merit of necessity, and pretended not to care who entered and who left the province. Considering the critical state of the relations of Denmark with Germany at the moment, I was much struck with the enlightened and civilised treatment which the traveller met with on both sides. Although pontoon-trains were rumbling through the streets of Rendsburg, and engineers were taking the preliminary steps to erecting batteries which should command the Kronewerke, and the town was full of Saxon and Hanoverian troops, and every outward indication was in favour of a speedy outbreak of hostilities, not the slightest suspicion attached to those who crossed or recrossed the frontiers. A drawbridge not twenty yards long separated the German from the Danish sentry; every time they paced it they almost met in the centre. At one end of the bridge floated the German, at the other the Danish, flag. Groups of Danish soldiers inspected groups of German soldiers, at twenty yards apart, as prize-fighters do before the fight begins; and the peaceable inhabitants of the town came to look at the combatants eyeing each other. One seemed to be standing on a volcano with a very thin crust indeed. Observing people pass both sentries unchallenged, I followed the example, and in two minutes found myself in Schleswig. Soldiers, with the little red-and-white cockade of Denmark in their caps, were far more occupied, it seemed to me, in making preparations to resist the expected attack than their opponents were in carrying out their aggressive works.

Two strong lines of palisades, loop-holed for musketry, flanked the bridge; and an erection of some description, the nature of which I could not exactly discover, was in progress on a commanding position. The Kronewerke is the *tête de pont* on the Schleswig side of the bridge which crosses the Eider; there were a few buildings used for barracks near it, and in a semicircular form surrounding it was the district claimed by Holstein, and which contained six villages, in most of which, at the moment of my visit, Danish troops were billeted. It was then reported to be the intention of General Hake, commanding the Federal army of execution, to summon the Danish General to evacuate the position; and the Danish General having announced his determination not to comply with this summons, a conflict was considered imminent. It did not ultimately take place, because the Federals were not in sufficient force, and the Saxon General did not wish to summon either the Prussian or Austrian contingents to his assistance. The jealousy which then existed between the Federals and the armies of the two great German Powers, might have been exasperated with immense advantage to the Danes at this early stage of the war.

It was never properly understood in this country that both the Federal-German army and the Danish army had a common enemy which they hated more even than they hated each other, and this was the Prussian army. They both had the same policy in one respect, and this was to keep their quarrel to themselves, and not allow the two Great Powers to interfere with overpowering force, and settle the matter off-hand in their own sense. It is most probable that, had Prussia and Austria never meddled in the affair, the Germans and Danes would have fought out the matter with pretty equal chances of success; but the moment these two absolute Governments were permitted to take the affair in hand and settle it according to treaty, they obtained the control of the situation, and the power of abusing to an unlimited extent the confidence reposed in them.

After an unmolested exploration of the Kronewerke, I returned to Holstein by way of the railway bridge. Here, too, German and Danish sentries were keeping amicable guard, and on each side the river expanded into a sort of lagoon, covered with ice, on which boys were skating; and firmly frozen-in were the small craft which represented the maritime commerce of Rendsburg. Although trains were running regularly at this time from Rendsburg to

Schleswig, I preferred making the journey in an open waggon, partly for the sake of seeing the country, and partly for the convenience of being able to choose my own hour of starting. Rumbling once more over the drawbridge, we soon found ourselves beyond the limits of the six villages, and traversed a hard frozen road, over which our well-roughed horses made good progress. The fields on each side were covered with a thin coating of snow, and divided with hedges as in England. Farmhouses were few and far between, and villages, or more properly hamlets, very rare. In the first one through which we passed we observed a battery of field-artillery; but soldiers were not moving along the line, and there did not seem any intention to reinforce the troops then occupying the Kronewerke. According to the usual habit of the country, we stopped at a half-way house, after an hour and a half's drive, for a glass of schnaps and a bait, and then, once more facing the bleak cutting wind, we trundled merrily along, by the light of a rising moon, into Schleswig. On the way we passed the railway junction of Kloster Krug, the scene of rather a sharp combat, a month later, between the Danes and the Austrians; then winding between the low hills crowned with the batteries of the Dannevirke, we entered the long town of Schleswig, and found its single street encumbered with troops, and its not very spacious hotels crowded with officers. We were upwards of an hour vainly trying to persuade inhospitable hotel-keepers to take us in. Being all German in sympathy, they were in no very amiable mood at finding themselves obliged to provide accommodation for their enemies; and it was only after much persuasion that my German companion induced a stanch patriot to turn his two daughters out of their bedroom, and place the accommodation at our disposal. This mark of friendship and confidence warmed our hearts to our host, and he and a waiter with strong political feelings entertained us with an account of their grievances till a late hour. Considering that the room in which we dined was crowded with Danish officers, and that our political conversation was by no means carried on in a subdued tone, I was struck with the proof which this episode afforded of the leniency of the Danish rule. As compared with the tyranny of despotic governments, the administration of these provinces by Denmark contrasted most favourably; but unfortunately there is no amount of political liberty which will satisfy the sentiment of national independence, which is in most instances unreasonable; for it may be safely laid down as an axiom, that people would rather govern themselves badly than let other people govern them well. However, I do not mean to imply by this that Holstein, as a sovereign German duchy separated from Denmark, would not be governed upon liberal and enlightened principles, nor can it be said that the rule of Denmark has been altogether unexceptionable. No doubt many serious grievances have existed: still at such a moment of political agitation, the freedom of speech and of action permitted to a population avowedly hostile was remarkable.

We were roused at an early hour the following morning by strains of martial music, and looking out of the window we observed regiments forming in the open space in front of the hotel, and the street already crowded with a train of artillery and ammunition waggons. Every outward indication betokened the confident anticipation of the speedy outbreak of hostilities; and the contrast with the German preparations which were going on at Rendsburg was very remarkable. There, it is true, things looked warlike, but it was in a sleepy, uncertain sort of way: here everything was activity and bustle. The men looked bright and cheery, the officers seemed in high spirits at the prospect of a fight. The laurels of their former campaign were still unwithered; and they believed they would reap a fresh supply whenever the attack from Germany should come. They little thought then that the overwhelming armies of the two great German Powers would be employed to crush them, and rightly judged that, so long as they only had the Federal troops to deal with, their chances of success were not unequal. Finding a battery of artillery bound apparently upon a military promenade, my friend and I followed it upon speculation, passing the old castle of Gottorp, a huge ugly building, like a factory, prettily situated. We found ourselves winding along some narrow country lanes, and afraid that the officer in command of the battery might imagine we were spies, we kept at a respectable distance, scrambling across ploughed fields and over deep-rutted country roads, until the glitter of bayonets in another direction revealed to us the objects of the promenade. On striking a highroad we found troops moving in large masses into the batteries of the Dannevirke, which crowned the hills we had been ascending. Although we were the only civilians, no notice was taken of us, and we were allowed to explore at leisure this celebrated fortification. As I walked along the covered-ways which connected together the nineteen or twenty separate forts, each bristling with cannon and surrounded by ditches and *chevaux de frises*, I thought I saw in prospective the grave of many of the brave men who were now drawn up within its lines in all the display of a grand military review; but even then the inadequacy of the force was apparent to the most unskilled in military matters. The defences of the Dannevirke consisted of no less than three different ramparts, one four miles long, one two miles long, and one fourteen miles long. When in addition to this twenty miles of earthwork is added, the position of Frederickstadt and the whole line of the Schlei, it is difficult to comprehend why the Danes should ever have seriously thought of making a stand against an overwhelming force, with the troops at their disposal. That a hundred thousand men could make the position impregnable is scarcely to be doubted; and from the earliest times this line of defence has been regarded by the Danes as their natural military frontier. Traditions as far back as the tenth century exist to prove that, even at that remote period, the military instinct of the people had led them to execute a line of defence which the most advanced stage of civilisation should adopt, and render celebrated in the future history of the country. The subsequent evacuation of the Dannevirke divested it, however, of that interest which, before the war began, it possessed in the eyes of those who considered that the tide of German invasion would meet here its first check.

I cannot say that, standing on the crisp snow which covered the heights of the Dannevirke, and looking on the proud array of men drawn up behind its intrenchments, I anticipated that in less than two months they would be struggling for bare life in Jutland. I have seldom seen an army which looked more business-like and full of fight; nor, it must be admitted, did they afterwards show themselves wanting in any of the finer qualities of a soldier. Numbers alone drove them to their last intrenchments, and the want of numbers alone compelled them to evacuate the strong position they were now holding. In a plain on the extreme right were drawn up the cavalry, and behind the batteries upon the heights were massed the artillery and infantry. About mid-day the King, surrounded by his staff, and accompanied by the Crown-Prince and the unfortunate General de Meza, who afterwards had reason to regret that he ever had any connection with the Dannevirke, rode along the line; but previous to his arrival, a general order, in the patriotic sense, was read by the colonels to each regiment formed into square. Then the King himself passed them in review, and addressed to each division a few stirring words, which were received with cheers and every appearance of enthusiasm. It was an interesting and exciting spectacle, not so much on account of the display itself, as from the political significance which attached to it. It was a hard day's work scrambling over the stiff half-frozen ground from one battery to another, along the ridges of hills for miles; but we were repaid as well by the good fortune which had led us so opportunely to the spot, as by the lovely view over the town of Schleswig, the broad frozen Schlei, and the wood-crowned hills in rear: and when at last we reached the town hungry and tired, we were more than consoled by our day's work, and gained much interesting information from a young

Danish officer, whose sanguine anticipations of the result of the impending hostilities have certainly not been realised. The trains continued to run between Schleswig and Rendsburg exactly as if those two towns were not occupied by hostile armies; and there was no hindrance to my walking straight out of the Dannevirke down to the booking-office, and being within an hour in the office of General Hake at Rendsburg narrating my experiences, if so it had pleased me. However, the liberality and unsuspiciousness of the Danes were so great, it would have been most unworthy to abuse it; and I went back to Holstein in a reticent frame of mind, with a higher opinion of the Danish army, and of their powers of resistance, than I had before, and with a stronger conviction of the inevitable certainty of a speedy outbreak of hostilities.

As, at this crisis in the Dano-German question, European diplomacy had taken the complication fairly in hand, and was disporting itself recklessly in its meshes, a residence in Kiel lost a good deal of the piquancy which the popular enthusiasm, and the uncertainty of political events, had imparted to it on the occasion of my first arrival. I got tired of skating out to sea, down the magnificent harbour of Kiel, over miles of unsurpassed ice; of listening to *canards*, which proved oftener false than true; and of getting up in my leisure hours the genealogical tree of the House of Oldenburg. But while Holstein was hushed in the calm which preceded the storm, the Prussian Prime Minister, Count Bismarck, was arranging some very lively combinations indeed at Berlin. The operations of so skilled an artist could not be other than a profitable study, so I repaired to that extremely dull and pedantic city, and watched with interest the progress of that diplomacy which resulted in the precipitate and unexpected crossing of the Eider. The general impression which prevailed in Berlin just before that event took place was, that it could not possibly come off until the middle of February. Indeed, a review of the army was fixed for the 2d, and announced as publicly as possible, in order that the Danes might be thrown off their guard, and the crossing effected on the 1st with less chance of opposition. The fact was, that Berlin had been worked up to a martial *furor;* the military element, which is largely preponderating and highly influential, was burning for distinction. It had found its only development, for many years past, in the tightness of the uniform which, in the mind of the Prussian officer, at once elevates him into a cherub, or some such superior order of being—though it did seem unnatural that, being already provided with wings, he should wish to add spurs. The fact is, that except in the last Holstein war, when they were beaten by the Danes, the Prussians had seen no fighting, and it would have cost even Bismarck his place had he attempted to stem the torrent of military ardour which his policy had excited, which carried away society, and which sent even the stalwart Prime Minister whirling down the flood rather faster than he originally intended.

As I found everybody of distinction going to Holstein, and as I had good reason to believe that the public was purposely left in error with reference to the crossing of the Eider, I started off once more to the scene of action, and arrived in Kiel on the night of the 31st of January.

The news brought in by the waiter, with coffee, was that a sanguinary battle had taken place at 5 A.M., and that the Danish army was routed and retreating. This ultimately dwindled down to two shots exchanged and a Dane slightly wounded. But the important fact remained—the Eider had been crossed, and the right thing to do was clearly to cross it also. So thought a knot of friends collected in the street, which, although the hour was early, was already full of gossiping groups; so, after swallowing a hasty breakfast, I found myself, with four eager patriots and Mr Hardman, the 'Times' correspondent, seated in an open cart of the country, provided with three cross benches, rattling over the hard frozen road as rapidly as a pair of stout nags could drag us.

In an hour we had reached the Eider, which here presented the appearance of a canal rather than of a river, and is spanned by a drawbridge to allow the passage of boats. The bridge-keeper, who had been accused of spying for the Danes, was already in custody, and his family, grouped around the door of their abode, watched the invading battalions crossing the narrow bridge. Since seven o'clock in the morning, when the leading regiments crossed without resistance, one incessant stream of troops had been pouring into Schleswig, and we arrived just in time to hear the triumphant cheers of the rear-guard as they passed out of one duchy into the other. Soon we overtook the artillery, and our pace was reduced to a walk. The roads were like ice, and the unroughed artillery and cavalry horses slipped about terribly; but every face beamed with animation, and it was easy to perceive in the ruddy youthful countenances of the men, full of hope and eagerness, that they were new to the work. Here were no rugged, furrowed visages, such as betoken a veteran army. The serious business of war was to these men as yet a holiday pastime: laughter and songs rang in the clear frosty air, and our unpretending waggon, with its six "civil" occupants, was the subject of an incessant volley of chaff as we squeezed our way to the front. There was a goodly sprinkling of Kielers on foot, making their way to see the fun; students of the college, with little red caps, trudged along with newspaper correspondents and amateur spectators. The boom of distant cannon sent a thrill down the line as it broke in upon the merriment, and a cart conveying a sick dragoon to the rear gave matters a serious look, for we supposed him to be wounded. Everybody was eager to push on, and a little after mid-day we entered the half-way village of Gettorf. Here the population was in a condition of frantic enthusiasm; the tap-room of the village inn was filled with a noisy multitude of soldiers and country people fraternising, drinking, and singing "Schleswig-Holstein meer umschlungen." Flags were waving, and Duke Frederick had been already proclaimed amid the applause of the populace. Taking advantage of a halt in the line, we pushed on through scenery less tame than that through which we had already passed; the country became more undulating, and at one point the road passed through a thick wood, and over a hill which would have afforded a defensible position. Probably the movement on the part of the Prussians had been too sudden to admit of the Danes profiting by it: the firing had long since ceased; indeed, we had only heard one or two shots; but now we met two carriages driving in all haste towards Kiel. These contained the Austrian and Prussian Ministers on their way from Copenhagen. We were also informed that the firing we had heard proceeded, in the first instance, from two Danish war-steamers, which had thus greeted the leading columns of the Prussian army as they debouched from the wood on to the shores of the bay. Except slightly wounding a horse, they did no damage; and on the artillery coming up and opening fire, the wooden ships were compelled to get under way; and when we came upon the scene of action they were no more visible. The artillery which had been so recently engaged were in position on a range of hills overlooking the harbour, and two or three round-shot were embedded by the side of the road which ran along their base. We had now passed the whole of the column which had originally impeded our progress, and drove into Eckernfiorde in style. As only quite the leading regiments had entered, and were still billeting themselves, we were fortunate enough to find accommodation, but not repose. The town presented a scene of confusion and excitement perfectly bewildering; the whole population seemed bent upon forcing the Prussian soldiers to share their patriotic emotion. They embraced them, drank with them, sang with them, cheered them, and paraded the streets with them. The population of the town is only about 6000; but they made noise enough for ten times that number. Flags were being hung out in every direction; provident patriots had brought some from Kiel; stripes of red, white, and blue were being hastily patched together, and fluttered from every house-top, except from the mansion immediately opposite the hotel, which was inhabited by a medical man with Danish sympathies — because, as I understood, his practice had been chiefly among Danish *employés*. However that may be, it spoke well both for Danes and Germans that he should at such a moment have the courage to stand alone. He could not, however, prevent a number of pretty daughters looking out upon, and taking a lively interest in, the animated scene below. For just in front of the hotel popular demonstrations kept going off like fireworks: every now and then a stern officer dashed through the crowd on special service, and scorned to notice the political excitement around him. Probably he had very vague ideas on the subject, and knew as little of the Schleswig-Holstein question as the British public or the officers of the Austrian army, who "wondered how it was that, being in an enemy's country, the people should all be so civil." Presently a great crowd gathered at the hotel door, and forming into a sort of procession, went off to the market-place singing the national anthem. I followed it, and was chiefly struck by the stern rebukes which respectable citizens administered to any member of the crowd disposed to be too boisterous, and the submissive way in which the more rowdy element received reproof. Still nothing could prevent the triumph of dragging Prussian soldiers along to assist in proclaiming Duke Frederick; for these simple people seemed to think that Bismarck might be touched by this exhibition of sympathy on the part of the Prussian army.

The town-hall of Eckernfiorde is a queer, ramshackle old place, with a broad flight of stone steps leading up to it; and on this the Corporation took its stand; while a band played vigorously, and people shouted themselves hoarse, until the order for silence was given, and a burly burgher addressed his fellow-citizens in a stentorian voice, congratulating them upon the recovery of their ancient liberties, complimenting the Prussian army upon having taken the matter so decidedly in hand, expressing his sense of the obligation they were under to them for rendering possible the proclamation of Duke Frederick, whose name was coupled with many endearing epithets, and was received with most enthusiastic applause. "Finally," said the speaker, "we have still in the town a rascally Danish Burgomaster, who must be instantly requested to leave; but of course the people will not think of meddling—my colleagues and myself are men enough for the task of ejecting him!" The band then struck up a sacred anthem, and every head was bared, while all joined in the well-known words of the hymn, "God our strong tower." After which the mob betook themselves again to parading the streets and singing; whilst, curious to see the result of the Burgomaster episode, I inquired where might be the residence of that worthy; and, having found it, lingered in a promiscuous manner at a neighbouring corner. I found a good many other persons similarly occupied; and in a few minutes the late orator and his friends entered the silent mansion, from which, of course, no popular flag was waving, and which was conspicuous by its gloomy aspect. I don't exactly know what there was to expect. I am half afraid I had thought a stand-up fight possible at the top of the steps. At all events, I felt rather ashamed of the idle curiosity which tempted me to wait for a report of the interview. It was satisfactory to those interested, as the Burgomaster promised to vacate the premises at 10 P.M.; meantime some citizens were left with him to take over the records. This man had contrived, apart from being a Dane, to make himself extremely unpopular in the province, and many were the stories current of his cruelty and injustice. As, however, I am not aware how far they are to be relied upon, and as whatever may have been his misdeeds he has suffered for them, it will be unnecessary here to repeat them. At a later period of the evening, when I passed the house, I saw two sentries at the door, so that he had applied for protection, fearing some popular ebullition of feeling; but the alarm was groundless. Even the Danes must render justice to the people of both the duchies for the moderation they displayed in the moments of their triumph. A very primitive description of illumination, consisting simply of candles in all the windows, closed the day's proceedings; but all night singing went on, and once the town was thrown into a state of excitement by the report of the return of the Danish men-of-war in the darkness, for the purpose of bombarding it.

As it was understood that the army was to continue its march on the following morning, and that the Danes were to be attacked in a position called Kochendorf, distant only a few miles from the town, we secured a light trap, and, with a pair of wretched-looking nags, started at an early hour in rear of the army. The weather was still cold, but raw and foggy, and the roads as slippery as ever, so that our progress was slow. We were somewhat puzzled, after getting past one division, to meet some batteries which had received the order to countermarch, and none of the officers whom we asked seemed to know the reason.

It turned out afterwards that Kochendorf was evacuated, and that Prince Frederick Charles, afterwards known as the Red Prince, rather than return to Eckernfiorde *re infecta*, had determined to attack Missunde. This necessitated another disposition of troops, and we shortly after came upon the vanguard at some cross-roads near the village of Kossel, and were brought to a halt. Thinking we should be more independent without it, we left our waggon at this point, and, when the order was given to advance, accompanied the head of the column on foot. Passing through the village, the inhabitants of which were all excitedly collected to witness from afar the coming engagement, I ascended a hill, on which stood a picturesque church, and from the churchyard, filled with spectators, was just able to distinguish with my glass the indistinct forms of the Danish skirmishers. Unfortunately the mist lay so heavy over the landscape that the fortifications of Missunde itself were not visible; and after leaving the churchyard, we felt very much as though we were groping our way in the dark as we approached the enemy's position. Soon a shot from the Danish batteries enlightened us as to their exact whereabouts, and our artillery was brought up into position, extending itself in the form of a semicircle along the crest of the hill. Fortunately the frost had hardened the surface of the ploughed land across which the guns were to be dragged. The fields were divided by mud-banks surmounted by hedges, and pioneers were actively employed cutting gaps through them. These banks afforded very comfortable shelter for amateurs; but the firing was not hot enough to drive one behind them for long. I afterwards understood that no fewer than seventy-four pieces of ordnance were engaged in the bombardment; but I only counted six batteries, and the fire was not kept up with much spirit. In fact, the fog seemed to exercise a depressing influence upon all concerned: our extremities were very cold; but there was not even excitement enough to make one forget one's "poor feet." The unhappy Danes did not the least know where the infantry was massed, and could only judge what to fire at by the flashes of our heavy guns. The flashes of theirs alone revealed the position of Missunde, and the consequence was that comparatively little damage was done on either side. The enemy's fire was necessarily feeble, as they had but few guns in position; but the sound of shot and shell was evidently new to the young soldiers who composed the Prussian army, and who paid the tribute of respect to a whistling shell common to novices. Once I perceived, advancing dimly through the fog, the line of Danish skirmishers, and thought that some life was about to be infused into the monotonous artillery-combat, which had lasted for about two hours; but they halted two fields distant, and retreated in good order, having apparently made themselves acquainted with our position. On the extreme right, picturesquely situated by the side of a small frozen *meer*, stood a mill; and we determined to explore in that direction, as the fire had slackened on the left. Making a short cut across the ice, which in one or two places had been split with round-shot, we found a regiment of cavalry galloping in hot haste along a narrow lane towards the enemy, and two regiments drawn up in a field, apparently waiting the order for an attack. The Danes had got the range pretty well, and their riflemen were keeping up a well-sustained fire. Though we could not make out the direction from which they came, so thick was the fog, their hissing little messengers went flying about like invisible grasshoppers; and wounded men went scrambling to the rear, or got their comrades to carry them there in their greatcoats; for no stretchers had come up, and ambulances were nowhere to be seen—in fact, nothing could have been worse than the arrangements for the wounded. Now and then one went to the rear attended by quite an unnecessary quantity of comrades; but, on the whole, the men behaved quite as well as could have been expected of raw troops; and when at last the order came to advance on the intrenchments, they skirmished up with alacrity to within three hundred yards of the enemy, losing in so doing a good many men. The object of the move was to cover the retreat of the artillery. It had never from the first been intended to storm Missunde. As the result proved, this, as well as every other fortification on the line, would inevitably have to be evacuated; and it would have been difficult to have suggested a more useless afternoon's amusement than was provided for the Prussian army on the 2d of February 1864. The men with whom I conversed, as we toiled back towards the village, seemed rather mystified, as well they might be, with the whole operation. We had neither achieved a success, nor been repulsed, nor done anything except stand to be fired at throughout the greater part of a raw misty afternoon. And now, the fact that our shells had set fire to some houses in Missunde, which were blazing luridly through the fog, was a poor triumph. Fighting on these terms was not such good fun after all. Though it had not been attended with much danger—for the official list only gave 40 killed, and 180 wounded—we had been the only spectators at all near the front, and we found a cloud of German newspaper correspondents and citizens of Kiel in the village eager for sensation intelligence, which, under the circumstances, it was difficult to provide. However, a great deal of sanguinary hand-to-hand fighting, which never took place, was reported, with many graphic details, to have occurred in the trenches. The Prussian army was supposed to have covered itself with glory, though, even at this moment of anti-Danish excitement, the anti-Prussian feeling was so strong among the Holsteiners, that there were many present who would have chuckled over any decided reverse which could have happened to the Prussian army.

The little village of Kosel did not promise well for a night's accommodation; the road back to Eckernfiorde would be impassable for some hours, and it was getting late enough to make us feel nervous at the prospect of a good deal of scrambling and discomfort before we should discover quarters. Fortunately we found our trap with the two rosinantes, and were sitting speculating in what direction to go, when we saw a road leading towards the enemy's position free of all encumbrance. Along this we determined to proceed, in hopes of finding a village unoccupied by troops. There was so much confusion that no one thought of preventing our taking a line which led us straight to the enemy; and in five minutes we had left the din and bustle of the retreating army behind us. There was something startling in the sudden change to solitude; and in about half an hour we began to wonder how far we might be from the nearest Danes. A clean little village, a charming old-fashioned roadside inn, and a group of peasants collected round the porch, was a welcome sight. They raised their hands in astonishment at our appearance, and in deprecation of our venturing any further. The Danes, they said, were not above a quarter of an hour distant, and we had better stay at the inn for the night. The driver, who, like a true patriot, had a cockade in his hat, was recommended to dispense with that little addition, and he became altogether very *piano* at the unpleasant neighbourhood in which he found himself. If any of the villagers had been spies, we might easily have been made prisoners, had that been worth anybody's while; but, so far from this being the case, the rustics seemed to take courage. We were the first "Germans" they had seen. Their faces beamed with joy at the proof which our presence afforded of the reality of a speedy deliverance from their present masters; and, to my great regret, they began to sing, in subdued voices it is true, that eternal "Schleswig-Holstein meer umschlungen," with the air of which by this time I had become disagreeably familiar. The *empressement* of our host and hostess, the alacrity of a neatly-dressed, sprightly Hebe, who lingered in the room a great deal more than was actually necessary, to gossip with us about the Danes, and to hear our news about the battle, made us congratulate ourselves upon our good fortune. While those with the army were lodging in barns, we had a most luxurious inn all to ourselves. And when, after the fatigues of the day, we had discussed an admirably cooked dinner, and drew round the fire, with the usual accompaniments to the digestive process, we thought that there were worse places in the world than Fleckeby, and that it was decidedly pleasanter to be in front of an advancing army than in rear. The line, it must be admitted, is rather a delicate one to hit: for armies in this relative position to each other are constantly performing the process known as "feeling each other"; and if they "feel you" between them, the results are not satisfactory. However, there is an excitement in being ahead of everything, which, added to the extra comfort, makes the alternative, even though the risk be added, the most agreeable. We had a long discussion, before "turning in," upon our plans for the morrow, the question being whether it was better to return to the Prussian army, on the chance of another attack on Missunde, and the crossing of the Schlei, or whether we should not make an exploration towards the Austrian headquarters, on the chance of an attack upon the Dannevirke coming off. We were about an hour's drive from the Dannevirke in our present position; and although our host gave us very precise information as to the whereabouts of the Danes, one was never sure of escaping reconnoitring parties. There is no doubt that, as amateurs, we should have been much better treated in the Danish than in the Prussian army, so that it would have been rather good policy to have "fallen" into the hands of the enemy, had it not involved a return to England by way of Copenhagen, an operation for which I could not afford the time. All our plans were frustrated next morning by the change in the weather. The mists of the day before were succeeded by hurricanes of wind, with a violent beating rain, that made campaigning a most unpleasant occupation. Another attack on Missunde or the crossing of the Schlei was clearly out of the question, so we decided in favour of the left wing. While we were standing watching disconsolately the storm-gusts succeeding each other, the familiar uniform of the Austrian army suddenly turned a corner of the road, and an officer in command of a picket rushed up the steps of our cheery hostel to find warmth and food. Although, when he gave his orders to the sergeant, his mouth was full of beef-steak, I understood the Italian in which they were conveyed; and he started when, after having allowed him to enter into details, I made a remark in the same language. He had not calculated upon this in a remote corner of Schleswig, and evidently at once set me down as a spy. It was in vain to attempt afterwards to extract a word of information from him. He would neither say where he had come from, where he was going to, which roads were safe, which occupied by the enemy. The more questions I asked, the more suspicious naturally did he become, and he declined at last even to condole with me on the state of the weather. Getting impatient of inaction, we determined on being storm-stayed no longer; and being assured by our host that the Austrian head-quarters were at a village called Lottorf, we ordered our driver to take us there. For more than an hour we followed lanes and cross-roads without meeting a soul: at last I became sceptical about the direction, and we stopped at a hamlet, and were informed that we had passed the turning to Lottorf some time since; that no troops had appeared in the immediate neighbourhood, but that firing had been heard. As whenever hostile armies are at all near each other, firing is always being heard by the country people, whether there is any or not, we did not believe this latter part of the story, and decided, as we had passed Lottorf, not to go back there, but to push on and trust to Providence. It afterwards turned out that, had we gone to Lottorf, we should have gone straight into the Danish lines, as the enemy was holding the position in force. However, in blissful ignorance of this narrow escape, we kept on, still wondering where any army was. We were in the very middle of the position, and could not see a uniform of any kind. It was not until we reached the village of Breckendorf that we observed some Austrian vedettes on the hill-tops, and saw men creeping about in the fields reconnoitring. Still we could not believe in the proximity of the Danes, unless, indeed, we had come through them without knowing it. We said as much to the Austrian officer in command, who replied that he did not know what had become of the enemy, and that he was going to call in his scouts. If we could only have suspected that we had actually been passing over ground which in another hour was to be one of the most hotly contested fields of the war, we should have looked at it with greater interest. If we had left Fleckeby an hour or two later, we should have tumbled into the middle of the battle of Ober Selk; as it was, the villainous weather and the absence of any sign of the enemy induced us to push on to headquarters, in the hope of getting some good information. The difficulty was to find out where headquarters were. Every officer we asked told us a different place: some thought we were spies, others did not know themselves, or pretended they did not; so we found our-

THE BATTLE OF MISSUNDE. 411

selves approaching Rendsburg, simply because there was no other place to go to.

The country through which we had passed since leaving Fleckeby was not devoid of a rugged beauty, and, from its diversified character, formed a pleasing contrast to other parts of Holstein. The hills, though not high, were in places scarped, and granite boulders lay strewn at their base; while here and there we observed tumuli, which had all the appearance of having been artificially constructed. However, we had neither time nor inclination for geological observation. From a military point of view, the country was admirably adapted for skirmishing, and the battle, which took place at mid-day, was a sort of running fight over the hills, the Danes slowly retreating upon the Dannevirke, some five or six miles distant, standing on the hill-tops, and pouring down upon the advancing Austrians destructive volleys of musketry. They disputed effectively one position after another all through the afternoon, the Austrians only achieving their day's success at the price of thirty officers and upwards of 500 men killed and wounded. It was in a narrow lane that we met the division of Gondecourt, on whom this loss was inflicted, marching unconsciously to their fate. We had as little idea as they seemed to have of the bloody work awaiting them; and as regiment after regiment passed, and the officers inquired of us how far it was to their night-quarters, neither they nor we suspected the long sleep on the hillside that was in store for many of them. At the head of the column rode Gondecourt himself, and splashing through the deep mire after him came regiments of Galicians, Hungarians, and Styrians, the latter with sprigs of pine in their caps. We were obliged to draw up for nearly an hour to let the long train of artillery and transport go by, and as we watched the various nationalities pass, we could not help being struck with the strange political inconsistency which enabled the oppressors to use the oppressed to fight against oppression. It was a curious feature of the Schleswig-Holstein question, that it should have reversed all our positions; and that while the Prussians and Austrians apparently found themselves contending for the cause of nationality, we should so vehemently have expressed our sympathies against it.

Having only the day before been present with the Prussian army, I had a good opportunity of comparing it with the Austrian troops who were now marching past. The difference was sufficiently marked. The youthful, light-hearted Prussian seemed to go into action as a new experience, but did not inspire much confidence in his steadiness; the Austrian, on the other hand, worn and rugged, often brutalised in expression, plodded on like a machine. The Prussian looked intelligent enough to understand the Schleswig-Holstein question: the Austrian looked as if brandy and tobacco constituted the sum total of his ideas; but he was every inch a "professional," the others looked like amateurs. Nevertheless, two years afterwards, the amateurs gave the professionals a bad time of it. How it was we did not hear the firing which took place a short time after we had passed the column, we could not make out, so close to it must we have been. However, we pushed on to Rendsburg, more for the purpose of dining than anything else; and afterwards having received definite information as to the locality of the headquarters, we started once more along by-lanes, which brought us out ultimately on the pretty undulating shores of the Wittensee, a very considerable lake. By this time it was getting dark, but we were far from the end of our fatigues. Following the somewhat vague directions of a jovial innkeeper, we finally, more by good luck than good management, discovered the remote hamlet of Damendorf, where General Von Wrangel had fixed his headquarters; but he and his staff, having heard the firing, were witnessing the battle which we had missed, and came back late with the news. As there was no corner in which to lay our heads, we had nothing for it but to push on to Eckernfiorde. Here, again, every table was occupied, to say nothing of the beds. Our horses were incapable of moving another yard, but we determined to struggle on to Kiel, and about midnight were once more *en route* with fresh nags. Our bad luck this night pursued us; for we met a train of no less than 1500 waggons, conveying stores to the army, and spent the whole night scraping past them, at the constant risk of finding an unexpected bed in a ditch. It was 4 A.M. before I was once more ensconced in a snug bed, after twenty hours spent in an open waggon—the greater number of them in storms of rain or sleet.

As we received positive information at Kiel that the grand attack on the Dannevirke was to take place on the following day, we made another night-journey by carriage to Rendsburg, reaching that town at three in the morning, and leaving it again shortly after daybreak in a pitiless snow-storm. We followed the highroad to Schleswig, the same which I had traversed more than a month before; but which, as we soon found to our cost, was no longer free to the traveller. To the Prussian guards which protected the rear of the army was assigned the duty of making war upon Germany, while the front was conquering the Danes. Not even officers of the Federal army in uniform were allowed by these jealous guardsmen to penetrate their lines, and every civilian was regarded either as a Danish spy, or, what was still more odious, a member of the National Verein. We were the first of a series who were subsequently expelled from the neighbourhood of military operations for our political opinions. Not that the intelligent colonel who refused to allow us to pass had the least idea what our sentiments were; but all Englishmen are, in the eyes of the Yunker, revolutionary, and a danger not merely to society, but even to the discipline of an army. The Prussian officer, as a rule—which, like every other, has brilliant exceptions—prides himself upon being a soldier and nothing else. He generally succeeds to admiration in this limited ambition, so far as his bearing to the rest of the world is concerned; but the fact to some extent accounts for the unpopularity of the class generally. One may affect military precision without allowing it to degenerate into rudeness, and maintain the dignity of one's profession without showing contempt for all who do not belong to it,—all which reflections were suggested to me by the extremely uncivil treatment I received, first from a colonel, and then from a general, simply because I asked to be allowed to go, as I had done two days before, to headquarters. The elements combining with the colonels to make any connection with the fortunes of the Prussian army most disagreeable, I determined to quit the scene of operations; and, as it turned out afterwards, I missed nothing, for the night I left Schleswig the Dannevirke was evacuated, and I should have been detained some time longer had I waited to see the subsequent operations in Jutland. I therefore lost no time in making the best of my way home.

CHAPTER XIX.

THE MORAL OF IT ALL.

ONE result of the erratic and somewhat turbulent life I had been leading, described in the foregoing pages, was to place me in communication with sources of political information of altogether exceptional value. The misfortune was that it was of so confidential a character that it was difficult to use it to advantage in any organ of the public press of which one had not absolute control. For instance, a conference was at that time sitting in London on the Schleswig-Holstein question, consisting of plenipotentiaries of all the European Powers who had been parties to the Treaty of London, the proceedings at which were kept absolutely secret; yet a few days after each meeting, I received from abroad an accurate report of everything that had transpired at it—and this, I hasten to say, through no one connected with our own Foreign Office. I felt bursting with all sorts of valuable knowledge, with no means of imparting it in a manner which suited me, when one day, at a little dinner at which Sir Algernon Borthwick, Mr Evelyn Ashley, and the late Mr James Stewart Wortley were present, when the denseness of the British public in matters of foreign policy was being discussed, it was suggested that a little paper should be started by way of a skit, in which the most outrageous *canards* should be given as serious, and serious news should be disguised in a most grotesque form. In fact, we wanted to see to what extent society could be mystified. Sir A. Borthwick kindly undertook to print the absurd little sheet, which appeared a week or two after under the name of 'The Owl,' and which, I think, was the only instance of a paper on record which paid all its expenses—which, if I remember right, amounted to £15—by the sale of its first number. When it was found that it was likely to be profitable, we arranged that the proceeds should be applied to our common entertainment; and while we intrigued politicians by the accuracy of our information, we excited the curiosity of society to the highest pitch, not merely by maintaining our anonymity, but by the evidences which our spasmodic little publication afforded that we were thoroughly behind the scenes. With the close of the season, 'The Owl' retired to roost for the time, and I made a trip into Italy to watch the progress of events in the Peninsula. In the following year a general election took place, and I entered Parliament.

Most people are, I suppose, more or less conscious of leading a sort of double life—an outside one and an inside one. The more I raced about the world, and took as active a part as I could in its dramatic performances, the more profoundly did the conviction force itself upon me, that if it was indeed a stage, and all the men and women only players, there must be a real life somewhere. And

I was always groping after it in a blind dumb sort of way
—not likely, certainly, to find it in battle-fields or ball-
rooms, but yet the reflection was more likely to force itself
upon me when I was among murderers or butterflies than
at any other time. Now that I found myself among politicians, I think it forced itself upon me more strongly than
ever. Here was a stage, indeed, on which I had proposed
to myself to play a serious part. It was for this I had
applied myself to the study of European politics, for this
I had supplied myself with valuable sources of information. I had learnt my part, but when it came to acting,
it seemed to dwindle into most minute proportions. It is
true that just at this juncture the British legislature was
far more occupied with the cattle-plague than with foreign
affairs, and that the disinfecting of railway trucks was regarded as a subject of absorbing interest, second only in
importance to the Reform Bill which followed. The
House of Commons does not yet seem to have learnt the
lesson that voters are like playing cards. The more you
shuffle them the dirtier they get. When it became clear
to me that in order to succeed, party must be put before
country, and self before everything, and that success could
only be purchased at the price of convictions, which were
expected to change with those of the leader of the party
—these, as it happened, were of an extremely fluctuating
character, and were never to be relied upon from one session
to another—my thirst to find something that was not a
sham or a contradiction in terms increased. The world,
with its bloody wars, its political intrigues, its social evils, its
religious cant, its financial frauds, and its glaring anomalies,
assumed in my eyes more and more the aspect of a gigantic

lunatic asylum. And the question occurred to me whether there might not be latent forces in nature, by the application of which this profound moral malady might be reached. To the existence of such forces we have the testimony of the ages. It was by the invocation of these that Christ founded the religion of which the popular theology has become a travesty, and it appeared to me that it could only be by a reinvocation of these same forces—a belief in which seemed rapidly dying out—that a restoration of that religion to its pristine purity could be hoped for.

I had long been interested in a class of psychic phenomena which, under the names of magnetism, hypnotism, and spiritualism, have since been forcing themselves upon public attention, and had even been conscious of these phenomena in my own experiences, and of the existence of forces in my own organism which science was utterly unable to account for, and therefore turned its back upon, and relegated to the domain of the unknowable. Into this region—miscalled mystic—I determined to try and penetrate. Looking back upon the period of my life described in the foregoing pages, it appeared to me distinctly a most insane period. I therefore decided upon retiring from public life and the confused turmoil of a mad world, into a seclusion where, under the most favourable conditions I could find, I could prosecute my researches into the more hidden laws which govern human action and control events. For more than twenty years I have devoted myself to this pursuit; and though from time to time I have been suddenly forced from retirement into some of the most stirring scenes which have agitated

Europe, the reasons which compelled me to participate in them were closely connected with the investigation in which I was engaged, the nature of which is so absorbing, and its results so encouraging, that it would not be possible for me now to abandon it, or to relinquish the hope which it has inspired, that a new moral future is dawning upon the human race—one certainly of which it stands much in need. As, however, this latter conviction has not yet forced itself upon a majority of my fellow-men, who continue to think the world is a very good world as it is, and that the invention of new machines and explosives for the destruction of their fellow-men is a perfectly sane and even laudable pursuit, I will refrain from entering further for the present upon such an unpopular theme. Perhaps the day may come, though it cannot be for many years, when I may take up the thread of my life where I have dropped it here, and narrate some episodes which have occurred since, which I venture to hope that the public of that day will be more ready to appreciate than those to whom, with the warmest feelings of attachment and compassion, I respectfully dedicate these pages.

THE END.

www.ingramcontent.com/pod-product-compliance
Lightning Source LLC
Chambersburg PA
CBHW030544300426
44111CB00009B/850